D1585675

ron

ONE WE

Lord Byron (1788–1824) was as famous in his time for his love affairs and revolutionary politics as he was for his trail-blazing Romantic and satiric poetry, which sold countless copies across Europe. Looking beyond the scandal, Byron leaves us a body of work that proved crucial to the development of English poetry and provides a fascinating counterpoint to other writings of the Romantic period.

This guide to Byron's sometimes daunting, always extraordinary work offers:

- an accessible introduction to the many interpretations of Byron's texts, from publication to the present;
- an introduction to key critical texts and perspectives on Byron's life and work, situated in a broader critical history;
- cross-references between sections of the guide, in order to suggest links between texts, contexts and criticism;
- suggestions for further reading.

Part of the *Routledge Guides to Literature* series, this volume is essential reading for all those beginning detailed study of Byron and seeking not only a guide to his works but also a way through the wealth of contextual and critical material that surrounds them.

Caroline Franklin is a Professor of English at the University of Wales, Swansea. She works in the area of Romantic-period literature on which she has published widely, including books on Byron and Mary Wollstonecraft.

Routledge Guides to Literature*

Editorial Advisory Board: Richard Bradford (University of Ulster at Coleraine), Jan Jedrzejewski (University of Ulster at Coleraine), Duncan Wu (St Catherine's College, University of Oxford).

Routledge Guides to Literature offer clear introductions to the most widely studied authors and literary texts. Each book engages with texts, contexts and criticism, highlighting the range of critical views and contextual factors that need to be taken into consideration in advanced studies of literary works. The series encourages informed but independent readings of texts by ranging as widely as possible across the contextual and critical issues relevant to the works examined and highlighting areas of debate as well as those of critical consensus. Alongside general guides to texts and authors, the series includes 'sourcebooks', which allow access to reprinted contextual and critical materials as well as annotated extracts of primary text.

Available in this series

* Some books in this series were originally published in the Routledge Literary Sourcebooks series, edited by Duncan Wu, or the Complete Critical Guide to English Literature series, edited by Richard Bradford and Jan Jedrzejewski.

Byron

Caroline Franklin

Routledge
Taylor & Francis Group

LONDON AND NEW YORK

First published 2007
by Routledge
2 Park Square, Milton Park, Abingdon, Oxon OX14 4RN

Simultaneously published in the USA and Canada
by Routledge
270 Madison Ave, New York, NY 10016

Routledge is an imprint of the Taylor & Francis Group, an informa business

© 2007 Caroline Franklin

Typeset in Sabon and Gill Sans by RefineCatch Limited, Bungay, Suffolk
Printed and bound in Great Britain by
Antony Rowe Ltd, Chippenham, Wiltshire

British Library Cataloguing in Publication Data
A catalogue record for this book is available from the British Library.

Library of Congress Cataloging in Publication Data
Franklin, Caroline.
 Byron / by Caroline Franklin.
  p. cm.—(Routledge guides to literature)
 Includes bibliographical references and index.
 1. Byron, George Gordon Byron, Baron, 1788–1824—Criticism and
interpretation. I. Title. II. Series.
 PR4388.F73 2006
 821′.7—dc22
                                            2006015968

ISBN 10: 0–415–26855–9 (hbk)
ISBN 10: 0–415–26856–7 (pbk)
ISBN 10: 0–203–96800–X (ebk)

ISBN 13: 978–0–415–26855–4 (hbk)
ISBN 13: 978–0–415–26856–1 (pbk)
ISBN 13: 978–0–203–96800–1 (ebk)

For my students at Swansea University

Contents

Acknowledgements

My thanks are due to the series editors, Professor Richard Bradford and Dr Jan Jedrzejewski for their careful and detailed commentary on the first draft, and to Liz Thompson at Routledge for her suggestions and advice. My students at the Department of English, Swansea University, have helped enormously by giving me feedback on the work in progress and challenging me with their reactions to Byron, and the book is dedicated to them.

Abbreviations and referencing

References to the letters, journals, poetry and prose of Byron are to the following texts:

BLJ   Leslie A. Marchand (ed.) (1973–94) *Byron's Letters and Journals*, 12 vols, London: John Murray.

CPW   Jerome J. McGann (ed.) (1980–93) *Byron: The Complete Poetical Works*, 7 vols, Oxford: Clarendon Press.

CMP   Andrew Nicholson (ed.) (1991) *Lord Byron: The Complete Miscellaneous Prose*, Oxford: Clarendon Press.

The Harvard system is used to key all references by author and date of publication to the bibliography.

Cross-referencing between sections is a feature of each volume in the *Routledge Guides to Literature* series. Cross-references appear in brackets and include section titles as well as the relevant page numbers in bold type, e.g. (see Life and Contexts, **pp. 14–15**).

Introduction

Byron is one of those writers whose scandalous and adventurous life has, in the past, tended to overshadow the fact that he was one of the greatest poets in English literature. However, in the past twenty-five years this neglect has begun to be remedied. Scholars have been engaged in a wholesale reassessment of the literary map of the Romantic period and this has resulted in a revaluation of the British writer whose work took Europe by storm in his own lifetime. Some of the most eminent Romanticist critics and scholars of the day have published on Byron. This guide is divided into three parts: Life, Works and Criticism. It aims to provide readers with information on the poet's life: vital in reading poetry which is sometimes confessional and which often comments on current affairs of the time; contextual and literary commentary on the major works, which consist of long narrative and dramatic poems; and suggestions for finding their way through this wealth of literary criticism. The reader new to Byron may like to read the short biography and then select the relevant sections of Part 2, where necessary, to introduce and assist their reading of the major poems. Critical issues raised by the verse will be briefly indicated. Students may then want to pursue some of the key arguments in more depth, and can consult Part 3, where they will find summarised the main discussions over and various critical approaches to the poetry from Byron's day to our own. Suggestions for further reading are given at relevant points in each section, and major criticism is listed in the bibliography. The clear signposting of the contents page, index and cross-referencing of the text, it is hoped, will make it easy for the reader to use the tripartite arrangement interactively to enhance their understanding and pleasure in the verse. For example, someone reading *Childe Harold's Pilgrimage* Cantos I and II might need to go back to the biography to find out the details of the poet's Grand Tour which inspired this poem, whose first draft was written while travelling. They should also use it to check out the political situation in Europe during the Napoleonic wars, the historical context for the poem. The commentary in the part on Works can be referred to if clarification is needed concerning the scenes being described, if, for example, confusion arises when the poet moves from present time into memory and back again. The reader will there be alerted to the vexed question of whether Harold is a self-portrait of the author and the even more tendentious issue of whether Byron sufficiently differentiates between the function of the protagonist and the narrator. After reading the poem, students may want to explore the views of the critics on this and other questions, and so consult Part 3 to guide them in their critical reading. They may be intrigued to find out more about why this poem was so extraordinarily popular in its time, and could contrast the view of Paul West that Byron was a fashionable poseur with that of William St Clair, whose study of the reading habits of the nation shows his appeal to the lower classes. Part 2 will have given them some basic information about the Philhellenism that inspired so much of Byron's output. But readers will also want to think about how this sentimental nationalism related to Byron's attitude to imperialism, for he was writing when the British Empire was expanding and consolidating. Part 3 will refer them to discussions between different scholars on how far Byron's Romantic Orientalism participated in the discourse of colonialism. Readers must make up their own minds on this and other issues, and the guide attempts to provide them with enough information to further their own study and research. It aims to be a reference book and companion to the reading of Byron's poetry in order to stimulate the asking of further questions, rather than providing closure and conclusions. Hopefully, the poet would approve.

1

Life and contexts

Introduction

This part attempts to sketch Byron's life as a *writer* and show how his poetry was produced through interaction with specific literary cultures in Regency London and abroad. The circumstances of the composition of the verse will be mentioned here briefly but the major poetry will be discussed in more detail in Part 2 and different critical views of it will be indicated in Part 3. Byron's adventurous life has inspired many biographies, discussed in the 'Further Reading' at the end of this section. Reference will be made to these in parenthesis and also to *Byron's Letters and Journals* (*BLJ*) and to accounts of the poet written by his contemporaries.

Childhood and family background, 1788–1805

George Gordon Byron was born on 22 January 1788 at 16 Holles Street, Cavendish Square, London, the son of aristocratic parents: Captain 'Mad Jack' Byron and Catherine (née Gordon). His father was a handsome English fortune hunter who soon ran through his plain Scottish wife's money, and the marriage disintegrated not long after the birth of the baby. Mrs Byron returned to Scotland and took lodgings in Aberdeen in 1789, then in 1791 rented an apartment at 64 Broad Street. Captain Byron died in the same year and she was left to bring up her son alone on only 150 pounds a year. At this time 500 pounds per annum was considered the minimum income for the gentry, and a nobleman needed 10,000 pounds per annum to participate fully in the social season, so this modest lower-middle-class standard of life was considered akin to poverty by an aristocrat such as Catherine Byron.

George had been born lame, perhaps with a club foot, and suffered throughout his childhood both from the stares and taunts of others and from the painful contraptions and treatments ordered by doctors who tried to straighten out his foot. He grew to be handsome like his father yet self-conscious about his disability and also about his tendency to put on weight because of the inability to take much exercise. Yet he loved swimming and riding and also cricket, where another boy ran when he batted. He was spoilt by his mother and did not take kindly to teachers' discipline but was an omnivorous reader with a retentive memory. He would later look back nostalgically on his Scottish childhood and occasional visits to the wild countryside of the Highlands (see Works, p. 32). In 1794 he had begun his education at Aberdeen Grammar School, but when the news came in May 1798 that, through a succession of unforeseen deaths, he had inherited the Byron title and family estates, he and his mother moved to England. When they arrived at Newstead Abbey, near Nottingham, they found the mansion to be near derelict but were nevertheless enchanted with the scene of picturesque desolation, which would later inspire Byron's earliest verses.

On both his Scottish mother's side (the Gordons of Gight) and his English father's (the Byrons of Lancashire and Nottinghamshire), the noble families from which Byron was descended had lost their wealth and importance. This was largely as a result of their own profligacy, but also because power was beginning to pass from the landed aristocracy to the mercantile classes in the nineteenth century (Rowse 1978: 117–52). His mother was a fervent Whig and supporter of the French Revolution, and the young Byron inherited both her aristocratic pride (made hypersensitive by their impoverishment) and the radical politics which seemed so incompatible with it.

Byron's social status is an important clue to his interest in creating characters who are proud outsiders or out of joint with the times. Because of his rapid transformation from middle-class schoolboy to becoming the sixth Baron Byron of Rochdale, Mrs Byron and her young son were both extremely sensitive about their rank. This was exacerbated by the fact that in the eighteenth century the Byrons had become a disreputable family and were, anyway, only on the lower rungs of the nobility, so young George would not have been welcome in the very highest circles had he not made a name for himself in literature. His income from the estate was inadequate to pay for the necessary repairs to the mansion and to fund an aristocratic lifestyle, so Newstead Abbey had to be rented out. His mother stinted herself to fund Byron's education at Harrow (1801–5) and then at Cambridge (1805–7) in accordance with his rank. But for all his early life, until Newstead was sold and the purchase money for the mansion finally paid in February 1819, Byron was plagued by lack of ready money and amassed large debts by attempting nevertheless to live in a suitably lordly style (Beckett 2001: 126–28). He was also uneasy for a long time as to whether a nobleman was lowering himself by engaging in the trade of publishing.

Religious heritage

Byron had been brought up by his mother and tutors in Scotland as a Presbyterian and knew his Bible inside out, particularly the Old Testament (Looper 1978: 287–95). Scots Presbyterians, like English Dissenters, identified with the Jews, having been persecuted and deprived of full civil rights in the historical past because of their religious beliefs. Byron would grow up to be critical of the way the Tory government made loyalty to the Anglican church and monarchy the cornerstone of British patriotism at this time of the Napoleonic wars, when Britain was at war with France. He advocated religious toleration instead. When he became sceptical about orthodox religion as a young man, Byron would vehemently reject the Calvinist belief in which he had been educated: that only a few, 'the Elect', were predestined by God to be saved, while the majority were consigned to eternal damnation regardless of their good works. Nevertheless, he could not entirely shake off the pessimism and fatalism which were the heritage of this austere theology.

This was exacerbated by his belief in aristocratic 'blood': he knew that his own father had been a dissolute rake, and his great uncle another, who had also killed his neighbour in a duel in dubious circumstances and was tried by the House of Lords and disgraced. When his volatile mother shouted at her headstrong son, she reproached him for following in the footsteps of the Byrons. She was superstitious and probably also saw his club foot as a taint. The lame boy was a prodigious reader (Moore 1860: 20) and particularly fascinated with Gothic fiction such as William Beckford's *Vathek* (1786), John Moore's *Zeluco* (1789) and Matthew Lewis's *The Monk* (1796), in each of which the sinful protagonist was drawn on by fate to commit evil deeds. He would later find decadent aristocrats portrayed as guilt-ridden villains in the Gothic novels of Mrs Radcliffe and Walter Scott's poetry, and the younger sons of minor aristocrats turning to banditry in the *Sturm und Drang* plays of Friedrich Schiller and Johann Wolfgang von Goethe. When he became a writer himself, he explored his own ambivalence towards aristocracy through elaborating and combining the characteristics of such anti-heroes, resulting in the creation of a succession of noble outlaws (see Works, p. 51). Critics have labelled this character 'the Byronic hero', not because it originated with Byron, but because he created a memorable series of such protagonists and many readers imagined they had something of the poet's own personality (Thorslev 1962).

Education and reading, 1794–1807

It was clear that Byron could not rely on an empty title to provide him with a place in the world. He needed to make his own way through merit. In Scotland, he had attended a day school and then the Grammar School at Aberdeen, but on inheriting the title he was sent to Dr Glennie's school at Dulwich to prepare him for entrance to public school. In 1803 his mother rented out Newstead and took a house at nearby Southwell, economising in order to provide him with the requisite upper-class education at Harrow and then Cambridge. Byron took some time to settle at Harrow, but eventually made close friends there and looked back nostalgically at his schooldays in his early verse (see Works, p. 31).

Byron was judged an indifferent scholar in the classics, then central to the curriculum at public school and university, by his chosen biographer; but the nineteen-year-old made a memorandum of an astonishing number of books he claimed to have read for his own amusement: mainly histories, biographies and literature in English and French (Moore 1860: 29, 46). History was then dominated by accounts of heroic men of action shaping the destiny of nations. Such a role seemed barred to a youth with a club foot. But a writer was an equally masterful figure: the French revolution had demonstrated the intoxicating power of ideas, disseminated in print, to inspire the populace to action.

The public schools of Byron's day, which trained their upper-class pupils to become leaders of their country, specialised in oratory. Many boys grew up to become statesmen, and the future prime minister, Robert Peel, was Byron's class-mate. Byron himself would be entitled to take his seat in the House of Lords at the age of twenty-one, and, though it was less important politically than the House of Commons, it was still a vital part of government. In fact, his mother cherished ambitions that he would become a political leader. Byron performed in three Harrow Speech Days, where the best boys gave recitations to an audience of their friends and relations. He chose passages from Virgil's *Aeneid*, Edward Young's *The Revenge* and Shakespeare's *King Lear* respectively. The scholar Paul Elledge has argued that Byron's self-creation in literature and in life began here, with 'a testing and accumulation of roles, a defining of identity through performance' (Elledge 2000: 3).

Whilst at Cambridge from October 1805 to December 1807, Byron did not spend much time studying, but enjoyed himself and got into debt. He indulged his love of animals and rebellious sense of humour. For example, when the college authorities objected to his keeping a dog, he obtained a bear instead and had it entered for a masters degree. He made some close friends, some of whom he kept for life. These included John Cam Hobhouse, Charles Skinner Matthews and Scrope Berdmore Davies, who were all witty liberal sceptics who shared his passions for literature and politics. Matthews, Hobhouse and Byron were also drawn together through a common gay identity at a time when homosexual acts were a capital offence and there was a rabidly homophobic climate (Crompton 1985: 129). Byron was bisexual: as a schoolboy and student, he experienced intense romantic friendships with boys, such as that for the Cambridge chorister, John Edleston (see Works, p. 37).

Byron was an avid theatre-goer and spent much of the time he should have been studying going to plays in London. In 1806 he also took the lead in organising and starring in two amateur theatrical productions at home in Southwell. For Byron the idea of making a speech to an audience and moving the listeners to action would perhaps always be even more important than the power of the printed word to transcend the historical moment of transmission. His love of theatre, his training in oratory and the examples, in the school and university syllabi, of classical rhetoricians who sought to persuade and move their hearers imbued him with a concept of poetry as performance.

Early writing

This performative aspect of Byron explains why he produced so much 'occa-sional' verse: short poems written on specific occasions to particular people. Through verse he attempted to seduce women, argue with friends, ridicule enemies or set down his response to events of the day. He passed his poems around in manuscript and literary friends would respond in kind. This began when he was a teenager. It was his interaction with the provincial circle at Southwell that inspired him to pay a local printer at Newark in 1806 to publish a collection of such verse, *Fugitive Pieces*. Second thoughts led him to revise the anthology and entitle it *Poems on Various Occasions* in 1807 (Pratt 1973: 29). The poems were originally meant only for the entertainment of those who recog-nised themselves or knew the recipients. Most were love poems, some of which were risqué enough to outrage the local worthies. The furore persuaded the ambitious youth to make great changes when launching the volume in London, now retitled *Hours of Idleness* (1807) and designed for the public at large (see Works, **p. 31** and Criticism, **p. 85**). Byron chose fewer erotic love poems now, concentrating more on melancholy lyrics exploring his innermost and mixed feelings about his ancestry and ruined mansion and regret on leaving behind the camaraderie of schooldays. The lyrics were not especially promising, but they were unusually personal. They were well reviewed on the whole, and a second edition was published in March 1808 as *Poems Original and Translated*.

However, Byron was enraged and humiliated when *Hours of Idleness* was remorselessly mocked in the leading periodical of the day, the *Edinburgh Review*, as the pretentious trifling of a dilettante whose preface had simultaneously attempted to overawe the public with his rank and obtain sympathy on account of his youth. The crusading Whig lawyer Henry Brougham was the anonymous reviewer, though Byron assumed it was the editor, Francis Jeffrey. The attack was the best thing that could have happened, for it galvanised Byron into declaring himself a serious writer with a moral purpose: the stance he now adopted in a withering riposte to the *Edinburgh Review*, a Popeian satire in rhyming couplets entitled *English Bards and Scotch Reviewers* (1809), which attacked the *Edinburgh Review* as well as many of the leading contemporary poets of the day for good measure (see Works, **p. 32** and Criticism, **p. 85**). The adoption of the Roman satirist Juvenal as a model also enabled the noble poet to retain a patrician persona in his condemnation of shoddy bourgeois culture. This boisterous and unsubtle poem made Byron's name, going through four editions before Byron suppressed it, for its attack on the Whig periodical eventually proved politically embarrassing for him. In July 1809 he now left England with his friend from Cambridge, J. C. Hobhouse, to make his Grand Tour.

The Grand Tour and the poetry of place

The Grand Tour was the conventional way an aristocrat completed his education, visiting sites associated with classical history, Renaissance art and European culture. Because Europe was ravaged by the Napoleonic wars, the two friends could not take the usual route to Italy to study the great masters. Since 1793 Britain had been at war with republican France, and at this point Napoleon Bonaparte seemed unstoppable in his conquest of Europe. In 1798 he had taken Switzerland, northern Italy and Malta, and in 1804 declared war on Spain and had himself proclaimed an emperor. Byron and Hobhouse were thus not able to travel through France or Italy, so they decided to follow in the steps of the British army who were supporting the Portugese and Spanish insurgents against the French invaders in the Iberian peninsula.

The aim of the two young men was to seek adventure, first by vicarious experience of the Peninsular war. Then they would strike east, into the Ottoman Empire, little known by Westerners, their destination being Turkey itself and also the outlying provinces which today constitute Greece and Albania, where their only British fellow travellers would be the occasional diplomat or military attaché. The Orient had long functioned for British artists as an imaginary realm of luxury, violence and sensuality (see Criticism, **pp. 111–14**). Byron and Hobhouse intended to find material for travel writing, in subjective poetry and antiquarian prose respectively. Byron's poetry would play a pivotal role in transforming the experience of the aristocratic Grand Tour into an exotic excursion into the cultural Other (Buzard 1993: 114–28) and would be instrumental in popularising travel amongst the middle classes later in the century.

Athens was Byron's and Hobhouse's ultimate destination. For both men were interested in Philhellenism, the idea of Western nineteenth-century intellectuals that the republican ideals of classical Greece could be recuperated by helping the Christian inhabitants of that part of the Ottoman Empire approximating to 'Hellas' to rebel against their Turkish masters and form a new nation-state. Byron would soon discover that the present 'Romaic' (Eastern Orthodox Christians) population of the region had no knowledge of the civilisation of the classical Greeks and certainly no more understanding of the modern concept of a nation-state than their city-state ancestors had done.

But first the friends would sample Orientalism nearer home in the Moorish influence on the Iberian peninsula, for they had taken a last-minute opportunity to depart from Britain on the Lisbon packet. Spain inspired Byron, as would Venice later, as a place where Christian and Islamic culture collided. Byron had been drawn to exotic places through his extensive reading of travel books and he was not the only one. Spain was to become mythologised by other poets such as Robert Southey, Walter Scott and Walter Savage Landor at this time. Spain became the focus of Romantic writing because 'Since the first explorations of the Mediterranean in remote times, this land was identified with the extreme Western limits of the known world, the *Finis Terrae*, the end of the organised cosmos and a place where order and disorder mixed' (Saglia 1996: 45). British readers were particularly fascinated with evocations of the peninsula at this moment because it was the scene of the protracted campaign which would be the turning point of the war with Napoleon. Byron and Hobhouse donned British military uniforms to identify themselves with the army, whose route they were following. They visited Sintra in Portugal and Cadiz and Seville in Spain before sailing to Gibraltar, arriving on 4 August 1809. From thence they sailed to Malta where Byron had a love affair with Mrs Spencer Smith, whom he would address as 'Florence' in a series of lyrics. These would be published in 1812 with Cantos I and II of the long topographical poem inspired by his travels and written in Spenserian stanzas, later entitled *Childe Harold's Pilgrimage*.

On 19 September Byron and Hobhouse departed for Patras in Greece. They journeyed over wild mountainous terrain to Janina in the Epirus, to visit the court of Ali Pasha, the cunning and unscrupulous Albanian governor who was just then disposed to welcome noble British visitors as he was courting British support against the French in his bid for control of the Ionian islands. Though supposedly governing his fiefdom under the suzerainty of the Sultan, Ali Pasha displayed near independence. He had risen from little more than a bandit leader and, having subdued the inhabitants of the region and even fierce tribes such as the Suliotes by ruthless warfare, ruled as a despot over the Epirus while his son controlled the Morea. On 5 October Byron and Hobhouse arrived at Janina, but the Pasha was away, so they travelled on an arduous journey through even more remote regions to Tepelene, where they arrived on 19 October. This was the high spot of their tour, surveying the unforgettable scene of the picturesque Albanian troops garrisoned before the Pasha's exotic palace and mosque, before being treated to a royal welcome from the romantic warrior leader himself.

By 31 October 1809 Byron had begun the first draft of the first canto of *Childe Harold's Pilgrimage*. The poem would make his name throughout Europe and in his lifetime was considered his best work. The protagonist was a world-weary young aristocrat weighed down by unexplained sorrow and guilt, who travels to relieve his *ennui*, meditating on the passing away of ancient heroism as he contemplates the ruins of past civilisations. The narrator gave way increasingly to lyric introspection of his own as the poem progressed, for Harold was too flat a character to express a great range of feeling. In later installments of the poem, the narrator would virtually abandon his protagonist, as his own volatile subjectivity coloured the reader's view of the landscapes. But even in the first two cantos, this poem was startlingly personal and intimate.

Harold's journey east in Cantos I and II took him deep into the fierce warrior culture of Albania which Byron depicted as stirringly picturesque. The poet would, from henceforth, set many of his romantic verse tales and even later comic episodes in *Don Juan* in the Ottoman Empire. His portrayals of tyrannical pashas and of the Greek brigands or *klephtes* who rebelled against Turkish rule were inspired by his time at Ali Pasha's court, and Byron's poetic fictionalisation of his travels can be usefully compared with the long, vivid letters he wrote to his mother at this time (*BLJ* Vol. I, 223–4, 226–31, 234–6, 242–3, 249–52; Vol. II, 3–4, 8–9, 17–18, 34–5).

The friends now travelled back to Prevesa by way of Ali Pasha's inadequately skippered armed vessel (which nearly sank) and then, accompanied by a contingent of his soldiers, they made their way to Missolonghi in Greece. As aristocrats, they travelled in style, so were in great danger of robbers in this wild country. But every night the picturesque Albanian soldiers sang and danced around their campfires, and Byron took phonetic transcripts of their war songs and ballads so that he could have them translated and incorporate them into his poem, as well as try his hand at imitating them. From Missolonghi, having crossed the gulf to Patras, they began the long trek to Athens which they would not reach till Christmas Day 1809. On their way, the young men saw Mount Parnassus, visited Delphi and many ancient sites their classical education had invested with significance. But they also heard more folksongs and patriotic war songs sung by modern Greeks. These included 'Greeks Arise' by Constantine Rhiga, who had founded a nationalist society, the Hetairia, and, as a result, had been executed by the Turks in 1798. Byron and Hobhouse's young host at Vostitza, Andreas Londos, though he was the governor of the town under the Turks, recited 'Greeks Arise' with tears streaming down his face. In time to come, Londos would be a leader of the Greek war of Independence, where Byron was to lose his life. These experiences were to be crucial in shaping the sort of Philhellenist verse Byron was writing at this time. Philhellenism had a long literary pedigree. But Byron's work would be different from that of most of his predecessors in that he conveyed his personal experience of the landscape and of the contemporary culture, rather than antiquarianism and book knowledge of classical civilisation.

Athens then was the size of a large village. Its population of 10,000 Greeks, Albanians and Turks was ruled by a *waiwode* or governor appointed by the *disdar aga*, an officer of the Sultan whom Byron later contemptuously described in the notes to *The Giaour* (1813) as 'the slave of the seraglio and guardian of the women . . . a pandar and eunuch'. However, as long as they paid their tribute, the Greeks were leniently treated, though, as Christians, they were second-class citizens. Their own aristocracy and bishops enjoyed the power to collect the taxes for the Turks and enriched themselves in the process.

Byron and Hobhouse had to obtain Turkish permission to visit the Acropolis which was being used as an arsenal and munitions store (the Parthenon would be greatly damaged by an explosion in 1827). They were accompanied by the Neapolitan painter Giovanni Battista Lusieri who was employed by Lord Elgin to make drawings of the Acropolis and then to dismantle and ship its famous sculptures to England. (They are, despite recent calls for their return from the Greek government, still displayed in the British Museum, which paid 37,000 pounds for them in 1816.) Byron became very indignant at this arrogant plundering of the Greek heritage, though supporters of Elgin argued that the British would at least preserve the marbles for posterity. He added an attack on Elgin to the second canto of *Childe Harold's Pilgrimage* whose first draft was finished on 28 March 1810. A year later he would compose a brief satire, *The Curse of Minerva* on the same subject.

The friends visited Sunium and Marathon and in March 1810 they sailed to Smyrna in Asia Minor, from where they travelled to Ephesus and the plains of Troy. In May Byron swam the Hellespont, in imitation of the Roman poet Ovid's legendary lover Leander, who did this nightly to meet his mistress. The lame poet boasted about this feat interminably in all his letters home, though he had to admit that, unlike Leander, he had only swum one way and hadn't made love either! On 13 May the friends visited Constantinople and saw gruesome evidence of Turkish despotism such as the heads of executed criminals displayed at the gates of the Seraglio. They attended an audience with Sultan Mahmoud II on 10 July, but left the city a few days later, when Hobhouse returned to England.

Byron stayed on in Athens for another nine months, lodging in a Franciscan monastery. He swam every day at Piraeus and one day witnessed a procession carrying a Turkish girl sewn up in a sack, who was to be ceremonially drowned in the sea as a punishment for illicit sex. Byron intervened but had to draw his pistol to stop the proceedings, and then to bribe the officials to procure her escape to Thebes. This horrifying incident was to inspire his verse tale, *The Giaour* (1813) (see Works, **pp. 51–4**). Byron's acquaintance, Thomas Medwin, who posthumously published somewhat unreliable accounts of his conversations with the poet, asserted that Byron had told him the incident was particularly chilling because the punishment was the result of the poet's own attempt to arrange an assignation with her, but there is no proof of this (Lovell 1969: 86–9).

In fact, one of the reasons Byron sojourned so long in the Ottoman Empire was to indulge his taste for young boys and to experience a culture that was tolerant of this. England, by contrast, had the most homophobic and intolerant laws in Europe or the USA, and hanged sixty men for sodomy in the first three decades of the nineteenth century and twenty more under its naval regulations (Crompton 1985: 17–18). When Byron returned to England in the summer of 1811, his emotional life came to a crisis. His mother died suddenly before he arrived at Southwell; then, two days later, he learned that his homosexual friend Matthews had been found drowned at Cambridge. Within the next two months, Byron discovered that John Edleston, the young Cambridge chorister with whom he had had an intense but almost certainly Platonic romantic friendship had also died. Byron wrote a series of elegiac lyrics in his grief for the latter, but when some of these were published with *Childe Harold's Pilgrimage*, their careful omission of personal pronouns and the use of a feminine name 'Thyrza' for the addressee misled readers speculating on their biographical source (see Criticism, **pp. 115–16**).

Politics

It was with some trepidation that Byron rejoined the literary world of London, not least because he had to make peace with many angry poets who had been mercilessly mocked in his satire *English Bards and Scotch Reviewers*. The Irish lyricist Thomas Moore even challenged him to a duel, but, after an exchange of posturing letters, the two met and became the best of friends. At this time, Byron also made the acquaintance of two older poets whose work he admired: Samuel Rogers and Thomas Campbell. All three literary men were Whigs and denizens of Holland House, where Lord Holland masterminded party affairs. Byron had joined the Cambridge Whig club in 1807, and, when he came of age in January 1809, he had taken his seat in the House of Lords and intended to take an active part in opposition politics. At first the Whig party was not sure what to make of him, as it had been assumed that the author of *English Bards and Scotch Reviewers*, whose main target was the Whiggish *Edinburgh Review*, had been a Tory. But after attending the house several times to listen to debates, on 27 February 1812 Byron made his maiden speech: a blistering attack on the Tory administration's proposal to make frame-breaking or 'Luddism' a capital felony.

As a Nottinghamshire landowner, Byron was intensely aware of the exploitation of the workers in the Midlands hosiery trade, their attempts to organise themselves to fight shoddy mass production that threw them out of work and their grinding poverty. 'Luddism', or the smashing of machinery designed to circumvent the need for skilled craftsmanship by manufacturing inferior cut-price goods for export, was at its height in 1811–12, as well as constitutional protest, in the form of petitioning parliament to pass a bill regulating the industry. Thousands of soldiers were prevented from swelling the army engaged in the Peninsular war, kept at home to maintain order in the riot-torn Midlands (Thompson 1963: 604–59).

Byron's speech was a passionate powerful piece of oratory in support of the workers which can only be described as 'radical' rather than Whig. It must have come as quite a shock to his drowsy audience of mediocre placemen that a nobleman could denounce the catastrophic effect on the poor of unfettered capitalism and reject the death penalty as the knee-jerk reaction of an unfeeling oligarchy. It certainly disconcerted Lord Holland and the Whigs, who planned merely to minimally amend the Government's proposals. Byron reminded his upper-class audience: 'It is the Mob, that labour in your fields & serve in your houses, that man your navy & recruit your army, that have enabled you to defy all the world, & can also defy you, when neglect & calamity have driven them to despair' (*CMP* 25).

Byron next spoke on 21 April 1812 when, according to Hobhouse, he kept the Upper House 'in a roar of laughter', in a witty speech advocating extending full civil rights to Roman Catholics. On 1 June 1813 he presented the tireless campaigner Major Cartwright's petition in support of parliamentary reform.

Byron's poetry has traditionally been considered as part of the radical tradition (Foot 1988). His verse certainly inspired young revolutionaries throwing off oppressive regimes throughout nineteenth-century Europe. However, his correspondence shows he was nervous of the new working-class agitators in his own country. Many of his views, it has been argued, were congruent with those of eighteenth-century aristocratic Whigs (Kelsall 1987: 5). Yet Byron was a revolutionary not a reformer, soon becoming bored with what he called 'parliamentary mummeries', for he preferred action to constitutionalism. But this is to anticipate.

The Murray coterie and the marketing of Byron

On 10 March 1812, less than a fortnight after his maiden speech, came the publication of the first two cantos of *Childe Harold's Pilgrimage*, by Byron's new publisher, John Murray. This event was enough to eclipse thoughts of his parliamentary career for the time being, for the poem became an overnight sensation (see Works, **pp. 34–7** and Criticism, **p. 85**). In three days, the first edition of 500 copies had sold out and 4,500 copies were sold within six months of publication. Byron became the literary lion of London. For the next four years he reigned supreme, and every poem he published increased his fame. He would in time write two more cantos of *Childe Harold's Pilgrimage*, the poem for which he became renowned throughout Europe, where it was translated into many languages.

He followed up the success of the first two cantos of *Childe Harold's Pilgrimage* with a series of extraordinarily popular adventure tales in verse, set in the Ottoman Empire: *The Giaour* (1813), *The Bride of Abydos* (1813), *The Corsair* (1814) and *Lara* (1814) (see Life and Contexts, **pp. 5–9**). In the early twentieth century, these tales were dismissed by British critics as mere fashionable entertainment. Yet, in Part 3 it will be shown how contemporary cultural historians have rediscovered this conflicted verse, seeing it as the product of a Romantic Orientalist who resolutely opposed imperialism yet who recognised that his own poetry participated in its discourse – by recommending the extension of the values of British liberty over the world (Leask 1993: 16).

Byron's contemporary popularity can hardly be overstated. Six thousand copies of *The Bride of Abydos* were sold in a month, and 10,000 of *The Corsair* on the first day of publication alone. Byron had modelled himself upon, but far surpassed, Walter Scott, whose verse romances in medieval settings had sold in huge numbers. Secular books were a highly priced luxury commodity in the first twenty-five years of the century, and exotic love poetry by a handsome young aristocrat particularly appealed to the aspirational mercantile classes and especially to women readers. The notes to Byron's orientalist poetry emphasised his personal experience of the East, and confessional lyrics included in *Childe Harold's Pilgrimage*, either put in the mouth of the hero or merely added at the end of the volume, encouraged the reader's interest in the poet's own personality and life story. The word 'commerce' in the eighteenth century meant communication in general; its secondary meaning was trade. But the Romantic poet's intimate relationship with the reader seemingly brought the two meanings into violent collision by making his frankness and self-revelation a selling point instead of a guarantee of disinterested sincerity (Martin 1982: 29; Christensen, 1993: xvii–xxi). John Murray, Byron's entrepreneurial young publisher, with the collusion of the poet himself, marketed the verse by shaping a Byronic image. Engravings adorned many a frontispiece, based on a famous portrait by Phillips, showing the dark-clad curly haired poet's white throat bared in an open-necked shirt. This instantly recognisable image imparted a dashing air of freedom which accorded with the exotic subject matter of the verse and its call for political and sexual emancipation. But because John Murray was a Tory who published the eminently respectable *Quarterly Review*, which had links to the Tory government itself, and because the poet's rank seemed incompatible with radicalism, then a façade of the utmost respectability was maintained.

This meant that from 1812 to 1816 Byron's poetry was favourably reviewed in virtually all the leading periodicals of the day, whether Tory or Whig, whether Evangelical, Nonconformist or Anglican, with only the mildest of censure for its religious skepticism or failure to sufficiently censure immoral characters (Walker 1979: 18). In order for the alliance to succeed, Byron had to work closely with Murray's team of literary advisers, sometimes by toning down objectionable passages or adopting self-censorship. He always wrote with an audience in mind: the addressee, his coterie of literary friends, his rivals and enemies, as well as the anonymous mass public. Byron did not write primarily for posterity: he wanted an immediate response from his readers. He tested his poems out on trusted advisers and an inner circle of friends before publication, and Murray targeted differently priced editions at different classes of readers (Franklin 2000: 37–60). Byron enjoyed this entrepreneurial aspect of authorship and the cachet of being able to command huge sums of money should he deign to accept them. Murray had offered him the fabulous sum of 1,000 pounds for *The Giaour* and *The Bride of Abydos* but, as an aristocrat, for many years he would only accept payment in order to confer it on other more impecunious authors such as his literary agent R. C. Dallas or the radical philosopher William Godwin (Smiles 1891: 1, 222). In this way he conflated the role of an aristocratic patron with the bourgeois business of authorship.

Amours

Literary fame achieved for Byron what his raffish ancestry could not: entry to the very highest echelons of aristocratic society. The poet became a sort of Whig anti-laureate and took all their women by storm, especially those in Melbourne House, the household of William Lamb – who would later become Queen Victoria's staid prime minister, Lord Melbourne. First Byron had a tempestuous semi-public adulterous affair with William's brilliant and eccentric wife, Lady Caroline Lamb, whilst making a confidante of his mother, Lady Melbourne, and proposing (unsuccessfully at first) to his heiress cousin, Annabella Milbanke. Then he dispatched Caroline and took as his mistress the political fixer, Lady Oxford, a middle-aged beauty with a bevy of handsome children by different fathers. Under her influence, he now joined the faction of Sir Francis Burdett, on the left of the Whig party. Byron would later reminisce about and fictionalise his experience of these years in high society in the English cantos of *Don Juan* (see Works, **pp. 73–5**).

But of most immediate significance for the direction his life and poetry would now take was the most controversial of his affairs: that with his own half-sister, Augusta Leigh. The theme of brother–sister incest had featured in the first draft of *The Bride of Abydos* (1813) and would be prominent in *Manfred* (1817) and *Cain* (1821) (see Works, **pp. 55–6, 59–62, 79–83**). Byron's literary depictions of sibling incest are usually explained as the therapeutic outpouring of self-revelation, but it should be borne in mind that several other Romantic and Gothic writers explored this theme, presumably without the benefit of personal experience. Byron and the motherly Augusta, who was five years older than him and was married with several children, had seen little of each other while growing up. Byron had no family except Augusta, and he enjoyed showing off his new acquaintances to her. Their warm, easy relationship seems to have become sexual in nature in 1813. It is even possible that Augusta's daughter Medora was her brother's child. Like many aristocrats in Regency society, they both had a permissive attitude towards sexuality; but, for Byron, breaking the incest taboo gave the relationship a special attraction. He now had a guilty secret like that of so many villains in Gothic fiction. However, the poet's ambivalence about his libertinism and the necessity of settling his mounting debts impelled him to marry an heiress and to reform forthwith. He married Annabella Milbanke, an earnest moralist with a penchant for mathematics, on 2 January 1815.

Marriage, separation and exile

Perhaps as a mark of his good faith, Byron now threw himself into a project to write biblical lyrics to settings of Jewish traditional airs arranged by musician Isaac Nathan, published as *Hebrew Melodies* in 1815. But he also infused into the collection an unmistakably Byronic championing of the Jewish people as victims both of the Roman Empire of old and contemporary anti-Semitism. He then wrote two more verse tales, *The Siege of Corinth* and *Parisina*, which were published early in 1816. The same year, 1815, he was also persuaded to join the amateur sub-committee running the newly rebuilt Drury Lane theatre (Lansdown 1992: 11–58). His role was to read scripts offered for performance and to commission new drama. This experience would undoubtedly influence his own poetic dramas in the years to come, for Byron became the most important dramatist of all the Romantic poets.

Byron's marriage was an unmitigated disaster. Though his Newstead estate was valuable, the poet was short of ready money, and bailiffs entered his Piccadilly house ten months after the wedding. On 15 January 1816, Annabella left her husband for a visit to her family, taking their month-old baby daughter, Augusta Ada (known as Ada), with her. Though Annabella wrote to him affectionately, she never returned or gave a reason for this. No one can be sure exactly what happened, but it is most likely that, in her naivety, she told her parents about Byron's incestuous relationship with Augusta in 1813, which he had confessed to her, and they persuaded her to separate. Byron had certainly vented on his pregnant wife the bad moods his volatile temperament generated, exacerbated by money worries and sexual guilt. During the acrimonious proceedings of a legal separation, an enormous scandal blew up, whose flames were undoubtedly fanned by the mischief-making Caroline Lamb circulating hints of her ex-lover's bisexuality. Rumours about the excesses of Byron's sex life and his brutal treatment of his wife split high society into two camps: those who championed the rights of the wronged wife and those who characterised her as a humourless prude. The society hostesses now ostracised Byron and made it impossible for him to stay in London.

Wives, in those days, were 'covered' by their husbands in the eyes of the law: in other words, treated as minors. Custody of a child was therefore normally awarded to the father; and, anyway, wives were very rarely allowed to instigate divorce. But incest was one of the few crimes that had persuaded courts to grant an aggrieved wife a divorce. It seems likely that an unspoken understanding or stand-off existed whereby Byron did not press for his custody rights as long as Lady Byron did not accuse him of incest. She did not; in fact, she continued to act as a 'friend' and sister-in-law to Augusta. Nevertheless, the scandal marked a watershed in British sexual mores, for Byron represented the aristocratic promiscuity which was no longer acceptable in the dawn of a new age of moralism and domestic virtue symbolised by his wife. The first canto of Byron's *Don Juan* would fictionalise and satirise the separation.

The newspapers and theatres became filled with lampoons of the poet in one of the greatest scandals in the nineteenth century. Byron was in the habit of passing round poems in manuscript to his inner circle, and his poems on the separation ('Fare Thee Well' to Annabella and satires on her friends) were pirated and printed in the newspapers. These then inspired broadsheet replies and imitations. Caroline Lamb represented him as a Gothic villain in her *roman à clef* (a novel fictionalising real people and events, sometimes for satiric purposes), entitled *Glenarvon* (1816). As the historian Thomas Babington Macaulay wrote in 1831: 'It is not every day that the savage envy of aspiring dunces is gratified by the agonies of such a spirit, and the degradation of such a name' (quoted in Massie 1988: 74).

The personal suffering the poet endured in the loss of his wife, daughter and sister, and the blackening of his reputation both as a man and a poet, did have the effect of stimulating him to prove himself once again in the face of adversity. So for poetry readers it turned out a fortunate fall. On 25 April 1816, Byron left Britain, never to return.

Writing poetry in Europe after the defeat of Napoleon

Byron's personal crisis had coincided with that of Europe, as 1815 was the year that Napoleon Bonaparte was finally defeated by the allies on 18 June at the battle of Waterloo. The egotistic poet didn't find this surprising; in fact he compared himself with the fallen military hero. When he had to adopt the forename 'Noel' to inherit a bequest, he enjoyed using his new initials and had a travelling coach made in imitation of that of the Emperor. In 1814–15, the Congress of Vienna was held to dismember Napoleon's empire and to restore the Bourbon monarchy to power in France. The four main powers, Britain, Russia, Prussia and Austria, bound themselves together into an alliance and attempted to create a balance of power so that war would not break out again in Europe. However, this meant that they ignored the emergent nationalist feelings of various territories, which were parcelled out to monarchical and dynastic rulers in an attempt to reinstitute the *ancien régime*.

Byron was in despair that the ideals of liberty, equality and fraternity that had inspired the French revolution and its republic had been first perverted into a bloodthirsty dictatorship and then finally extirpated by the forces of conservatism, and that his own country was enforcing the restoration of monarchies throughout Europe. He now adopted Europe as his stage and became the self-appointed spokesman of all heterogeneous peoples ruled over by imperial dynasties and absolutist regimes.

The poet embarked upon a sort of second Grand Tour, visiting the region now known as Belgium, Germany and Switzerland in the spring of 1816, accompanied by Hobhouse. As during their first travels together, they were keen to vicariously experience the recent warfare. One of the first places they visited was the 'place of skulls', the battlefield of Waterloo, where Byron collected some helmets and sabres as souvenirs. That May he resumed his travel poem, *Childe Harold's Pilgrimage*, and would publish the third canto on 18 November 1816 (see Works, pp. 37–43 and Criticism, pp. 86, 102). The figure of the solitary wanderer now became a portrait of the exiled Romantic genius, exploring the creative springs of his own imagination in nature and art. Byron dramatised himself through ironic analogy with Napoleon, whilst questioning the possibility of heroism in the modern world (Bainbridge 1995: 134–82).

The poet had already expressed his mixed feelings obliquely about this military genius in the series of portraits of renegade leaders in the oriental tales, overtly in his journal 1813–14 (*BLJ* III, 204–58) and publicly in the 'Ode to Napoleon Bonaparte' and a series of short poems ventriloquising different views of Bonaparte's abdication and subsequent return to power, the romantic episode of the 'Hundred Days'. Now he began to set down his imaginative evocation of its climax in the battle at Waterloo and his considered evaluation of Bonaparte's demonic overreaching energy in stanzas soon to become famous. Reading them, Walter Scott would speak for many when he declared himself shocked at Byron's startling omission: his lack of patriotic pride in Wellington's victory. In the preface to Canto IV of *Childe Harold's Pilgrimage*, Byron would respond by deploring 'the bacchanal roar of the songs of exultation still yelled from the London taverns, over the carnage of Mont St. Jean, and the betrayal of Genoa, of Italy, of France' (*CPW* II, 124). He even defiantly puffed Hobhouse's Bonapartist history, *The Substance of Some Letters Written by an Englishman Resident in Paris during the last Reign of the Emperor Napoleon* (1816) (see Works, pp. 43–51 and Criticism, pp. 87, 92, 102).

Dialogues with Shelley

After travelling up the Rhine, Byron settled for a while in Switzerland. At Sécheron on 27 May he met Percy Bysshe Shelley and now commenced the most important literary friendship of his life (Robinson 1976). That summer, Byron rented the romantic Villa Diodati on Lake Geneva near Shelley's house, and the two men spent the next three months constantly in each other's company. Their meeting was no accident, for Shelley admired Byron's verse and had sent him a copy of his own youthful poem, *Queen Mab*. His eighteen-year-old mistress and later wife, Mary Godwin (daughter of the philosophical anarchist William Godwin and feminist writer Mary Wollstonecraft), had already been introduced to Byron in London by her younger step-sister Mary Jane 'Claire' Clairmont, who had instigated an affair with the poet before his departure. Byron was a magnet for other British writers who flooded into Italy, now that the end of the wars made travel possible, and especially for disappointed liberals who now made the liberation of the Italians from their Austrian imperial government a new cause to set alongside Philhellenism.

Shelley and Byron were both aristocratic radicals self-exiled because of their politics and sexual permissiveness. But Shelley's atheism and Godwinian progressivism were in contrast to Byron's dark pessimism, which consisted of Humean skepticism in uneasy dialectic with a Calvinist conviction of damnation (Priestman 1999: 238–44). Shelley was perhaps the first intellectual who both took Byron seriously as a poet and challenged him to defend his philosophy. Their conversations that summer influenced the second half of the third canto of *Childe Harold's Pilgrimage*, the most idealistic and Wordsworthian of Byron's poems (see Works, pp. 37–43). Even the returning pessimism of 'The Dream', 'Darkness', 'The Prisoner of Chillon', 'Prometheus' and the agonized *Manfred* may be seen as generated by Byron's need to answer Shelley's visionary liberalism with philosophical depth of his own. Also, both poets were inspired by each other's literary experimentation and preoccupations, for example, with orientalism, the Gothic, the myth of Prometheus, the representation of sibling incest, and subjectivity and solipsism.

One thundery June night, Byron instigated a ghost-story competition amongst the group. The only successful attempt was Mary Shelley's *Frankenstein* (1818), though Byron's doctor, John Polidori, later published *The Vampyre*, which would become one of the inspirations behind Bram Stoker's *Dracula*. The week following the competition, Shelley and Byron read the work of Jean-Jacques Rousseau together, explored places associated with the Swiss philosopher and visited the Chateau de Chillon (see Works, p. 41). The Shelley party departed at the end of August. Claire went on to bear Byron a daughter, Allegra, on 12 January 1817, whom her father brought up until her death in 1822, but Byron and Claire's relationship was a short and acrimonious one.

After the Shelleys and Claire had returned to Britain, Byron toured the Bernese Alps with Hobhouse in September 1816 and kept a journal of his impressions for his sister (*BLJ* V, 96–105). Shelley delivered the manuscript of Canto III of *Childe Harold's Pilgrimage* to Murray, together with *The Prisoner of Chillon*, a moving dramatic monologue spoken by an inmate of the castle dungeon. The publisher paid the enormous sum of 2,000 guineas for the manuscript. By now, Byron was accepting remuneration for his verse and even haggling for more. At this time also, Byron renewed his acquaintance with the novelist and cultural theorist Madame de Staël at her country house at Coppet. The poet had long been an admirer of Staël's work, and her travelogue-novel *Corinne, or Italy* (1807) influenced the fourth canto of *Childe Harold's Pilgrimage* which would be published on 28 April, 1818 (Wilkes 1999: 100–38). He met many of her circle of European intellectuals, which included literary critic August Wilhelm von Schlegel, whose *Lectures on Dramatic Art and Literature* (1815) Byron read in translation.

Byron may have been partly inspired by Schlegel's enthusiasm for Renaissance theatre in composing his first experimental lyrical drama, *Manfred* (1817), as well as by hearing the Gothic novelist, M. G. Lewis translate passages from German poet Johann Wolfgang von Goethe's verse drama, *Faust* (see Works, p. 59). However, in the 1820s, he would react against Schlegel's idolisation of 'Romantic' or Shakespearian drama by adopting a neo-classical stress on the unities in his later plays.

Italy, its culture and politics

On 5 October 1816, Byron and Hobhouse travelled to Italy, which would remain the poet's chosen domicile for seven years. It was a collection of regions and city-states, never having been a unified 'country', except in the eyes of classically educated tourists and its conqueror, Napoleon. Much of it had been given to the Hapsburg Austrian Empire by the Congress of Vienna (1815). The experience of colonialism was beginning to generate patriotic feeling, but, as with 'Greece', local rivalries impeded the development of this into nineteenth-century nationalism. Byron was instrumental in promoting the concept of nationalism in Italy through rhetorical verse, such as the fourth and final canto of *Childe Harold's Pilgrimage* (1818) (see Works, pp. 43–51). This fictionalised his own tour of Italy, which country became the focus of his political ideals for some years. He had already studied the language and history and now saturated himself in Italian literature past and present (Vassallo 1984: 1–23). As with his predecessors, Chaucer and Shakespeare, the influence of Italian poetry was the key to Byron's greatest verse. Until his death he experimented with Italian forms and metre: *terza rima*, *ottava rima*, neo-classical tragedy and extempore burlesque comedy, for example.

The friends stayed in Milan in October 1816, meeting literati and 'patriots' such as Ludivico de Breme, dramatist Silvio Pellico, poet Vincenzo Monti, writer Pietro Borsieri and the French novelist Henri Beyle, later known as 'Stendhal'. With the help of these new friends, Byron read some satires of Pietro Buratti in Venetian dialect. He learned to appreciate the different local cultures of northern Italy. Then he travelled to Venice itself, whose melancholy decayed grandeur appealed greatly to Byron's mood. Like many Britons, he thought of his native land as a successor to Venice in founding its own maritime empire. He continued his study of the dialect with Marianna Segati, his landlord's young wife, who rapidly became his mistress. That winter, while his antiquarian friend Hobhouse toured Italy, Byron lived quietly at Venice, reading much and keeping his mind sharp by studying Armenian at the monastery of San Lazzaro. He enjoyed explaining to friends back in puritan Britain that so relaxed were Italian sexual mores that Venetian wives could openly take one declared lover or *cavalier servente*. He experienced the colourful carnival and regularly attended literary salons.

The poet resumed sightseeing in spring 1817, visiting Padua, Ferrara, Bologna, Florence and then exploring Rome with Hobhouse. When he returned to Venice in June, Byron rented the Villa Foscarini at La Mira and devoted himself to reading and writing. He had completed his first verse drama, *Manfred*, which was published on 16 June, and now began writing a series of important poems inspired by the landscape, culture and politics of Italy. 'The Lament of Tasso' was an example of his continuing preoccupation with ventriloquising exiled, imprisoned or misunderstood genius. The theme was continued in the elegiac fourth and final canto of *Childe Harold's Pilgrimage*, completed that year.

This began with a meditation on Venice and then followed a sort of secular pilgrimage to Rome. The third canto had hymned nature, but in the fourth Italy is apprehended via art, as the narrator remembers its representation in literature by the great medieval and Renaissance poets Petrarch (Francesco Petrarca), Giovanni Boccaccio, Alighieri Dante, Ludivico Ariosto and Torquato Tasso, as well as the eighteenth-century dramatist Vittorio Alfieri. The shape of the fourth canto was determined more by the conventions of travel than the subjectivity of the traveller. Also, as we shall see in Part 3, critics have felt that Byron's later incorporation of many additional stanzas to the first draft made this last canto more disjointed and dislocated in mood than its predecessor (see Works, **p. 43** and Criticism, **p. 105**). On the other hand, Byron found his own voice in embracing such disjunctions, when the melancholic narrator views Italy's ruins, contemplating the discrepancy between its cities' former republican glories and degraded present. As the French revolution passed into history, art was seen as the only hope of preserving the ideals of freedom for the future.

Hobhouse published his antiquarian notes on the sites mentioned in the poem in a separate volume. The canto and the accompanying *Historical Illustrations to the Fourth Canto of Child Harold's Pilgrimage* were both published by Murray on 28 April 1818. Cantos III and IV of *Childe Harold's Pilgrimage* were greater poems than anything Byron had ever written before, and the best British critics acknowledged as much. But the vituperation of Byron in the press increased in intensity because of his outspoken criticism of British foreign policy and reputation as a libertine. He eventually made Italy his home until he departed for Greece in 1823.

In August 1817 Byron took or was taken by another mistress, Margarita Cogni. In fact he threw himself into a frenzied round of pleasure and sexual dissipation for the next two years that shocked his English friends. That October, Byron wrote an experimental poem inspired by the Venetian carnival, *Beppo* (1818). This was the poet's first attempt at a burlesque comic tale in the style of the fifteenth-century Italian writer, Luigi Pulci, who wrote in a disarmingly digressive manner in *ottava rima* metre. Byron had been visited in September 1817 by his friends Douglas Kinnaird and William Stewart Rose, who presented him with a copy of John Hookham Frere's poem, *Whistlecraft* (1817). This was a very mildly satiric mock-heroic in the style of Pulci, with a garrulous narrator and medley style. Byron seized upon the Pulcian maner, which he knew would admirably suit his own confessional writing persona, with its 'mobility' of temperament that changed mercurially from melancholy to passionate joy. He aimed to recreate in English verse an impression of the Italian art of improvisation.

But Byron wanted to sharpen not blunt the edge of Pulcian burlesque. He was inspired by the example of another Italian poet, the eighteenth-century satirist Giambattista Casti, whose subject matter was the sexual hypocrisy of the *ancien régime*. In March 1818 he read W. S. Rose's free translation of Casti's *Animali Parlanti* published anonymously in 1816 as *The Court of Beasts*. Though he pronounced it 'excellent', Byron, who spoke and read Italian, was doubtless aware that Rose had toned down the politics of the original, which had been inspired by the French Enlightenment philosopher Voltaire's contempt for all political systems and condemnation of imperial warfare (Vassallo 1984:111). These were Byron's views too, and, if *Beppo* succeeded, he decided to use his new writing style in composing an ambitious indictment of the *ancien régime* in Europe on the eve of the French Revolution. Byron published *Beppo* anonymously, for it was a trial balloon to see how the public responded. It was an immediate success. Quite a few readers took some persuading that the melancholy poet mocked as 'Mr Cypress' in comic novelist Thomas Love Peacock's *Nightmare Abbey* (1818) had written this bawdy comedy.

Byron began his sexual satire *Don Juan* in July 1818, when he knew for certain *Beppo* had been acclaimed, and he would publish the poem in various installments so that he could ascertain its popularity before continuing (see Works, **pp. 62–5**). Percy Shelley visited him on 23 August, and they rode together along the lido discussing poetry, philosophy and politics. Shelley fictionalised the occasion in 'Julian and Maddalo'. Shelley had urged his friend to consecrate his powers to a great epic on the subject of the French Revolution. But since *Don Juan* was not the type of work he had in mind, the younger poet attempted the task himself (*The Revolt of Islam* 1818). Nevertheless, Shelley was one of the few of Byron's contemporaries to recognise and respect the originality of *Don Juan*: the startling combination of Romantic idealism with bitter irony.

Of course, the new satire was inspired by personal grievances as well as by politics and philosophical skepticism. Byron wrote this sexual satire to revenge and justify himself after British society had turned its back on him because of his libertinism. For the same reason, he began to write his memoirs in the summer of 1818 for posthumous publication (*BLJ* VI, 261). By October 1819 he had entrusted them to his friend Thomas Moore, who was allowed to show them to whomever he pleased. In September 1821, he instructed Murray to request copies of his letters from early correspondents, so that Moore could use them in composing a biography. We can see that – expecting obloquy – Byron was consciously attempting to shape and control the construction of the image he would leave posterity. That summer, as well as beginning *Don Juan* and the memoirs, the prolific poet had written another verse tale, *Mazeppa*, in which an old soldier wryly tells the story of his youthful passion.

The myth of the legendary lover Don Juan had originated in the Spanish monk Tirso de Molina's morality play *El Burlador de Sevilla* (1630), but had been adopted and adapted by various European playwrights, including the eminent

French dramatist Jean-Baptiste Poquelin (Molière). At Venice, Byron would certainly have seen the opera *Don Giovanni* by Wolfgang Amadeus Mozart and Lorenzo da Ponte, and Goldoni's comedy, adapted from Molière's, *Don Giovanni Tenorio, o sia Il Dissoluto* (Boyd 1958: 35). Neither was the legend merely the preserve of high art: during Byron's lifetime there was a craze for the character in popular London theatres, which rivalled each other with numerous burlesques and pantomimes, where the Don had metamorphosed from an impious overreacher, thankfully consigned to Hell, into the pasteboard villain of musical comedy (Haslett 1997: 36–51). Byron's poem is different from most manifestations of the legend in portraying the Don sympathetically and having the women, more often than not, taking the sexual initiative.

Byron saw an opportunity here for fictionalised autobiography and self-justification. He may well have been responding to poet and critic Samuel Taylor Coleridge's criticism of the deleterious morality of seductive Byronic anti-heroes, glamorised and excused by their authors. Coleridge, in Chapter 23 of *Biographia Literaria* (1817), called instead for a contemporary update of the seventeenth-century dramatist Thomas Shadwell's didactic tragedy *The Libertine*, where Don Juan is a straightforward villain shown being sent to Hell. Coleridge speculated that the anarchy into which the French Revolution had descended would be an appropriate modern version of Hell, demonstrating where religious skepticism and sexual promiscuity led. Byron answered this appeal with a version of the myth which denounced not libertinism but hypocrisy. He began with an attack on his wife and all the female moralists of the nineteenth century, whose passion for reforming the world, he thought, was a disguised play for power. But he did plan to have Juan eventually guillotined in the Terror, though, not as a villain, but as a naïvely utopian aristocratic idealist (*BLJ* VIII, 78).

By 19 September Byron had completed the first canto of *Don Juan*, together with a satirical prefatory 'dedication' to the Tory poet laureate, Robert Southey, with whom Byron had commenced a feud. He abominated Southey (as well as his fellow Lake poets, William Wordsworth and S. T. Coleridge) because he saw him as a renegade who had abandoned his earlier radical views (he had supported the French Revolution) in order strenuously to support the Church, King, Tory Government and Empire (see Life and Contexts, pp. 23–4 and Works, pp. 64–5). As always, while he waited for the reaction of Murray and his circle, Byron sent on extra stanzas and emendations. Though he was an egoist, Byron also needed reassurance about new work. The heavily revised manuscript is evidence that his mastering of the new stanza and style, and his carefully crafted impression of extempore careless writing, had actually cost him much effort.

By mid-January 1819, Murray's coterie had sent the poet news of their unanimous decision that the poem was unpublishable because of its sexual freedom, its radical politics and its satirical attacks on individuals. After a battle by post where the poet defended his new work and defined his intentions in it (see *BLJ* VI, 67, 76, 91, 94–9, 101, 104–7), Byron made some concessions, such as omitting the mock dedication and stanzas castigating the foreign secretary Viscount Castlereagh, for allying himself with dynastic imperialism in the Congress of Vienna. He had meanwhile written a second canto and both were published on 15 July 1819 after an exciting advertising campaign. But the poet had to agree to the indignity of the poem being published anonymously and without even the publisher's name, in an attempt to avoid prosecution. Even then, Murray disobeyed Byron's instruction of 'no more gelding' by substituting asterisks for some passages.

Don Juan was written at a time of working-class turbulent agitation for reform. Now that the war against France was over, it could no longer be painted as unacceptably unpatriotic to criticise the Establishment. Chartists and early socialists criticised British society as corrupt from top to bottom: from the profligate Regent, the Prince of Wales, to the unrepresentative Houses of Parliament, to the rapacity and brutalities of empire and unrestrained capitalism's creation of urban slums and poverty in the newly expanded cities. The year 1819, when the poem was published, saw the 'Peterloo Massacre' when the government congratulated the yeomanry for charging a peaceful meeting of men, women and children at St Peter's field, Manchester, and killing and injuring several. Radicals, such as Byron and Shelley, were outraged. However, the Government was terrified that lower-class demands for democracy meant that a repetition of the French Revolution was on hand, and they blamed the power of print for spreading inflammatory ideas. The infamous Six Acts were passed, which included measures against the circulation of political literature and increases in paper tax and stamp tax to prevent cheap newspapers. Already harsh penalties of long imprisonment for seditious and blasphemous libel were augmented; now a second offence incurred banishment for seven years.

What did all this have to do with a Romantic poem by an expatriate nobleman? Byron's *Don Juan* put the authorities in an awkward position. The work of an aristocrat, it was published by a staunchly Tory publisher whose periodical, the *Quarterly Review*, had links with the government. But when the poem wasn't prosecuted, despite its liberalism and libertinism, radical propagandists – such as William Hone – were quick to point the finger at the double standard and renew their calls for a free press and an end to censorship. The pirates took advantage of Murray's timorousness and undercut his expensive editions. He initially hesitated to sue them for infringing his copyright, since the poem had come out minus the author's or publisher's names, to protect the publisher from being prosecuted and imprisoned for obscenity or sedition.

Byron received the handsome sum of 2,000 guineas for *Mazeppa*, the 'Ode on Venice' and the first installment of *Don Juan*. But since his disgrace and because of his radical politics, Byron had lost favour with the wealthy readers of his 'years of fame' (*BLJ* VI, 237). He was in great demand, however, from a burgeoning lower-class readership, and *Don Juan* would become a staple text of working-class reformers in the years before 1832. However, the respectable Murray would be very reluctant to publish any more of the poem in the future, especially as it caused an outcry in the conservative and religious periodicals.

At the beginning of April, Byron met and fell in love with the teenage Countess Teresa Guiccioli, who was married to a sixty-year-old wealthy and slightly sinister aristocrat. They lived in Ravenna, the capital of the province of Romagna, in north-eastern Italy. He wrote her, 'Now I love *you*, there is no other woman in the world for me' (*BLJ* VI, 112), gave up his libertine lifestyle and became her acknowledged *cavalier servente*. In June Byron visited Ravenna to be with Teresa. In August he followed the Guicciolis to Bologna, then returned to Venice with Teresa in September. At the end of 1819 he stayed with the Guicciolis in Ravenna before finding his own house there, opposite the tomb of Dante. He identified with the medieval Italian poet, whom he saw as an Italian patriot. Dante, like Byron, had been exiled from his home city and misunderstood in his own lifetime. By July 1820, Teresa formally separated from her husband and would live with Byron until he departed for Greece.

Byron steeped himself in the literature, culture and politics of his adopted country. He continued *Don Juan*, boasting to friends about the poem's unique burlesque conversational style (*BLJ* VI, 232); discussing his plans for the hero (*BLJ* VI, 206–8); and trying to persuade the reluctant Murray to continue publication of more stories of the epic lover. He also set himself some tough exercises. He began a close translation of the first canto of Pulci's sprawling epic poem, *Morgante Maggiore*, to get more attuned to the literary techniques of one of his models (Vassallo 1984: 143–55). He had been reading Dante's *Divine Comedy*, both in translation and in the original Italian. In the summer of 1819 he began writing *The Prophecy of Dante* in the tricky *terza rima* metre. As with *ottava rima*, the metre is easier in Italian which has more rhyming words than English. Byron had also long admired the patriot dramatist Vittorio Alfieri, and he adopted him as a model when he began a strict neo-classical tragedy, *Marino Faliero*, conforming to the unities. All these literary enterprises may be seen as evidence of the serious and disciplined honing of his craft and extension of his range and belie the poet's pose of aristocratic indolence and carelessness, affected whenever he wrote of poetry to his friends.

By early 1820 Byron had completed *The Prophecy of Dante*, where the medieval poet is made to speak from beyond the grave: the very embodiment of Italian patriotism. The poem appeals to the Italians to forget their local rivalries and to unite in revolution. He had also completed the third and fourth cantos of *Don Juan*. But Murray had now applied for an injunction to suppress the piracies of the first installment, and Byron himself became worried that if this was denied on grounds of obscenity and blasphemy, he might lose paternal rights to custody of his legitimate daughter Ada, as had happened to Shelley over the publication of *Queen Mab*. He even offered to refund the money he had already received for the copyright of the first two cantos. In the event, the Chancellor granted the injunction. But Byron was nervous enough to urge that anonymity be continued in publishing Cantos III and IV. However, Murray procrastinated. He had no wish to publish any more of *Don Juan* or any overly contentious verse, yet could not bring himself to sever his flatteringly close relationship with his most prestigious and aristocratic client.

Later, Byron's enthusiasm for the poem revived. He began the fifth canto in autumn 1820 and by the end of the year had sent the completed manuscript to his financial adviser, Douglas Kinnaird, preparatory to negotiations with Murray in publishing Cantos III, IV and V together. The poet defiantly refused to consider killing the Don off. In fact, he ebulliently sketched for Murray his further plans for the hero, who was to have many more adventures in Europe before being guillotined in the French Revolution (*BLJ* VIII, 78). But Murray was silent. All was at a standstill regarding publication.

Meanwhile Byron was becoming involved in Italian revolutionary politics. Teresa's father, Count Ruggero Gamba Ghiselli and brother Pietro were the leaders of the Romagnan Carbonari, a secret society plotting to overthrow the

Austrian government. In summer 1820, Byron, who was popular amongst the poor because of his charity, had become initiated into the Carbonari as honorary leader of the *Turba* or section of working men. He allowed his mansion to be used as their arsenal and helped to plot an uprising. Despite this, when the district commandant was assassinated outside his house, he had the body carried inside and described the incident in *Don Juan* V, 33–9. The poet was watched closely by spies and his letters were opened by the authorities. The fourth canto of *Childe Harold's Pilgrimage* and *The Prophecy of Dante* were proscribed in Italy because they fomented Italian nationalism. Byron's letters were full of guarded references to his hopes for the revolution, but then the leaders were betrayed just in time to stop the plot, on 24 February 1821. The Ravenna journal which the poet kept from 4 January to February 1821 (*BLJ* VIII, 11–51), and 'Detached Thoughts' intermittently from 15 October 1821 to 18 May 1822 (*BLJ* IX, 11–52) give a detailed impression of his day-to-day life, reading and reminiscences at this time.

In despair over the failure of the uprising, Byron threw himself into finishing *Marino Faliero*, an historical play set in Renaissance Venice, which nevertheless echoes this contemporary context of revolution. Byron had been struck by the black-veiled empty space amongst portraits of the doges when he had visited the Ducal Palace at Venice, and felt inspired by the story of the duke who had conspired with the artisans to overthrow the aristocratic oligarchy and restore true republicanism (see Works, **p. 78** and Criticism, **p. 117**). He personally identified with this romantic idea of a noble but charismatic leader of the People, both in Italy and even (in fantasy anyway) in Luddite Nottinghamshire.

The year of 1821 saw the death of Byron's fallen hero, Napoleon Bonaparte. Though the French Revolution had been extinguished, its ideals were invoked that year in the Greek War of Independence, in Simón Bolívar's Venezuelan war of independence against Spain and in the uprising of Naples, which was suppressed like that of Romagna. It was the year in which Byron devoted himself to writing disciplined tragedy to express his political and liberal views. He had decided that he himself and the other poets we now label 'Romantics' were on the wrong tack in embracing the lyrical impulse so wholeheartedly in their verse, because it could lead to solipsism and sentimentalism. He felt that the satiric tradition, so prevalent in the eighteenth century, had endowed the poet with the valuable role of critic of society and should therefore be preserved. He wrote two letters in defence of Alexander Pope to the sonneteer Revd William Lisle Bowles, who had disparaged Pope's poetry, and published a letter to Murray on 31 March 1821 on the same subject.

Byron also fulminated against 'bardolatry' and the pseudo-Elizabethan plays of his contemporaries. Though Byron was not a very impressive theorist and critic of poetry, he was sincere in his attempt at this time to embrace a severe neoclassicism in his historical dramas, which he thought more appropriate to their politics, and he wanted each play to focus on one moral dilemma rather than an extravagant web of story (*BLJ* VIII, 57, 210). In spite of his intentions, the plays do have strongly Romantic elements, however, such as an intense concentration on the psyche of the protagonist. Byron's experience as a member of the Drury Lane subcommittee had convinced him that an irremediable fracture had developed between page and stage. Serious dramatists could rarely now please the popular audience. Therefore, experimental drama, especially with political or religious themes, could only be produced for the private reader in his study (Simpson 1998).

These issues came to a crisis when four days after its publication on 21 April 1821, a severely censored version of *Marino Faliero* was staged in Drury Lane without Byron's or Murray's permission. Though the lower classes cheered such liberal sentiments as had been left in, the performance was not a tremendous success, mainly because the actors were under-prepared. Though he might have been swayed had he tasted the honey of popular acclaim, Byron always firmly declared himself to be writing for the 'closet' (*BLJ* VIII, 59, 64). He continued writing two more historical dramas: *Sardanapalus* and *The Two Foscari*.

Teresa objected to his writing the bawdy *Don Juan*, and Byron used this as an excuse to discontinue the poem. The announcement of this seems to have broken the stalemate with the reluctant Murray, who eventually published Cantos III, IV and V on 8 August 1821. They were a great success, causing a traffic jam outside Murray's offices in Albemarle Street, Piccadilly, where copies had to be thrown out of the window to the booksellers' messengers. Byron wrote a series of letters to the publisher and his circle, in which he reasserted his belief in the value of the poem which they so much deplored (*BLJ* VIII, 192, 198, 209; IX, 54).

The Pisan circle, *The Liberal* and the break with Murray

In July 1821 Teresa's father and brother were banished from the Romagna because of their suspected involvement in the failed uprising. As a separated woman, Teresa was compelled to live under her father's roof, so she left with them for Florence. Byron stayed on in Ravenna until October in a frenzy of writing. He began the iconoclastic biblical dramas *Cain* and *Heaven and Earth*. In these plays Byron used biblical stories to question the notion of original sin and the function of evil and suffering in the world and to imagine a universe ruled by an authoritarian tyrannical Old Testament deity. Sceptical questioning of religious precepts was interwoven with an acceptance of the inevitability of sinfulness and damnation, producing a dark vision of an irrational cosmos.

These plays were so tendentious in their questioning of orthodoxy that Byron had to write to Murray denying that Lucifer's speeches in *Cain* reflected the author's views (*BLJ* IX, 53–4, 103). On 19 December 1821 were published *Sardanapalus*, *The Two Foscari* and *Cain*. The skepticism of the latter caused an outcry among the clergy and immediately attracted the attention of radical publishers and pirates (see Works, **pp. 79–83**). Murray appealed to the Chancellor, but the poem was declared to be blasphemous and was therefore free to be pirated without prosecution. (This was an unintentionally absurd effect of the laws of the time.) The plays were harshly criticised by Jeffrey in the *Edinburgh Review*, and even Hobhouse denounced *Cain* in a letter to his friend. Byron felt that the educated public had turned against him.

The poet also completed two satires: *The Blues* was a weak squib, but *The Vision of Judgment* was a brilliant parody in *ottava rima* of Poet Lareate Robert Southey's pompous and clumsily written apotheosis of the late King George III's beatification and entry into Heaven. Byron had been incandescent with rage at the preface to Southey's poem which referred obliquely to him as the leading light of 'the Satanic school' of poetry, whose obscene poem (*Don Juan*) was poisoning the waters of literature. Southey even pictured Byron repenting on his deathbed in vain! Byron was careful, therefore, to use Horatian geniality, not Juvenalian harshness, in his satiric riposte, in order the better to bring out the intolerant sectarian hatred underlying Southey's religiosity (*BLJ* IX, 62). He intended the satire for anonymous publication. Southey had already written to *The Courier*, protesting against an earlier attack on him in a note appended by Byron to *The Two Foscari*. The feud had been fuelled by rumours and gossip. For the exiled poet had been told that Southey had circulated rumours that Byron and Shelley had formed a 'league of incest' with Shelley and the 'two daughters of Godwin' in Switzerland in 1816, while doubtless Southey had been informed by the Murray circle of Byron's suppressed satiric dedication of *Don Juan* to him, where his attempts at poetic sublimity were likened to a man having intercourse without being able to achieve climax.

Shelley visited Byron that August, and the friends decided to settle in Pisa, where they would form an expatriate community with other liberal writers such as Edward Williams, John Taaffe and Edward Trelawny (Cline 1952). Byron's writing career post–1816 should be seen in the context of his perception that he could take on the leadership of a new generation of Romantic poets on the liberal/ radical side in politics and make war on the older generation who had become supporters of the Tories and enemies of reform. The irony was that his own publisher, Murray, ran the *Quarterly Review*, of which Robert Southey and the pro-Establishment acerbic critic John Wilson Croker were the leading lights.

Byron had always enjoyed the cut and thrust of competition amongst the literary coteries and cabals of literary London. In Regency times the hugely influential periodicals were intensely ideological, and reviewing could be brutal. Byron and Shelley were impatient with the opponent of the *Quarterly Review*, the heavy, Whiggish *Edinburgh Review*, which was old-fashioned in its literary judgements. Byron had long thought of founding his own more radical and lively periodical, and Shelley was equally keen. Shelley, and now even Byron, experienced difficulty in having radical works published. Both wanted some control over the publication process. It was becoming painfully obvious that Murray was unwilling to publish more of Byron's increasingly radical poetry, such as *Heaven and Earth* or *The Vision of Judgment* (*BLJ* IX, 118, 136, 163). Murray had set up the former in press but after the outcry about *Cain*, he could not bring himself to print. Byron wrote to him repeatedly without effect. The successful partnership of many years was about to break up.

In 1822, the two poets invited Shelley's friend, the poet and journalist Leigh Hunt, to join them. Byron knew Hunt and had visited him in prison in 1813 when he was serving a two-year sentence for libel on the Prince Regent, for contradicting in rudely explicit detail a sycophantic Tory newspaper which had described the corpulent heir to the throne as 'an Adonis of loveliness'. Leigh and his brother John Hunt had run the brilliant radical newspaper, *The Examiner*, for fourteen years. This supported many humanitarian causes. It also drew attention to a whole panoply of abuses from the dissolute royal family and unreformed parliament, to the corruption and patronage running through the professions and administration. Hunt combined radical politics with cultural commentary. He was an astute and influential literary critic and had been a mentor to Shelley as well as the younger John Keats. His influence was sufficient to stimulate the Tory wits of *Blackwood's Edinburgh Magazine* to lampoon and deride the 'Cockney School' at every opportunity (Cox 1998: 30–7).

Shelley wrote to Hunt on 26 August 1821 to invite him to help them run the journal, and Hunt arranged for his nephew to edit *The Examiner* in his absence, since his brother John had again been imprisoned for libel. Meanwhile, in November, Byron took up residence in a grand and historic mansion, the Casa Lanfranchi in Pisa. In January 1822 he received an addition to his coffers on the death of his mother-in-law, to add to the comfortable income he received from interest on the capital realised following the sale of Newstead. Hunt therefore saw him as an aristocratic patron. But Byron was becoming miserly and was especially unwilling to be regarded as a bottomless purse, when he realised, on getting to know Hunt better, that the latter was incapable of managing money. Nevertheless, in February 1822, he paid for the Hunt family to travel to Pisa and invited them to stay with him. They arrived at the beginning of July. But within days of this, tragedy struck. On 8 July, Percy Shelley and Edward Williams were drowned in a sailing accident.

Byron, Hunt, and Shelley's friend, the adventurer Edward Trelawny, searched the beaches for Shelley's body, until they were informed on 18 July that it had been found with Hunt's copy of Keats's *Lamia* still in his jacket pocket. They ceremoniously cremated the body on the beach, so the ashes could be interred in the Protestant cemetery in Rome. Byron's grief, coming on top of the recent death of his natural daughter, Allegra, was channelled into writing and into making a success of the journal. This was fuelled by disgust at the gloating treatment of the accident by Tory newspapers.

Byron tried hard to get his friend Thomas Moore to contribute to the new periodical, which he had named *The Liberal* (*BLJ* IX, 183, 197). But Moore, Hobhouse and all Byron's Whiggish old friends disapproved of the Hunt circle as too radical. Hunt and Byron had more success when they invited left-wing journalist and brilliant essayist, William Hazlitt, to contribute to the new magazine. Byron also wrote to Leigh's brother John, newly released from gaol, instructing him to collect miscellaneous manuscripts from Murray, including *The Vision of Judgment*, for publication in the journal. Out of spite, Murray disobeyed Byron's written instructions to include the preface, in which Byron attempted to evade prosecution by explaining that the poem's target was Southey rather than the Monarch. This action facilitated the prosecution of John Hunt when the satire appeared in the first number of *The Liberal* on 15 October 1822. Murray also published the innocuous popular play, *Werner*, without Byron's permission on 23 November. Simultaneously, he showed around some gossipy letters previously received from Byron, which spoke disrespectfully of Hunt and the journal, thus causing maximum embarrassment to the venture. This spelt the end of Byron and Murray's business relationship, and Byron withdrew from him on 18 November 1822, though he continued to write to him as a friend. Byron told Hunt he believed Murray was being used by the establishment to muzzle him.

Murray certainly did all he could to scupper the new periodical by relaying and exaggerating adverse criticism of it and of Hunt. In this he eventually succeeded, for Byron's name was its main draw and the poet lost heart with it too soon, as we shall see. For all his swagger, his confidence was easily dented. The first number featured one of his best poems, *The Vision of Judgment*, together with some scurrilous epigrams on Castlereagh and a boyish spoof addressed to the editor of the reactionary *British Review*. Also included were Percy Shelley's fine translation of the Walpurgisnacht scene from Goethe's *Faust*, together with a stirring preface, chatty travelogue and other satirical and humorous pieces from Hunt. The periodical was an original and lively miscellany, much in contrast with the heavy quarterlies of the day. It caused enormous controversy: producing the prosecution of John Hunt for seditious libel on account of the *Vision* and inspiring right-wing parodies (see Criticism, p. 90). In consequence, it sold very well, though Hunt had overestimated the number of copies needed, so the first number made a financial loss (Marshall 1960: 118–34).

Byron had also been newly inspired by the presence of Shelley, Hunt and the excitement of the journal scheme to resume *Don Juan* that July. He had decided 'in the present clash of philosophy and tyranny, to throw away the scabbard' (*BLJ* IX, 191). The centrepiece of the new cantos he now wrote was 'a technical description of a modern siege' and 'satire upon heroes and despots' of dynastic imperialism (*BLJ* IX, 196). By Christmas 1822 he had seven more cantos ready for publication and now offered them to Leigh's brother, the publisher John Hunt, for publication at the author's risk (see Works, p. 62). Byron wanted to try retaining the copyright and taking a proportion of any profits instead. By May 1823, eleven unpublished cantos had mounted up. Before he left for Greece Byron arranged for Hunt to publish them all and to provide cheap editions to rival the pirates. He had written a searing new preface, championing the freedom of the press on behalf of the radical publishers as well as himself and rededicating the poem to the liberal cause (see Works, p. 71). Hunt was the most respectable of the radical publishers, but he was still beyond the pale as far as the conservatives of the literary world were concerned. Murray's coterie completely failed to understand why a British lord would ally himself with such people. They could only suppose he was a poseur who courted singularity.

On 1 January 1823 the second number of *The Liberal* was published with Byron's Biblical drama on Noah's Flood, *Heaven and Earth*, the leading piece (see Works, p. 79). Contributions from Mary and the late Percy Shelley, William Hazlitt, Hunt and others provided a medley of poetry, essays, fiction, and discussions of Italian culture. By February 1823, Byron finished a satire, *The Age of Bronze*, and a verse tale, *The Island*, on the mutiny of *The Bounty*, both of which he wrote for the periodical. But ironically, though the second number would be extremely well received, reports only now began to arrive in Italy of the ferocious attacks in literary London mounted on the first number.

Instead of riding out the storm, Byron began to panic. Rather than realising that the furore was an indirect compliment, he decided that the journal was a failure and that his own personal unpopularity was to blame. He withdrew the *Age of Bronze* and *The Island* from it, so that the next two numbers contained only his weak satire *The Blues* and the translation from Pulci. It was widely assumed that he had pulled out of the venture, and this rumour sounded the death knell of *The Liberal*.

The Greek War of Independence

Byron now decided to consecrate his remaining energies to supporting the war for Greek independence from the Ottoman empire. He was visited by Edward Blaquiere, from the London Greek committee, who flattered him that he could become a leading man of action on this heroic scene. Actually the committee wanted to use his magnetic personality as a figurehead to attract others to the cause. Byron agreed to depart and provide them information on the course of the war. He instructed Kinnaird to raise ready money, and chartered a brig, the *Hercules*, then ordered showy uniforms and helmets in which to make his entrance on the theatre of war.

In all the emotional upheaval that his imminent departure caused for Teresa, and in tying up his financial support for Leigh Hunt and for Mary Shelley, tempers flared, recriminations began, and Byron managed to alienate both the latter. He went on board on 13 July, with Teresa's brother, Pietro Gamba, and Trelawny, and they eventually landed at Argostoli, Cephalonia on 3 August. His arrival caused a sensation. If Greece was exotic terrain to the poet, then the British lord was in turn a picturesque sight to the inhabitants. He became a magnet to all parties wanting funding and support. Byron took on some tough Suliote tribesmen as his bodyguard, but they soon became unruly. He now put the shrewd Scottish practical side of his personality into action, discarding his dreamy idealism and taking stock of the situation.

The year previously, after initial successes, the Greeks had elected Alexander Mavrocordatos their first president. However, the Greeks were riven by factionalism which was intensified when the Turks began to reassert themselves. The leaders of the provisional Greek government and churchmen lacked control over the local chiefs, who constituted Greek military strength, but who were short on nationalistic feeling and saw the conflict in purely religious terms as the extermination of Muslims. The Romaic population would have been content merely to drive out the Turks, leaving their regional governments untouched. It was Westerners and expatriate Greeks who had been educated in Europe who imagined a nation embodying the supposed restoration of Hellas (St Clair 1972: 150–94).

Byron was joined on 22 November 1823 by another agent of the London Greek committee, Colonel Leicester Stanhope – a radical influenced by the Utilitarian ideas of philosopher Jeremy Bentham, and great believer in enlightenment through education. A greater priority for this doctrinaire army officer than military supplies was the setting up of printing presses. He was nicknamed the 'typographical Colonel' by the poet, who, paradoxically, thought action should take precedent over words. Though their Philhellenism was of differing moulds, Byron tried to work with Stanhope. They set sail for the mainland and arrived in Missolonghi on 30 December 1823, after being menaced by Turkish ships and being blown onto rocks by a storm.

Byron soon met Mavrocordatos and settled himself into the officers' quarters where he and Stanhope began to plan forming an artillery corps and raising a loan for the provisional government to be administered by the British. Byron was glad when the fire master William Parry arrived with a consignment of military supplies and much practical experience. The plan was to take the nearby fortress of Lepanto.

The previous August the poet had helped some refugees, a Greek woman and her daughters who had been caught up in the fighting. The mother asked if her fifteen-year-old son, Lukas Chalandritsanos, could join them. Lukas became Byron's favourite, and what little poetry he wrote in the last months of his life were bittersweet lyrics, inspired by his patriotic desire to die nobly for the cause and his unrequited love for the boy. The most well known of these is the poem written on his birthday, 'On This Day I Complete My Thirty-Sixth Year'.

On 15 February 1824, Byron had a serious seizure, the first sign of the illness that would eventually prove fatal. His depression at the disunity of the Greeks, the unruliness of the Suliotes, the naivety of the Western Philhellenes and the continual call on his money from all quarters contributed to his continuing poor health. On 21 February there was an earthquake. The following month Byron was invited to meet the military leader Odysseus in Salona. Mavrocordatos would accompany him. Byron hoped to use the occasion as an opportunity to unite the military and governmental parties. He was then invited to visit the Greek Government at Kranidi in the Morea and to accept the office of Governor General of Greece (Marchand 1971: 444–60).

Whilst he was delayed by bad weather from the first of these projected journeys, Byron was laid low by a severe fever. As long as he had power to command, Byron resisted all attempts to bleed him. But, as he weakened, the doctors contributed to his end, as Byron guessed they would, with their purgatives and leeches, which drained his remaining strength. On Easter Monday, 19 April 1824, he died.

Byronism

Byron had done much to forge his own image and to encourage the cult of personality that made him a 'star'. However, the myth of Byron had a life of its own which outlasted the poet himself. His fine head and open-collared shirt was a recognisable image used not only by Murray to sell the poetry, but also adopted by the radical publisher and pirate William Benbow for his shop sign – for it had become an emblem of liberty. When the poet's literary executors and family decided to have the manuscript of Byron's memoirs, not published but cast into John Murray's fireplace, they unwittingly fed the flickering flames of scandal they intended to smother. Would-be readers probably imagined more salacious revelations than they actually contained. Byron would never be accepted by the Establishment and had to wait until the permissive 1960s before being commemorated in poets' corner, Westminster Abbey. Though Byron was the most popular British poet of the nineteenth century, quite soon after his death his poetry began to be unfavourably compared with that of Wordsworth by professional critics, engaged in forming the canon of English Literature now to be taught at schools and universities for the first time (Chew 1924: 258–62).

Byron was extremely influential, especially on his female contemporaries, Felicia Hemans and Letitia Landon: the former's evocation of Italian patriotism was accomplished enough to sting him into competitive jibes in his letters. His experiments with the dramatic monologue would inspire further innovation by

Victorian poets, Alfred, Lord Tennyson and Robert Browning. Women novelists were ambivalent about the poet's aristocratic individualism: his contemporaries Caroline Lamb and Mary Shelley fictionalised the poet himself in sinister portraits. The Brontë sisters, who read Byron's poetry avidly as girls, produced their own Byronic anti-heroes in their 1847 novels: Heathcliff of *Wuthering Heights* and Mr Rochester of *Jane Eyre*.

In 1869, the year of John Stuart Mill's feminist classic *The Subjection of Women*, the American novelist Harriet Beecher Stowe reactivated the gendered debate on the separation scandal by publishing for the first time the story of Byron's incest with his sister: information that her friend Lady Byron had confided to her. The Byron marriage was for Stowe, as for many women moralists and Victorian feminists, an illustration of the inequity of the marriage laws, and Byron an example of the domination of art by male libertinism. Other writers and artists assumed the Byronic pose and reworked it in their own Bohemian style. Some, such as novelist and dramatist Edward Bulwer Lytton and novelist and statesman Benjamin Disraeli, emulated the sexual ambiguity which shadowed the poet's performance of the Regency dandy (Elfenbein 1995), while the glamour of the fallen anti-hero became a staple of popular culture that has lasted into contemporary times (Wilson 1999).

Was Byron a Romantic?

This may seem a strange question, but up until twenty years ago, British and American scholars often defined Romanticism very narrowly. Though nominally included in the 'big six' male canonical British poets, Byron had become marginalised and even categorised as an anomaly (see Criticism, **p. 107**). The ostensible reason for this was Byron's use of satire and irony, which was construed as backward-looking and 'Augustan' rather than Romantic (see Criticism, **pp. 91–2, 100**). Of course, Byron mocked Romantic writing at times, including his own. He certainly vociferously championed Pope and experimented with neo-classical drama. Bernard Beatty has argued that Byron identified particularly with the 'exploratory pessimism and exuberant energies' of a particularly British unruly strand of eighteenth-century writing (in Bone 2004: 239). However, the uneasiness which some critics have felt about including Byron in the Romantic canon also stemmed from Byron's philosophical pessimism and scepticism, which were not congruent with Wordsworth's belief in the inspiration of Nature: the younger poet represented an unacceptably dark side of Romanticism (see Criticism, **p. 101**). Byron's revolutionary and nationalistic rhetoric continued to epitomise the ideology of Romanticism to European readers, even when mid twentieth-century British and American critics began cynically to cut the poet down to size, either as a poseur or as hopelessly backward-looking (West 1960, Martin 1982, Kelsall 1987). As we shall see in Part 3, Byron's critical fortunes changed when feminism and New Historicism together forced a much more inclusive view of writing in the period (see Criticism, **p. 107**). At last, Byron was once again acknowledged as one of the leading voices of European Romanticism.

Further reading

The best way to find out about Byron's life and times is to dip into his inimitable and lively letters: *Byron's Letters and Journals*, ed. L. A. Marchand, 13 vols (1973–94). A one-volume paperback selection, edited by Marchand, was published in 1982. Byron's friend Thomas Moore's *The Life, Letters and Journals of Byron* is a classic nineteenth-century biography, essential for Byronists (Moore 1860). Many other contemporaries wrote accounts of the poet's conversations, and Ernest J. Lovell, Jr. has arranged selections from these chronologically in a useful volume: *His Very Self and Voice, Collected Conversations of Lord Byron* (Lovell 1954). The most up-to-date reliable one-volume biography is Fiona MacCarthy's well-written *Byron: Life and Legend* (2002), though this is an account of the man rather than the poet. For a scholarly day-by-day chronology of the facts of Byron's life, consult for reference Leslie A. Marchand, *Byron: A Biography*, 3 vols (1957). There is also a condensed one-volume version (1971). For a medium-length account of the poet's writing life and participation in literary coteries, see Franklin (2000).

On Byron's ancestral home, see John Beckett with Sheila Aley's *Byron and Newstead: The Aristocrat and the Abbey* (2001). Allan Massie's *Byron's Travels* (1988) gives a brief but sound account of the poet's tours, with background information on the decline of the Ottoman Empire and the sporadic support for its Greek Christian subjects of Western powers, especially Russia, France and Britain who hoped to take advantage of their desire to rebel against the Turks. For information on Byron's marriage and the separation and its aftermath, consult Ethel Colburn Mayne's *The Life of Lady Byron* (1929). Margot Strickland gives brief entertaining biographies of the most important women in Byron's life in *The Byron Women* (1974), and his relationship with Teresa Guiccioli is portrayed in Iris Origo's *The Last Attachment* (1949). Byron's bisexuality is set in historical context in Crompton's critical biography *Byron and Greek Love* (1985). Studies of specific periods of the poet's life include Peter Quennell's readable *Byron: The Years of Fame* (1935) and *Byron in Italy* (1941). Scholarly accounts of Byron's participation in the Shelley and Leigh Hunt circle are provided in C. L. Cline, *Byron, Shelley and their Pisan circle* (1952), W.H. Marshall, *Byron, Shelley, Hunt and the Liberal* (1960) and in Nicholas Roe's recent biography of Hunt, *Fiery Heart: The First Life of Leigh Hunt* (2005). The role played by Byron in the Greek War of Independence is addressed by William St Clair in *That Greece Might Still Be Free* (1972); and Stephen Minta, *On a Voiceless Shore: Byron in Greece* (1998). Two books by Doris Langley Moore shed interesting light on Byron's life by taking unusual angles. *Lord Byron: Accounts Rendered* (1974) examines his finances and *The Late Lord Byron* details the events following the poet's death.

2

Works

Introduction

This section aims to introduce Byron's major works, to indicate the principal themes and literary features of the poems and to give suggestions for further reading. Byron was a prolific writer, so it has been necessary to be selective: for example, *The Giaour* is discussed in more detail than the other Oriental tales and *Cain* taken as an example of one of Byron's verse dramas. Quotations from the poetry are either by canto and stanza (in the case of a long poem such as *Childe Harold's Pilgrimage*), by act, scene and line in the dramas or by line number in poems not divided into stanzas. The text cited is *Lord Byron: The Complete Poetical Works* edited by Jerome J. McGann (abbreviated to *CPW*), whose notes should be consulted for more detailed information than is given here on likely dates of composition and the textual history of the poems. This will be especially necessary when studying *Childe Harold's Pilgrimage* and *Don Juan*, as they were published in parts over many years. McGann's notes on the different stages of publication provide evidence that the popularity of Byron did not just happen but came about as the result of the poet's deep immersion in the literary scene, especially when in professional collaboration with the firm of John Murray. Before he left England in 1816, Byron was closely involved in the publishing process and extremely responsive to readers' reactions. He was sometimes persuaded to tone down or remove contentious passages by Murray or his advisers. On the other hand, the poet habitually made additions, emendations and corrections not only while a work was being prepared for the press but to each of its early editions.

Hours of Idleness

Hours of Idleness, as its teenaged author readily admitted, was not a particularly original collection of lyrics (see Life and Contexts, p. 5 and Criticism, p. 85). Byron sometimes modelled himself, for example, on Thomas Moore's pseudonymous versifier 'Thomas Little' in his amorous verses to the beauties of Southwell or, in poems such as 'Childish Recollections', he emulated the youthful poet Henry Kirke White's nostalgia for schooldays, while in the stirring heroic prose of 'The Death of Calmar and Orla' he also imitated James Macpherson's 'translation' from the Gaelic of Ossian. He tried out his hand at a variety of forms and genres, from the verse epistle addressed to Edward Noel Long, a friend from Harrow, to satiric epigrams such as that on the school's new headmaster, 'Portrait of Pomposus', while schoolboy translations from the classics jostled the Romantic medievalism of a verse tale set in the Highlands, 'Oscar of Alva'. As Brian Nellist comments, the strength of the volume lies not in the individual compositions, but in the capacity to ventriloquise such a wide range of poetic voices (Beatty and Newey 1988: 44). In his title and preface, Byron emphasised this virtuoso impression by affecting the stance of the aristocratic dilettante, who only wrote for the perusal of his friends and 'to divert the dull moments of indisposition, or the monotony of a vacant hour' (*CPW* I, 33).

This defensive posturing is contradicted, however, by the combative language Byron employs in the preface when describing his own daring in crossing 'the Rubicon' from amateurism to the professional sphere of publication. By reminding the reader that he was 'accustomed, in [his] younger days, to rove a careless mountaineer on the Highlands of Scotland', and denying he is able 'to enter the lists with genuine bards' who still enjoy its pure air, Byron unsubtly hints at his ambition to rival Walter Scott, currently enjoying unprecedented popularity for poetic romances such as *Lay of the Last Minstrel*, set in Scotland's heroic past. In 'Lachin Y Gair' Byron portrays himself as a child clad in plaid set against the foaming cataracts of the Highlands, where his ancestors 'dwell in the tempests', having been 'destin'd to die at Culloden' in 1745, fighting for Bonny Prince Charlie and the Jacobite insurrection against Hanoverian rule (*CPW* I, 103–4; see *BLJ* I, 75). The notes to the poem inform the reader of Byron's mother's descent from the Gordons of Gight and thus connect him, as a real historical personage, with the mythical Scotland conjured up by the forgeries of Macpherson and the fictions of Scott.

This guarantee of 'authenticity' is where *Hours of Idleness* was exceptional. As McGann has remarked, its disparate lyrics are arranged into a coherent self-portrait of the author (McGann 1968: 21): sometimes heroic, sometimes self-ironising. Many, such as 'I Would I Were a Careless Child', look back nostalgically on the lost innocence of childhood. However stylised the mode and mood, the notes and epigraphs that frame the verse insist on the factual reality of the poet whose autobiography is sketched in the collection, by familiarising us with his lineage, the part played by the Byrons in history, his ruinous ancestral home, friendships, loves and student days. The egotism of authorship, uneasily combined with pride in his aristocratic origins, provoked the contempt of the radical critic Henry Brougham as it has many readers since. Yet, poems such as the opening lyric of the volume, 'On Leaving Newstead Abbey', testify to the poet's determination to maintain the honour of his forefathers through his writing.

Further reading

Byron's lyric poetry has been relatively neglected by critics, but many note that even in the juvenilia his poetry oscillates between the poles of sentiment and satire (Rutherford 1961: 15; Marchand 1965: 18). McGann argues that Byron seems to have consciously striven to publicise and mythologise his character in this his first book of poetry intended for general circulation (McGann 1968: 8–28). Gleckner points out Byron's preoccupation with the death of the young, separation and the loss of love (Gleckner 1967: 1–26).

English Bards and Scotch Reviewers

Byron had suppressed the satiric side of his poetic personality in choosing mostly melancholic lyrics for *Hours of Idleness*. But now he took Alexander Pope's *Dunciad* (1712) as a model, by castigating the Romantic poetry and drama of his own age as inferior to the Augustans in this anonymous poem written in heroic couplets. Aesthetically conservative poets often made use of this satiric tradition (Dyer 1997: 43), but Byron's motives were less purist than boisterous and self-assertive. Byron hailed his own contemporary, William Gifford, as the master of the genre (*CPW* I, 251, ll. 701–3) because his *Baviad* (1794) and *Maeviad* (1795) had successfully skewered the Della Cruscans, a group of liberal minor poets, who were lovers of Italy and forerunners of Romantics such as Byron and Shelley. As critics have pointed out, Della Cruscan writers, such as Charlotte Dacre, had actually been strong influences on *Hours of Idleness*. This turn-about evidenced Byron's self-defensive posturing. Byron's mockery of his contemporaries, such as Wordsworth, Southey, Coleridge, Scott and Moore, was unoriginal yet hilarious. Brougham's contemptuous review of *Hours of Idleness* inspired him to extend the first draft of the satire both in length and range to include critics, especially Francis Jeffrey, the editor of the *Edinburgh Review*, amongst his targets (see Criticism, **p. 85**). The success of the first edition stimulated him to bring out a revised, greatly extended version, with a preface and his name on the title page. The tone was now more scathing: modelled on that of the Roman satirist Juvenal and the Augustan satirist Charles Churchill. *Ad hominem* personal attacks targeted sycophantic or mercenary writers as hacks participating in a corrupt political system. When he returned from his Grand Tour, Byron prepared minor additions for a fifth edition of this popular poem. He intended to print it together with two more satires: *Hints from Horace*, in the less severe style inspired by the Roman poet's *Ars Poetica*, and *The Curse of Minerva*, which attacked Lord Elgin for his appropriation of the Parthenon marbles. However, when he realised that the attack in *English Bards and Scotch Reviewers* on the links between the *Edinburgh Review* and Holland House, the headquarters of the Whig party, would endanger his attempt to enter politics as a Whig peer, he suppressed the volume.

Further reading

Frederick L. Beaty situates the poem in the context of the classical and Augustan satiric traditions (Beaty 1985: 17–42). See also Claude Fuess, *Lord Byron as a Satirist in Verse* (1912). For the poem's allusions, consult Peter J. Manning, 'Byron's *English Bards and Scotch Reviewers*: The Art of Allusion' (1970). On the Juvenalian aspects of the poem, see Mary Clearman, 'A Blueprint for *English Bards and Scotch Reviewers*: the First Satire of Juvenal' (1970) and Steven E.

Jones, 'Intertextual Influences in Byron's Juvenalian Satire' (1993). On the attack on Jeffrey and possibly confused satirical aims of the poem, see William Christie, 'Running with the English Hares and Hunting with the Scotch Bloodhounds' (1997) and 'Byron and Francis Jeffrey' (1997); also Muriel Mellown, 'Francis Jeffrey, Lord Byron, and *English Bards and Scotch Reviewers*' (1981).

Childe Harold's Pilgrimage, a Romaunt

Cantos I–II

This phenomenally successful poem which made Byron internationally famous was a travelogue (see Life and Contexts, **pp. 5–9** and Criticism, **pp. 85, 102, 112**). More than that, it was also the modern sceptic's version of pilgrimage: a quest for meaning in a Europe no longer centred on Christianity or fired with the French revolutionaries' secular belief in human perfectibility. The protagonist, Harold, was the poet's alter ego, a libertine satiated with sin, whom the narrator treats with distanced irony and sometimes outright moral condemnation, as he travels across the Iberian peninsula and through the Ottoman Empire. The tone varies between sardonic mockery and serious concern in its use of Harold for self-dramatisation. Harold leaves behind his mother, sister, mistresses, home, his home and homeland, domesticity and duty, to set out on a masculine quest of adventure which will substitute for the sense of purpose and destiny he lacks.

The poem is written in the interlaced Spenserian stanza ABABBCBCC which uses only three rhymes in nine lines and concludes with a couplet. Byron thought it would be flexible enough to produce a range of moods: 'droll or pathetic, descriptive or sentimental, tender or satirical, as the humour strikes me' (*CPW* II, 4). However, Paul West has commented that it sets up 'a closed circuit of sounds in ninety-two syllables: they echo each other too quickly for too long' sometimes producing an unwanted sonority (Jump 1973: 156). Byron initially deployed the Spenserian stanza in the same way as did his eighteenth-century models, Scots James Thomson, James Beattie and the English Johnsonian, William Shenstone, whose archaisms produce a deliberately quaint burlesque of epic romance:

> Ah me! in sooth he was a shameless wight,
> Sore given to revel and ungodly glee;
> Few earthly things found favour in his sight
> Save concubines and carnal companie,
> > (*Childe Harold's Pilgrimage* I, 2)

A libertine, an embittered sceptic, an anti-hero, Harold is the obverse of the Christian knight idealised in the Middle Ages. Yet he is also a man of feeling, performing spontaneous lyrical effusions of his own in ballads, such as his last 'Good night' to his native land of England or the song 'To Inez' on his 'secret woe', sung to explain his *Weltschmerz* to a kindly Spanish maid. He is the earliest version of the 'Byronic hero', who had evolved out of the Gothic villain, with a dash of the child of nature and the gloomy egoist: types found in eighteenth-century literature (Thorslev 1962: 138–9). Many readers have seen the character as a self-portrait, though Byron strenuously denied this (see *BLJ* IV, 13–14). Philip W. Martin comments on the staginess of this alter-ego device by which Byron can watch himself perform (Martin 1982: 21). As we shall see in Part 3, Martin and other twentieth-century critics have criticised Byron as a poseur (see Criticism, p. 100). Ironically, they judge the poet by the criteria he himself helped produce, for he would take confessional poetry further than ever before in order to produce an impression of sincerity. We see this happening as the narrator's moralistic travelogue becomes increasingly self-referential in *Childe Harold's Pilgrimage*: interspersed by melancholy asides, referring to the deaths of friends and family members the poet had suffered during composition. One lost love especially intrigued readers, in lines we now know were probably inspired by the death of Byron's friend the Cambridge chorister, John Edleston:

> There, thou! – whose love and life together fled,
> Have left me here to love and live in vain –
> Twin'd with my heart, and can I deem thee dead,
> When busy Memory flashes on my brain?
> (*Childe Harold's Pilgrimage* II, 9)

The narrator's act of composition is made to seem spontaneous by the diary-like use of the present tense: 'Full swiftly Harold wends his lonely way' (*Childe Harold's Pilgrimage* I, 45). Yet he reminds us he has been imagining not viewing the scene when he interrupts a paean to Spanish beauties with an address to the Greek mountains supposedly before his eyes as he writes:

> Oh, thou Parnassus! whom I now survey,
> Not in the phrenzy of a dreamer's eye,
> Not in the fabled landscape of a lay,
> But soaring snow-clad through thy native sky,
> In the wild pomp of mountain majesty!
> (*Childe Harold's Pilgrimage* I, 60)

Jerome McGann comments that by the end of these two cantos the narrator has gradually become as introspective and brooding as Harold, who correspondingly declines in importance. Indeed, he will fade away entirely after the Rhine journey of Canto III (McGann 1968: 67–93). McGann admits that the use of Harold as ego-projection was a clumsy device and that contrasting Romantic and satiric/sceptical points of view in the poem were not handled with assurance or consistency. On the other hand, the importance of the development of the poem in Cantos III and IV will lie in the fact that Byron's fragmented poetic identity is foregrounded and shown in process. The pilgrim's paradoxical search for an ideal in spite of his pessimistic awareness of the tarnished nature of the fallen world, his elegiac lament for the heroism of the past, this very contradictory mixture of fervour and despair was the essence of Byronism, which encapsulated the mood of disillusioned liberals at the time of the end of the Napoleonic wars. Byron himself commented: 'If ever I did anything original it was in C[hil]de H[arol]d' (*BLJ* IV, 107). In a recent essay, Philip W. Martin comments that the poem is difficult for a modern reader, not because of hidden meanings, but because of its surface: its 'complex movements back and forth through time', as it questions the nature of heroism and the way history is made (Bone 2004, 79).

The poem was innovative, too, in turning an Augustan topographical poem into an expression of Romantic orientalism (see Criticism, **pp. 111–14**). For Harold travelled East, experiencing 'Greece': so-called by classical scholars, even though the area had never been a unified state and had long formed part of the Ottoman Empire. He even journeyed into the Islamic heart of the little-known and dangerous land of Albania. Byron had been influenced by other poems describing travels in Greece such as Richard Polwhele's *Grecian Prospects. A Poem. In Two Cantos* (1799), William Falconer's *The Shipwreck* (1804) and Waller Rodwell Wright's *Horae Ionicae* (1809). But *Childe Harold's Pilgrimage* followed up the familiar Philhellenist narrator's meditations on the ruins of classical civilisation, his anguished address to Athena, 'Where are thy men of might? thy grand in soul?' (II, 2), with a brilliant portrait of the contemporary inhabitants, 'The wild Albanian kirtled to his knee' (II, 58). The depiction of Ali Pasha's court at Tepelini (II, 55–64), its minarets and harem, the picturesque scene of his warriors preparing an evening feast, the dancing and singing of the wild Suliote tribesmen around their fire (II, 71–2): all evoked a primitive, tribal culture with a Barbarian beauty of its own.

> On the smooth shore the night-fires blaz'd,
> The feast was done, the red wine circling fast,
> And he that unawares had there ygaz'd
> With gaping wonderment had star'd aghast;
> For ere night's midmost, stillest hour was past
> The native revels of the troop began;
> Each Palikar his sabre from him cast,
> And bounding hand in hand, man link'd to man,
> Yelling their uncouth dirge, long danc'd the kirtled clan.
>   (*Childe Harold's Pilgrimage* II, 71)

In a recent brilliant essay on this poem, Nigel Leask has shown that there were two somewhat contradictory aspects of Byron's Philhellenism: mere melancholic musing over past greatness, which was a great selling point of the poem; and, in dialogue with this, an embryonic streak of revolutionary political activism (Bone 2004: 99–117). In this rousing celebration of Ali Pasha's military prowess, Byron's poem challenged the merely nostalgic type of Philhellenism with a realistic vision of what a contemporary uprising would look like.

As was his wont, Byron continually made additions and adjustments to *Childe Harold's Pilgrimage*, to which miscellaneous lyrics, informative and combative footnotes and information on the contemporary Greek language were appended. It was not until the tenth edition of Cantos I and II was published that he ceased making changes. Contemporary readers were particularly intrigued by the addition of lyrics addressed to a mysterious Thyrza, Harold/Byron's dead love ('Without a stone to mark the spot', 'Away, away, ye notes of woe', 'One struggle more, and I am free', 'And thou art dead, as young and fair', 'If sometimes in the haunts of men', 'On a cornelian heart which was broken'). Scholars have shown that though the addressee seems feminised, these poems had actually been inspired by news of the death of John Edleston, for whom Byron had experienced intense feelings of protective and idealised love but also sexual guilt (see Life and Contexts, **p. 4** and Criticism, **p. 115**).

Further reading

The most important study of the poem as a whole is the very detailed second chapter of Jerome McGann's *Fiery Dust*, though its author has subsequently rejected some of the conclusions of this book. John Jump's anthology of nineteenth- and twentieth-century criticism, *Byron*: Childe Harold's Pilgrimage *and* Don Juan: A Casebook (1973) is now dated. On the character of Harold, consult Peter L. Thorslev Jr., *The Byronic Hero: Types and Prototypes* (1962). Peter J. Manning considers the poem's popularity as a travelogue in 'Childe *Harold* in the Marketplace: From Romaunt to Handbook' (1991).

When considering Cantos I and II specifically, Byron's letters to his mother while travelling on his Grand Tour set the scenes the poem dramatises, especially that of 12 November, 1809 (*BLJ* I, 226–31). McGann gives a crisp summary of the ideology of the poem in *The Beauty of Inflections: Literary Investigations in Historical Method and Theory* (1985b: 258–64). Gleckner gives a detailed reading of the poem, emphasising its pessimism (Gleckner 1967: 39–90). Paul Elledge examines forms of valediction in his essay 'Chasms in Connections: Byron Ending (in) *Childe Harold's Pilgrimage* 1 and 2', reprinted in Stabler (1998: 123–37). On the depiction of Spain, see Diego Saglia, *Byron and Spain: Itinerary in the Writing of Place* (1996). For a feminist reading, see Caroline Franklin's 'Cosmopolitan Masculinity and the British Female Reader of *Childe Harold's Pilgrimage*' (1997). On homoeroticism and the 'Thyrza' poems, see Louis Crompton (1985: 158–95). For a postmodernist view, see William H. Galperin, *The Return of the Visible in British Romanticism* (1993). Two recent excellent essays on the first two cantos are: 'Heroism and History: *Childe Harold* I and II and the Tales' by Philip W. Martin (Bone 2004: 77–98), and 'Byron and the Eastern Mediterranean: *Childe Harold* II and the "Polemic of Ottoman Greece" ' by Nigel Leask (Bone 2004: 99–117).

Canto III

The next section of the poem was published in 1816 and was inspired by the poet's later tour, following on from the collapse of his marriage (see Life and Contexts, **pp. 14–15** and Criticism, **p. 86**). Europe was at last at peace with the end of the Napoleonic wars in 1815. The poem however, is anything but peaceful – it is an agonised expression of inner turmoil. We are immediately plunged into the poet's innermost thoughts on the baby daughter he will never see again:

> Is thy face like thy mother's, my fair child!
> Ada! sole daughter of my house and heart?
> When last I saw thy young blue eyes they smiled,
> And then we parted, – not as now we part,
> But with a hope. –

> Awaking with a start,
> The waters heave around me; and on high
> The winds lift up their voices: I depart,
> Whither I know not; but the hour's gone by,
> When Albion's lessening shores could grieve or glad mine eye.
>
> (*Childe Harold's Pilgrimage* III, 1)

But exactly halfway through the stanza, the focus is abruptly jarred, all the more effectively by way of a misplaced participle, from the inner mind's eye to a willed refocusing on exterior reality. This dichotomy indicates the theme explored in this canto: the narrator will attempt to find an escape from the inner self through meditating on the most picturesque rivers, lakes and mountains in Europe. The poet was by now a well-known public figure, and his readers would know all about the separation scandal that drove him to leave England in 1816, never to return. Nevertheless, the openness with which he spoke in the opening and closing stanzas to his baby daughter and about his own emotional turmoil was something new and shocking. There are also allusions in the poem to the speaker's 'sin' (III, 73), his imagining 'a sister's voice' (III, 85); while the lake and river are compared to a nursing mother (III, 71) and the steep cliffs of the Rhine valley to 'lovers who have parted/ In hate' (III, 94). Readers are therefore reminded of the biographical context of the speaker's melancholy. Byron later said of the poem: '[I]t is a fine indistinct piece of poetical desolation, and my favourite. I was half mad during the time its composition, between metaphysics, mountains, lakes, love inextinguishable, thoughts unutterable, and the nightmare of my own delinquencies' (*BLJ* V, 165).

The poetic voice is much more confident now than in the earlier cantos: freer in the rhetorical control of the Spenserian stanza, using enjambment more frequently and even running on from one stanza to the next. The poet begins by clearly differentiating between himself and the misanthropic Harold, 'The wandering outlaw of his own dark mind' (III, 3). He explains that it is through moulding such creatures of his imagination the artist can intensify and distil the experience of life and make something worthwhile even out of his misery. That way he transcends mere self:

> 'Tis to create, and in creating live
> A being more intense, that we endow
> With form our fancy, gaining as we give
> The life we image, even as I do now.
> What am I? Nothing; but not so art thou,
> Soul of my thought! with whom I traverse earth,
> Invisible but gazing, as I glow
> Mix'd with thy spirit, blended with thy birth,
> And feeling still with thee in my crush'd feeling's dearth.
>
> (*Childe Harold's Pilgrimage* III, 6)

Harold is then brought on stage and the narrator portrays him as a solitary intellectual rebel who refused to conform:

> He would not yield dominion of his mind
> To spirits against whom his own rebell'd;
> Proud though in desolation;
> (*Childe Harold's Pilgrimage* III, 12)

The poet next demonstrates his determination to universalise the human condition by bringing the Childe up sharp against something greater than merely his own sorrows as an object for contemplation: 'Stop!- for thy tread is on an Empire's dust!' (*Childe Harold's Pilgrimage* III, 17).

Harold is standing on 'this place of skulls, / The grave of France, the deadly Waterloo!' (III, 18) (see Life and Contexts, **p. 13**). For the spiritual desolation marking the opening of the poem is political as much as it is personal. The defeat of Napoleon also meant the end of the ideals of the French revolution and the restoration of monarchical or imperial dynastic rule over most of Europe. For the reader, the poem acted as an on-the-spot report from the battlefield itself. Byron's exciting recreation of the night before the battle (III, 21–6), his elegiac mourning for all the young men cut down (III, 27–31) and meditation on the human capacity for endurance of sorrow (III, 32–5) bring him to an analysis of the titanic figure of Bonaparte himself (III, 36–45).

> There sunk the greatest, not the worst of men,
> Whose spirit antithetically mixt
> One moment of the mightiest, and again
> On little objects with like firmness fixt,
> Extreme in all things!
> (*Childe Harold's Pilgrimage* III, 36)

In empathising with Napoleon, the artist's own subjectivity colours his interpretation, for he paints a Romantic overreacher comparable with himself, an extreme example of humankind's paradoxical mixture of grandeur and the contemptible.

> . . . there is a fire
> And motion of the soul which will not dwell
> In its own narrow being, but aspire
> Beyond the fitting medium of desire;
> (*Childe Harold's Pilgrimage* III, 42)

Byron was later criticized for giving too favourable a portrait, and thus being unpatriotic, but he declared: 'I have spoken of him . . . as a man of great qualities and considerable defects' (*BLJ* V, 202) (see Criticism, **p. 87**). Byron would go on in the third and fourth cantos to examine many such prototypes of the Romantic individualist, which would take over the function of Harold, in enabling the writer to project his own *Weltschmerz* as an aspect of the spirit of the age.

McGann suggests that Canto III is the first poem Byron wrote in which he was able completely to subdue his own Haroldian scepticism (McGann 1968: 165). This view has also been recently endorsed by Alan Rawes (Rawes 2000: 50–79). To achieve this, Byron has Harold turn to 'maternal nature' as he journeys along the river Rhine.

> There Harold gazes on a work divine,
> A blending of all beauties; streams and dells,
> Fruit, foliage, crag, wood, cornfield, mountain, vine,
> And chiefless castles breathing stern farewells
> From gray but leafy walls, where Ruin greenly dwells.
>   (*Childe Harold's Pilgrimage* III, 46)

The delineation of the fertility of the Rhine landscape, with its empty castles indicating the passing of all conquerors, is one of the conventional topographical set pieces of the canto. Others are the sea voyage, and the contrast between the sublime Alps and the stillness of deep lakes. For the modern sceptic, though, who, like Harold, has abandoned orthodox religion and whose political ideals have been overthrown, Nature offers more than moralised topography or picturesque beauty: it connects him with forces greater than the self. Harold therapeutically 'gazes on a work divine' and obtains restorative solace. He remembers too the human beauty of his forbidden but pure secret love (III, 55) and is inspired to sing 'The Castled Crag of Drachenfels'. But as Joseph remarks, it is the more complex narrator not the flat character Harold who later in the canto experiences a pantheistic communion with nature reminiscent of that in Wordsworth's 'Tintern Abbey', when contemplating Lake Leman (Joseph 1964: 77).

> I live not in myself, but become
> Portion of that around me; and to me,
> High mountains are a feeling, but the hum
> Of human cities torture . . .
>   (*Childe Harold's Pilgrimage* III, 72)

By the middle of the canto the poet has abandoned Harold, the figure in the landscape which helped direct our view. Now the artist's own subjectivity is the subject as well as the medium of the poem in lyrical first-person narration. The external tour has been subordinated to the poet's psychological journey. Canto III has sometimes been judged severely because of the failure to maintain the use of the protagonist, as well as its lack of structural coherence. Gleckner comments that it is possible to see the merging of Harold and the narrator in two ways: 'first, as the poet absorbing into himself his own metaphor of fallen man, for properly such a metaphor remains a mere counter, a figure in a tableau, unless it is made articulate through the imagination of his creator; and secondly, as Harold finally become articulate, not merely in lamentations of his own personal plight but as the visionary historian of man's eternal lot amid the ruins of a universe not well lost and a nature glorious and beautiful but flatly indifferent' (Gleckner 1967: 229).

Not all critics would go as far as Gleckner in stating that the quasi-Wordsworthian vision of a pantheistic nature is depicted as illusory. In meditating on nature the poet/narrator loses his separate identity – if only temporarily – within the 'eternal harmony' (III, 90) of the universe, and is reconnected with the spirit of love. True he questions the pantheistic vision even as he asserts it:

> Are not the mountains, waves, and skies, a part
> Of me and of my soul, as I of them?
> (*Childe Harold's Pilgrimage* III, 75)

But when he describes Lake Leman at night (III, 85–93), the narrator strongly affirms the unity and beneficence of a sacred nature:

> From the high host
> Of stars, to the lull'd lake and mountain-coast,
> All is concentered in a life intense,
> Where not a beam, not air, nor leaf is lost,
> But hath a part of being, and a sense
> Of that which is all Creator and defence.
> (*Childe Harold's Pilgrimage* III, 89)

Byron makes this Wordsworthian vision of nature his own, for he immediately follows this scene of mystical stillness with a violent storm to show nature as essentially changeable, and as capable of violence and destruction as of peace.

> And this is the night: – Most glorious night!
> Thou wert not sent for slumber! let me be
> A sharer in thy fierce and far delight,–
> A portion of the tempest and of thee!
> (*Childe Harold's Pilgrimage* III, 93)

The Byronic poet delights in the revolutionary energy of nature and its changeability mirrors his own 'mobility' of temperament.

Throughout the canto, the narrator attempts to sublimate his personal misery through his own act of imaginative creation, thereby producing the poem itself. Byron projected that Haroldian part of himself which seemed cut off from humanity into his depiction of thinker and novelist Jean-Jacques Rousseau – who was reclusive, a botanist who idealised nature and whose political writings helped inspire the French Revolution (see Life and Contexts, **p. 15**). When the poet described the Swiss landscape where the philosopher had lived, he mythologised the artist as a suffering hero:

> Here the self-torturing sophist, wild Rousseau,
> The apostle of affliction, he who threw
> Enchantment over passion, and from woe
> Wrung overwhelming eloquence, first drew
> The breath which made him wretched; yet he knew
> How to make madness beautiful, and cast
> O'er erring deeds and thoughts, a heavenly hue
> Of words, like sunbeams, dazzling as they past
> The eyes, which oe'r them shed tears feelingly and fast.
> (*Childe Harold's Pilgrimage* III, 77)

Byron portrayed Rousseau's Platonic concept of 'love as passion's essence – as a tree / On fire by lightning', a search for an 'ideal beauty, which became / In him existence' (III, 78) in his creation of the heroine of his influential novel of sentiment *Julie, ou La Nouvelle Heloïse*. Byron portrays himself in comparable imagery in Stanza 97, in his intense but vain desire to condense into one word with all the force of lightning all the contradictory elements of his selfhood: 'Soul, heart, mind, passions, feelings, strong or weak'. But Byron's lightning is not self-consuming passion, but a weapon made of language he wishes he could wield against his enemies. For he hopes 'there may be / Words which are things' (III, 114): thoughts which can materialise and inspire revolutionary action.

The poet was also influenced by the idealist philosophy of Percy Shelley, who had accompanied him on his pilgrimage to Clarens, at the upper end of Lake Geneva, the area described in Rousseau's novel (see Life and Contexts, **pp. 14–16**). Stanzas 94–104, the last to be incorporated into the finished canto, were composed on the spot (*CPW* III, 311).

> Clarens! sweet Clarens, birth-place of deep Love!
> Thine air is the young breath of passionate thought;
> Thy trees take root in Love; the snows above
> The very Glaciers have his colours caught,
> (*Childe Harold's Pilgrimage* III, 99)

This passage shows Byron's capacity for a mystical apprehension of the spirit of place, and he appended a note which strongly asserts that the artist does not imagine but is merely the conduit for such a spirit: 'if Rousseau had never written, not lived, the same associations would not less have belonged to such scenes . . . they have done that for him which no human being could do for them' (*CPW* II, 312).

Yet hard on the heels of his Shelleyan assertion that love 'is the great principle of the universe' (*CPW* II, 312), the poet-narrator turns to more Haroldian intellectual heroes. For Ferney and Lausanne, near Lake Geneva, were respectively associated with the 'Titan-like' giants of scepticism, the freethinking French Enlightenment philosopher Voltaire and the ironic historian Edward Gibbon. The former excelled in ridicule: 'Now to o'erthrow a fool, and now to shake a throne' (III, 106); whereas the latter was 'the lord of irony' which sapped 'a solemn creed with solemn sneer' (III, 107). Byron admires these sceptical Enlightenment thinkers as much as the visionary Rousseau who expressed the spirit of love which inhered in the landscape of Clarens. It is not that the poet now rejects the redemptive possibilities of nature, but that this ideal has tempered rather than entirely replaced Haroldian scepticism.

For, as Vincent Newey suggests, the third canto is 'no drama of maturation, but a holding operation' (Beatty and Newey 1988: 164), and as it draws to a close the poet returns to his sense of personal bitterness at the vituperation he has received in the press during the separation scandal: 'I have not loved the world, nor the world me' (III, 113). Switzerland had long been idealised by republicans as the refuge of exiled or unpopular radical thinkers, amongst whom Byron now counts himself. Yet he has not merely returned full circle, for it is with a renewed sense of poetic vocation he can now confidently address his daughter, who also represents his future readers, posterity. However much she has been taught to hate him she will rebel, 'I know that thou wilt love me' (III, 117):

> Albeit my brow thou never should'st behold,
> My voice shall with thy future visions blend,
> And reach into thy heart,—when mine is cold,—
> A token and a tone, even from thy father's mould.
> (*Childe Harold's Pilgrimage* II, 115)

Further reading

For Byron's changing aims during composition, see McGann (1968: 112–21, 165–73). On the literary relationship of Byron and Shelley, see Charles E. Robinson, *Shelley and Byron: The Snake and Eagle Wreathed in Fight* (1976: 421–4). For a reading that situates the canto within a dialectic of pessimism and benevolism, see M. K. Joseph, *Byron the Poet* (1964: 76–83); while Alan Rawes argues that the canto is primarily comedic because its movement turns away from the tragic vision of the earlier verse in *Byron's Poetic Experimentation: Childe, Harold, the Tales, and the Quest for Comedy* (2000: 50–79). Vincent Newey examines Byron's creation of doublings of himself in 'Authoring the Self: *Childe Harold III and IV*' (1988). Stephen Cheeke examines ideas concerning the spirit and body of place in *Byron and Place: History, Translation, Nostalgia* (2003: 68–81).

Canto IV

Byron dedicated the final canto to J. C. Hobhouse and heads the poem with a personal letter to his dedicatee, in which he pays him a heartfelt tribute for his loyalty and support in the separation crisis. This bitter mention of his marriage indicates that the new section of the poem will continue the theme of the poet's resentment at his blasted reputation, from the conclusion of Canto III. The poet declares Hobhouse had been an even older and better friend to him than Harold and his poem, and had accompanied him on many of the travels on which it had been based. Hobhouse had collaborated with Byron on the notes to the canto, which he amplified and which were separately published as *Historical Illustrations to the Fourth Canto of* Childe Harold (1818). These provide invaluable information on the literary and artistic sources that inspired the poetry, and also often give a political gloss relating its generalities to specific current issues. Hobhouse would become a radical MP by 1820 (see Life and Contexts, **pp. 16–17**).

Just as Percy Shelley had inspired the Romantic tendency of Canto III, which gives direct access to the poetic imagination in its mystic apprehension of a spiritualised exterior world, so the influence of Hobhouse on Canto IV saw something of a return to a more conventionally topographical and antiquarian mode with the traditional theme of *sic transit gloria mundi*. Before returning to *Childe Harold*, in the verse drama *Manfred* and the dramatic monologue *The Prisoner of Chillon*, Byron had set out with a critique of materialism (nature as empty of spirit), yet concluded with a vision of the independent mind as rising above the determinants of place and time and a renunciation of the idea, posited in Canto III, that the physical world was infused by spirit (Cheeke 2003: 89). Gleckner describes Canto IV as an 'extraordinary imaginative journey into nothingness and despair' (Gleckner 1967: 297): even when it rises to prophetic heights this poetry is never utopian, always grounded in the real.

The protagonist, Harold, is now entirely dispensed with. Byron announced,

> [T]here will be found less of the pilgrim than in any of the preceding, and that little slightly, if at all, separated from the author speaking in his own person. The fact is, that I had become weary of drawing a line which every one seemed determined not to perceive.
>
> (*CPW* II, 122)

His fame meant he could now rely on readers' familiarity with the world-weary melancholic personality he dramatised as his public image and could thus dismiss the apparatus of a fictionalised persona (see Criticism, **p. 86**).

Italy was both the traditional destination of a Christian pilgrimage and the art-lover's Grand Tour. To the modern Haroldian sceptic, particularly a Briton who had been brought up in a Protestant rational culture, a pilgrimage to Rome meant surveying a culture riddled with a superstitious religion, which had been superseded by scientific and historical thought, and the ruins of past empires, which mocked the ambitions of rulers. The alienation and nihilism produced by secular, historical relativism could, however, be offset by the hope that Italy – the cradle of republicanism in the ancient world – would provide a rebirth of political liberty and enshrine it in the creation of a new nation-state. For Republicans such as Byron and his friends, the ruins of ancient Rome were of a more than antiquarian interest. After the defeat of the French republic, young idealists turned to Italy (most of which was ruled by Austria) as well as Greece (part of the Ottoman Empire), and fixed on them their dreams of revolution against imperial, monarchical tyranny. Indeed, the aristocratic Grand Tour tradition of which the poem is a product, had been an important contributory factor in engendering the concept of Italian nationalism. For it was classically educated tourists who had first conceptualised the peninsula as one entity, rather than a collection of city-states and regions. It then took the Napoleonic occupation to provoke a spirit of defensive patriotism amongst the inhabitants.

Byron's epistolary dedication to Hobhouse concludes with a deliberately provocative antithesis between the 'bacchanal roar of the songs of exultation still yelled from the London taverns, over the carnage of Mont St. Jean' (Waterloo) and the British 'betrayal of Genoa, of Italy, of France, and of the world' in the Congress of Vienna, which had reinstituted monarchical and dynastic regimes over Europe. The way Byron referred to the British in the third person and scoffed at their 'permanent army and suspended Habeas Corpus' indicated he was now taking up the cudgels against his homeland and its Tory government in no uncertain manner. His poem would inculcate the opposite of British jingoism: cosmopolitanism. This was the Enlightenment virtue promulgated by travel. Italy had now become Byron's adopted country.

The poem opens in Venice (IV, 1–19), then follows the usual tourist route from northern Italy to Rome via the cities of Arqua, Ferrara and Florence and the contrasting picturesque landscapes of Lake Trasimene, the river Clitumnus, the cataract of Velino and the Appenine mountains. More than half of the canto is devoted to Rome: 'Oh Rome! my country! city of the soul!' (IV, 78). Rome in Byron's day was a tranquil and overgrown site of ancient ruins, not a large city. Within this section are set-piece meditations on the Colosseum in moonlight (IV, 128–45), and Saint Peter's and the art gallery of the Vatican (IV, 153–63). Byron was writing in a well-known, well-worn aristocratic tradition in his reflections on the civilisation which was the source of European culture. But meditating on the ruins of its imperialistic grandeur implicitly brought comparisons to mind with both the recently defeated Napoleonic and the currently burgeoning British empires.

Most readers regard the fourth canto as the most impressive, and Byron himself wrote to his publisher: 'I fear that I shall never do better' (*BLJ* V, 265). However, some critics comment that it is poorly organised in that its basic structure has been overlaid by digressions and the addition of sixty stanzas to the first draft (see Life and Contexts, **p. 17** and Criticism, **p. 105**). Rutherford suggests that the lack of unity and coherence is also due to the way this canto expresses contradictory emotions of gloom and delight inherent in Byron's volatile personality (Rutherford 1961: 97–102). McGann, however, argues that Byron deliberately avoided Wordsworthian ethical consistency, preferring to embrace constant change in the psyche (McGann 1991: 55). He has also analysed the additions, and comments that many of these are not caused by Hobhouse's insistence that various antiquities be mentioned, or Byron's self-indulgence, but result from the poet's attempt to emphasise art and the artist as the spearheads of the movement towards nationalist consciousness or *risorgimento* (McGann 1968: 130). The medieval and Renaissance poets Petrarch, Dante and Tasso are regarded as the prophets of love and liberty disregarded in their own time, to whose roll-call, Byron implicitly suggests, his own name could be added.

This theme is announced in the opening of the poem in Venice, when the poet stands on the 'Bridge of Sighs', which he described in a letter as

> that which divides or rather joins the palace of the doge to the prison of the state—it has two passages—the criminal went by one to judgement—& returned by the other to death—being strangled in a chamber adjoining—where there was a mechanical process for the purpose.
>
> (*BLJ* V, 244)

This bridge symbolised the tyranny that accompanied even a Republican empire. The fall, first to Napoleon and then to the Austrians, of Venice, whose government had once been hailed as an ideal combination of the classical republican tradition with Christian culture is a warning most of all to her successor – the maritime empire of Britain. From a distance Venice 'looks a sea Cybele' (IV, 2), 'a ruler of the waters', but when one approaches there is an uncanny silence. Now the narrator sees that 'Her palaces are crumbling to the shore' (IV, 3) and 'The Bucentaur lies rotting' (IV, 11). Venice has lost her freedom and the whole city now 'Sinks, like a sea-weed, into whence she rose!' (IV, 13). It is only through 'Otway, Radcliffe, Schiller, Shakespeare's art' (IV, 18), that we can repeople

Venice in the days of her glory: it is literature which endows her memory with immortality. Indeed the poet-narrator himself is implicitly the latest 'enchanter' whose magic wand of poetry causes the wings of the centuries of Venetian history to expand in the daylight (IV, 1).

> The beings of the mind are not of clay;
> Essentially immortal, they create
> And multiply in us a brighter ray
> And more beloved existence:
> (*Childe Harold's Pilgrimage* IV, 5)

This recapitulates Canto III, 6, and the poet refers directly to his earlier poetry which 'came like truth, and disappeared like dreams' but promises 'I could replace them if I would' (IV, 7), from his teeming mind. Like the titanic poets of Italy's past who were unappreciated or banished, Byron is a lonely wanderer and an exile: 'I've taught me other tongues' (IV, 8). Yet he puts himself on a par with Shakespeare when he declares he twines his 'hopes of being remembered in my line / With my land's language' (IV, 9). His detachment from Britain endows him with the independence to speak the truth on European politics. The decay of Venice:

> Is shameful to the nations,—most of all,
> Albion! to thee: the Ocean queen should not
> Abandon Ocean's children;
> (*Childe Harold's Pilgrimage* IV, 17)

The melancholy and bitterness of Canto III still erupts, but expressed stoically and defiantly rather than in anguish. Indeed the poet comments that just as the tannen grows best in barren soil, and into a giant tree on Alpine peaks where it is blasted by the elements, 'the mind may grow the same' (IV, 20). His sufferings have made him 'A ruin amongst ruins', most fit then:

> to track
> Fall'n states and buried greatness, o'er a land
> Which *was* the mightiest in its old command,
> (*Childe Harold's Pilgrimage* IV, 25)

And the poem expands to hymn Italy in her ruined state, where the fertility of nature outstrips the survival of creations of human culture, yet also suggests art's potentiality to revive and flourish.

> Thou art the garden of the world, the home
> Of all Art yields, and Nature can decree;
> Even in thy desart, what is like to thee?
> Thy very weeds are beautiful, thy waste
> More rich than other climes' fertility;
> Thy wreck a glory, and thy ruin graced
> With an immaculate charm which cannot be defaced.
> (*Childe Harold's Pilgrimage* IV, 26)

The ego-projection which had been accomplished through the persona of Harold, is now achieved through elegiac meditations on graves or places associated with poets who had been what Shelley termed 'unacknowledged legislators' for Italy. The medieval love poet and pioneer of the sonnet form, Petrarch, had raised the Tuscan language to prominence and inculcated the beginning of political nationalism: he reclaimed his land 'From the dull yoke of her barbaric foes' (IV, 30). The sixteenth-century epic poet Torquato Tasso is painted as an even greater Byronic hero, unquelled despite imprisonment in a madhouse in Ferrara by a despotic ruler (IV, 36), though the sensitivity of the artist makes his own mind an instrument of torture. The great Renaissance poets – exiled Dante, author of the *Divina Commedia*; Ariosto, who wrote *Orlando Furioso*; Boccaccio, poet of the *Decameron* – all had shaped the common culture which bonded Italy and receive tribute from Byron, though they are still not sufficiently appreciated in their native 'ungrateful' Florence (IV, 57).

Stanzas 42 and 43 incorporate a translation of Vincenzo da Filicaja's sonnet 'Italia, Italia, O tu coi feo la sorte' (which had also been translated by Robert Southey and Felicia Hemans) in which Italy is imaged as a helpless woman, whose beauty seems to invite rape. Byron was influenced by his friend Madame de Staël's novel *Corinne, or Italy* (1807), which had protested against Napoleon's incursion through an allegorical representation of Italy as a woman poet deserted by her soldier lover (Wilkes 1999: 100–31). He paid fulsome tribute to her genius in the notes (*CPW* II, 235–6). Throughout the canto, Byron deploys images of vulnerable femininity to rouse his readers' chivalric determination to fight in her defence. Italy is 'Mother of Arts ... Parent of our Religion' (IV, 47). Rome is 'Lone mother of dead empires!' (IV, 78), 'The Niobe of nations' (IV, 79) mourning for her dead children.

Yet the founders of Rome had been suckled by a she-wolf, 'Mother of the mighty heart' (IV, 88) and this thought leads the poet into a moralising commentary on the masculine desire for conquest: from Rome's armies to those of Napoleon: 'a kind / Of bastard Caesar' (IV, 90). The next eight stanzas explore the hard lesson of the French Revolution: that those who conquer tyrants seem to turn tyrant in their place. The despairing poet turns back for comfort to the image of the endurance of the lone tree, now also a symbol of liberty like those trees planted to commemorate the French revolution.

> Yet, Freedom! yet thy banner, torn, but flying,
> Streams like the thunder-storm *against* the wind;
> Thy trumpet voice, though broken now and dying,
> The loudest still the tempest leaves behind;
> Thy tree hath lost its blossoms, and the rind,
> Chopp'd by the axe, looks rough and little worth,
> But the sap lasts, – and still the seed we find
> Sown deep, even in the bosom of the North;
> So shall a better spring less bitter fruit bring forth.
> (*Childe Harold's Pilgrimage* IV, 98)

This stanza must have been an inspiration behind Shelley's 'Ode to the West Wind', and scholars have suggested that both poems are probably indebted to

Thomas Paine's imagery of a budding twig at the conclusion of the second part of *The Rights of Man* (1969: 273). The energy of Byron's metre makes it a stirring trumpet-call for liberty, yet its imagery of nature's inevitable capacity for revival encapsulated in a buried seed also implies the many bleak years which lie ahead before that new tree of liberty is mature.

Canto IV is a political poem which makes an impassioned plea for Italy to be recognised as a cultural whole, on account of its shared linguistic, literary and artistic traditions, and which protests against its rule by the Austrians. Both the notes and the poem perform the cultural memorialising and celebration which Byron and Hobhouse thought necessary to prepare the ground for a *risorgimento* (Cheeke 2003: 99). The poem stops short of calling for revolution or putting forward a programme of action. McGann has even suggested that 'Italian *risorgimento* and the great artists of Italy's past and present are only mirrors in which we perceive the struggle of the poet of *Childe Harold's Pilgrimage* to offer a general redemptive vision to mankind at large' (McGann 1968: 131). Readers must decide how far they see the poem as narcissistic. Certainly, in Canto III the self-aggrandising poet had placed himself on the page of history by traversing the battlefield of Waterloo, and in Canto IV he situates himself within the pantheon of European high art. Yet we might see him representing the isolated heroic individual, especially the artist, as left with the unenviable task of handing on the torch of liberty in an age of repression and conservatism. His self-dramatising technique works to invite us to share his visionary poetic inspiration in action and his feeling for the special qualities that make up Italy.

Standing by the ivied tomb of an unknown Roman matron he is inspired to make the dead live in his words (IV, 99–104). Meditating by the fountain where a nymph Egeria 'the genius of the place' (IV, 116) loved and inspired the philosopher Numa, the poet finds that he can no longer believe in Love as an external spirit, but recognises that artists project into their works the beauty that emanates from and dis-eases the human mind (IV, 115–22). This capacity to imagine perfect beauty can be seen as a torment and a curse. For man and his endless desire is not part of the harmony of nature since the Fall:

> This uneradicable taint of sin,
> This boundless upas, this all-blasting tree,
> Whose root is earth . . .
> (*Childe Harold's Pilgrimage* IV, 126)

The poet satanically situates his own psychic drama within the greatest arena in Rome, that of the Coliseum at night, where he dramatically calls upon Time and Nemesis to witness the curse of vengeance he calls down upon his enemies, only to turn it into forgiveness (IV, 130–7).

> But I have lived, and have not lived in vain:
> My mind may lose its force, my blood its fire,
> And my frame perish even in conquering pain,
> But there is that within me which shall tire
> Torture and Time . . .
> (*Childe Harold's Pilgrimage* IV, 137)

By implication he associates himself and his poetry with the mighty building which will stand as long as Rome (IV, 145), as well as the heroism imbued in its stones from those such as the gladiator Byron imagines seized from the banks of the Danube, whom he pictures 'Butcher'd to make a Roman holiday' (IV, 141). The Coliseum had been consecrated by the Church in order to commemorate the Christian martyrs who had died there, but Byron adapts the notion of pilgrimage to sacralise his own secular quest to fight back against oppression and injustice. Individual self-renewal is thus linked with the wished-for renewal of the independence of Italy. So the matter-of-fact material reality of the tourist's visit to a famous place goes hand in hand with an almost supernatural apprehension of the Coliseum as a 'magic' spot (Cheeke 2003: 104–7) in which the poet communes with the spirits of the dead.

As he contemplates the magnificent Pantheon, the temple built in Hadrian's reign which was conventionally the most admired building of the Grand Tour, the narrator now conjures up a greatly contrasting scene of selfless love, though perhaps just as grotesque as the curse of forgiveness. He was inspired by the 'Caritas Romana' story of a young mother who had kept her aged patriot father alive by feeding him from her own breast when they were imprisoned together in one cell by the Emperor (IV, 148–51). A version of it had been dramatised by Arthur Murphy as *The Grecian Daughter* (first performed at Drury Lane in 1772), and was regularly performed starring Mrs Siddons. The story was an allegorical representation of the keeping alive of republican ideals even when these had been overthrown. It also links with the conclusion of Canto III (117–18) where Ada is imagined loving her father after his death through reading his verse, and thus keeping his spirit alive. If the reader identifies with Ada, the verse creates a sense of intimate relationship with the poet and thus exerts a great emotional pull.

The conclusion of the poem finds the narrator at St Peter's basilica, whose grandeur always impressed Protestant tourists. But, as an experienced traveller, he can compare the mighty dome with the wondrous architecture of what Byron had thought was the Temple of Diana at Ephesus and the church turned mosque of St Sophia at Constantinople (see *Childe Harold's Pilgrimage* II, 79). It is unique: a fitting successor to the temple at Jerusalem and the effect of its sublimity on the visitor is described in imagery of swelling expansion:

> Enter: its grandeur overwhelm thee not;
> And why? it is not lessened; but thy mind,
> Expanded by the genius of the spot,
> Has grown colossal, and can only find
> A fit abode wherein appear enshrined
> Thy hopes of immortality; and thou
> Shalt one day, if found worthy, so defined,
> See thy God face to face, as thou dost now
> His Holy of Holies, nor be blasted by his brow.
> (*Childe Harold's Pilgrimage* IV, 155)

The next four stanzas take the reader with the poet into the basilica to experience the sense of immensity 'increasing with the advance / Like climbing some great

Alp' (IV 156); the senses taking in only an impression of 'Rich marbles—richer painting—shrines'. The act of perception cannot be totalising: 'Thou seest not all; but piecemeal thou must break, / To separate contemplation, the great whole' (IV, 157). This breaking down of the act of perception into its constituent parts serves as an analysis of the way the whole poem has functioned, as an example of loco-descriptive writing. But it is also an indication of Byron's view of nature and human life as always fragmented and in flux. McGann comments of this passage: 'The poet is made aware of the necessity of a "piecemeal" apprehension of a life which we never fully comprehend precisely because it involves us in constant passage and possibility' (McGann 1968: 38). So this, the culmination of the pilgrimage comes to no climax, but merely encapsulates the way the perceiving mind (both poet and reader) participates in the ongoing process which is life by momentary epiphanies and endless self-renewal rather than by one unifying vision or philosophy.

The poem concludes with descriptions of famous sculpture in the Vatican: the Laocoon, a statue of a father's agonising attempt to save his sons from the coils of sea serpents, illustrates the blend of a 'mortal's agony' with 'an immortal's patience' in the human condition (IV, 16). The contrasting Apollo Belvedere, 'a dream of love', like the Venus de' Medici described earlier (IV, 49–53), encapsulates not merely real human beauty, but rather: 'a dream of Love':

> All that ideal beauty ever bless'd
> The mind within its most unearthly mood,
> > (*Childe Harold's Pilgrimage* IV, 162)

Art, the poet concludes, is immortal because it is created by the 'fire which we endure', that 'Prometheus stole from heaven', and consequently 'if made / By human hands, is not of human thought' (IV, 163).

The poem ends in the Romantic wooded landscape beside Lake Albano, where the poet meditates on the ocean – symbol of eternal change yet 'Unchangeable save to thy wild waves' play' (IV, 182). We might think of his image of himself in almost sculptural terms, as a Neptune figure riding the untamed billows:

> And I have loved thee, Ocean! and my joy
> Of youthful sports was on thy breast to be
> Borne, like thy bubbles, onward: from a boy
> I wantoned with thy breakers—they to me
> Were a delight; and if the freshening sea
> Made them a terror—'twas a pleasing fear,
> For I was as it were a child of thee,
> And trusted to thy billows far and near,
> And laid my hand upon thy mane—as I do here.
> > (*Childe Harold's Pilgrimage* IV, 184)

This is a daring stanza with its wordplay punning on child/Childe, and mane/main, which blend the figure of the pilgrim with the child at play in the sea. The last words, in their present tense and immediacy of place 'here', give a dramatic sense of the poet's real presence. The poem has sought to do this in all the scenes visited, where places are rendered of particular significance, not only because of their existing historical or picturesque associations, but because they are now being newly associated with the composition of this poem by Byron. The last word 'here' seems to indicate the poem as well as the billows and leaves the reader with a reminder of his/her intimate connection with the author through the act of reading.

Further reading

On the influence of Hobhouse on this canto, see Andrew Rutherford, 'The Influence of Hobhouse on *Childe Harold's Pilgrimage, Canto IV*' (1961). On Cantos III and IV as a mediation on the theme of time and mortality, see especially Joseph (1964: 70–102). Malcolm Kelsall situates the poem in the context of Augustan and especially Whig representations of Italy in *Byron's Politics* (Kelsall 1987: 57–81). Gleckner sees the canto as a culmination of the total pessimism of the whole poem (Gleckner 1967: 267–98). But Alan Rawes argues, in opposition to Gleckner, that the canto, by exiling the Byronic hero and renewing a sense of Byronic rather than Wordsworthian idealism, is primarily positive, opening the way to the writing of comedy (Rawes 2000: 117–38). For a postmodernist reading, see William H. Galperin, *The Return of the Visible in British Romanticism* (1993: chapter 8).

THE ORIENTAL TALES

During 'the years of fame', Byron wrote six verse tales: *The Giaour* (1813), *The Bride of Abydos* (1813), *The Corsair* (1814), *Lara* (1814), *The Siege of Corinth* (1816) and *Parisina* (1816). They can be thought of as a series, most are set in the Ottoman Empire in the eighteenth century, and all of them are variations on similar themes. The Orient is here the domain of Gothic excess: violent, despotic, sensual. The male protagonists are often outlaws or renegades, competing with a patriarchal ruler for possession of a woman. The poems are full of stirring adventurous action, but all end tragically. The first three are of most importance, and so will be dealt with in more detail.

The Giaour

This poem is a famous example of Byron's habit of accretion. The first version was 375 lines long; the first published edition was 684 lines, but he did not cease adding to it until the seventh edition in December 1813, which reached 1,334 lines (*CPW* III, 413). It is an experimental, fragmented poem made up of snatches of narrative from different points of view. The fictional verse is framed by factual notes in which Byron cites his personal experience of the East and situates himself as an authority on Greek and Turkish culture, though he also acknowledges the help of Barthelemi d'Herbelot's invaluable reference work, *Bibliothèque Orientale* (1697), and Samuel Henley's scholarly notes to the English translation of William Beckford's Orientalist Gothic novel, *Vathek* (1784). Byron didn't expect the poem to be popular, but it had run to fourteen editions by 1815, the first thirteen of which amounted to 12,050 copies (CPW III, 413). The fact that the poem was dedicated to Byron's friend Samuel Rogers is a tribute to the inspiration of the latter's *Voyage of Columbus* (1812), which had suggested the fragment form.

The story of the poem was inspired by the incident in which Byron, whilst swimming at the Piraeus, had seen and intercepted a religious procession which was about to drown a girl sewn up in a sack for sexual misconduct (see Life and Contexts, p. 8). Byron decided against revealing this background to the public, but his final note to the poem testifies to its basis in fact, as well as acknowledging another literary influence. This was the ballads he had heard in Romaic (modern Greek), some of which sung of this subject. 'The fate of Phrosine, the fairest of this sacrifice, is the subject of many a Romaic and Arnaut ditty' (CPW III, 423).

In his development of the 'Byronic hero' character, Byron was influenced by the anti-heroes of Walter Scott's phenomenally successful adventurous verse tales, *Marmion* (1808) and *Rokeby* (1813). But whereas Scott's nostalgic romances mythologised the making of Britain out of the joining of the kingdom of Scotland with the more powerful England, Byron turned to the East to show the crushing of a culture by colonial powers in a much less positive light. In his Advertisement, Byron indicates that the story is set just after the Russian invasion of Greece in 1770. From the rising in the Peloponnese, inspired by this, we can date the beginnings of the Greek struggle for independence from the Turks, who had ruled them since the fifteenth century. The Russian Empress Catherine II only had her own interests at heart, but the Russians successfully fanned the revolt. By 1774, however, they had abandoned the Greeks and concluded the treaty of Kuchuk Kainarji with the Turks. So by 1779, as Byron explains, the Pasha Hassan Ghazi was able to restore Turkish rule by beating back the Arnauts (Albanians) from the Morea which they had been ravaging for some time. The Mainotes (people of the Peloponnese) deserted the Greek side because they were only interested in plunder. The whole area was plunged into unparalleled savagery for several years. No wonder that the memory of the savage reprisals after this first major attempted uprising was enough to deter the Greeks from listening to the Russians' blandishments to rebel in the mid-1780s and later. This is one reason that Philhellenes such as Byron would not succeed in spurring on the movement for independence until 1821.

Byron's poem is an attempt to represent the handing down of such a folk memory through oral culture. He thus dramatises the telling of the tale as a performance for a variety of voices. The poet claims

> The story in the text is one told of a young Venetian many years ago, and now nearly forgotten.—I heard it by accident by one of the coffee-house story-tellers who abound in the Levant, and sing or recite their narratives.—The additions and interpolations by the translator will be easily distinguished from the rest by the want of Eastern imagery; and I regret that my memory has retained so few fragments of the original.
>
> (CPW III, 423)

So the written text is supposedly fragmentary because of the poor memory of the transcriber: this is an attempt to convince the reader of its authenticity. It is also split into several points of view: the comments of the Western Philhellene 'translator' of the present time; the fragments of Turkish memories and eye-witness accounts of the 1780s, which have survived; the Christian monks' memories of the Giaour; and his dying words many years after the main events.

The plot itself is very simple, but has to be pieced together by the reader. A Turkish fisherman tells of a mysterious Venetian, known to Muslims as 'the Giaour' or infidel, who fell in love with Leila, a Circassian (a fair-skinned person from the Caucasus) odalisque in the harem of Hassan, the Turkish ruler. The Pasha has Leila executed for infidelity by being drowned in a sack and sets off on a journey to obtain a new wife. Hassan is ambushed by a band of Greeks and brutally murdered by the Giaour, their leader. Many years later the Giaour, who is residing in a Christian monastery, though he refuses to participate in Christian rites, retells the story from his own point of view before he dies.

The first 126 lines of the poem are in the melancholy and moralising voice of the Western translator, remembering classical heroes such as Themistocles, whose tomb overlooks a still-beautiful landscape. An extended simile likens Greece to the disturbing sight of a corpse of a young girl (ll. 68–102). Man mars this natural 'paradise' with brutal violence: such as a pirate murdering a returning fisherman (ll. 36–45), whose song was perhaps the same one that the ballad singer now recites. Lines 168–79 tell us of one fisherman who did return safely, and from lines 180–797 he is our main narrator. However, we are to imagine the coffee-house bard taking on as many roles as he needs to tell the story (McGann 1968: 145).

The poem is typically Byronic in style: an impression of spontaneity is created by frequent use of the present tense; the metre is urgent, with loose tetrameter couplets whose four insistent beats a line echo the clattering of horses' hooves in our first view of the mysterious Giaour:

> Here loud his raven charger neighed—
> Down glanced that hand, and grasped his blade—
> That sound had burst his waking dream,
> As Slumber starts at owlet's scream.
>   (*The Giaour*, ll. 245–8)

The reader's imagination is encouraged to enter into the gaps and fissures of the poem, not merely to piece together the fragments, but to puzzle over them because the wondering fisherman is partial to the Muslim point of view, isn't omniscient and does not know what to make of what he has seen:

> The hour is past, the Giaour is gone
> And did fly or fall alone?
>   (*The Giaour*, ll. 277–8)

Another complication is that the narration moves between present time, when Hassan's palace is in ruins (ll. 288–351) and memory of the time when the Emir commandeered the fisherman's boat for the casting of Leila, alive, into the sea (ll. 353–87), then back further still to an account of Hassan's search for Leila (ll. 439–72), and then to the lyrical description of her remembered beauty (ll. 473–518). The short scenes create a montage effect like the flashbacks of a film. We then leap forward to the climactic scenes of Hassan's murder, viewed perhaps by a Greek merchant resting on the hill (l. 541). The graphic violence and gloating of the Giaour over his revenge for Leila's death (ll. 675–88) contrasts with the tragic viewpoint of Hassan's mother, looking for his return with a new bride, but met with the sight of a Tartar bearing the body of her son on his horse (ll. 689–722). The Turkish account concludes with a bloodcurdling curse on the 'false Infidel', that he will be consumed with the everlasting fires of hell, after being condemned to 'suck the blood of all thy race' as a vampire (ll. 747–86). This reinforces Hassan's curse on his murderer (l. 619).

The Giaour, all this time, has been seen from the outside, a lonely figure of mystery. To the Muslim fisherman, a supporter of Hassan, he inspires fear at the opening of the poem. Though 'young and pale', he is a man of strong passions, one 'Whom Othman's sons should slay or shun' (l. 199). Compared to a meteor (l. 197), and a demon (l. 202), he mesmerises observers with his 'evil eye'. He is then absent from the poem until Hassan recognises the leader of the ambush as Leila's lover:

> I know him by the pallid brow;
> I know him by the evil eye.
> (*The Giaour*, ll. 611–12)

Even when he is in the European monastery, the monks describe him as solitary, brooding 'within his cell alone' (l. 806). Ironically he seems just as much a 'renegade' (l. 812) and infidel in Christian surroundings as in the Ottoman empire, for the monk comments that he 'shuns our holy shrine' (l. 814). One monk is afraid of the scowl 'That glares beneath his dusky cowl' (l. 834), but he has bought his way in to the monastery (ll. 902–4).

The usual markers of identity are absent: name, religion, cultural or dynastic affiliation. The Giaour therefore represents the rootless individual in modern society, who answers only to himself. The narrator sees him as the ruin of a noble soul (l. 869). All this encourages the reader to look for explanation to the substantial final first-person section where the dying man makes an anti-confession to the Friar, for he has no remorse (ll. 971–1,318). Ironically, what we find out is how similar are Hassan and the Giaour, driven by intense emotions of sexual possessiveness and revenge. The latter is no chivalric knight (ll. 1,103–4), but love for Leila is the overriding value of his life, equivalent to a religion (l. 1,131). He wants no paradise but sees a vision of Leila beckoning to him just before he expires (see Criticism, **p. 111**).

The world of Hassan and the Giaour has proved to be a fateful closed circle like a revenge tragedy. When the Turkish ruler is attacked, we find no patriot has led the raid – only a renegade European with his own agenda. The struggle over Leila has an obvious allegorical reference to the Turkish–Russian war over Greece. But while the Western 'translator's' Philhellenic rhetoric evokes our sympathy, the Satanic figure of the Giaour warns us that intervention has hitherto been tainted with imperialist aspirations which resulted in endless carnage.

The Bride of Abydos

This was begun on 1st November 1813 and the first draft was completed in only ten days, though Byron subsequently made a mass of corrections and amendments until publication at the end of the month. As with *The Giaour* and all the Oriental tales, sexual guilt is a strong theme. Byron's affair with Augusta was the immediate biographical impetus, and he originally intended Selim and Zuleika to be brother and sister (*BLJ* III, 199) (see Life and Contexts, **p. 12**). His intense 'platonic' affair with the married Lady Frances Wedderburn Webster was another contributing factor. The name 'Zuleika' relates to the Turkish version of the biblical story of Potiphar's wife (*CPW* III, 435). Byron often spoke of poetry as a therapeutic relief from private torment, but this must be seen as partly a defensive pose. Beckford's *Vathek* influenced all the tales, but the representation of Selim initially as an androgynous youth who 'falls' into masculinity is particularly reminiscent of the childhood idyll of Vathek, Nouronihar and Gulchrenrouz in the novel.

This is a much more straightforward narrative, with none of the fragments and gaps of *The Giaour*. An emphasis on dialogue, soliloquy and dramatic form is noticeable (Gleckner 1967: 121). The story is now set entirely within the patriarchal household of a Turkish pasha where both the girl and boy are oppressed. The Byronic hero, Selim, is not a static figure like the Giaour, but evolves from passive youth to warrior when he challenges the father-figure, Giaffir, in an Oedipal struggle for power reminiscent of *Hamlet*.

The narrator concentrates on exotic intensity, the verse supported by a panoply of notes. Sensual details of costume and setting evoke the perfumed East:

> She snatched the urn, wherein was mixed
> The Persian Atar-gul's perfume,
> And sprinkled all its odours o'er
> The pictured roof and marble floor.
> (*The Bride of Abydos* I, 269–272)

The fragility of their childhood idyll is smashed when Zuleika is consigned to an arranged marriage. Then Selim reveals that he is not her brother but her cousin and declares his love. Not only that, but he has been plotting with the partisans against the Pasha. Ironies abound as Selim seems set to replicate his enemy's military values and possessiveness over Zuleika (I, 349–50) as the Giaour had Hassan's. When he casts off his robe to reveal his armour and weapons, at first Zuleika thinks he means to kill her (II, 165–75). The renegade Selim paints to her his vision of their love, their freedom and their life with his 'lawless brood' (II, 363): 'The spoil of nations shall bedeck my bride' (II, 413). But their brief dream of escape and happiness is soon cut short as Selim is betrayed and shot down and Zuleika expires through shock and grief. Again the driving pessimism suggests the hopelessness of the utopian dream of a free Greece.

The popularity of this poem can be gauged by the fact that 10,000 copies of the next Oriental tale, *The Corsair*, were sold on the first day of publication. *The*

Bride of Abydos went through eleven editions by 1815 and the first six made up 12,500 copies (*CPW* III, 435).

The Corsair

Byron began this tale on 18 December 1813 and finished the proof corrections on 16 or 17 January 1814 (*CPW* III, 444). The first edition appeared on 1 February but could not remotely sate the public's appetite: the fifth edition was ready by 15 February. This was the height of the poet's popularity with the fashionable world. Perhaps no poet has ever equalled it (see Criticism, **pp. 110–11**).

So far, despite the fact that Byron was a radical Whig, this had been not too obvious to the reviewers, who were dazzled by his rank and knew his publisher to be the acme of respectability and a prominent Tory. The attack on the *Edinburgh Review* in *English Bards and Scotch Reviewers* had misled the public into thinking Byron a Tory also, and nothing he had published so far was too contentious. *The Corsair*, however, nailed Byron's colours to the mast. He added to the second edition the lyric 'Lines to a lady weeping', sympathetically addressed to the Princess Charlotte. This indicated Byron's disgust with the Prince Regent who had changed allegiance from the Whigs to support the Tory government, as had his father the King, whose illness had made him incapable of rule. The Prince's daughter, Princess Charlotte, had wept at the news, and thus became a Whig heroine.

Byron had earlier taken a keen interest in politics (see Life and Contexts, **pp. 9–10**), but by now he was disillusioned, feeling that the Whigs were a feeble opposition. He felt their cause was hopeless, for even when the ailing George III eventually died, it was now clear that his successor would not support a Whig government. Britain's unreformed parliament and corrupt Establishment seemed unassailable. *The Corsair* may be seen as a poetic expression of the poet's intense desire for political liberty to be extended at home and abroad, yet his pessimistic fear that this would never happen. Byron appended a dedicatory epistle to the Irish poet, Thomas Moore, which alluded to 'the wrongs of your own country' (*CPW* III, 148), thus making a parallel with Oriental despotism and British colonialism. The Tory Murray had resisted both the inclusion of the lyric and this preface.

The Byronic heroes of all these tales are aristocrats leading rebellious factions against their rulers and express the poet's desire for revolution in Britain as well as in Greece, but directed by an individual charismatic leader whom the people revere and obey. They may also be seen as expressing Byron's ambivalent feelings about Napoleon Bonaparte, a magnificent yet deeply flawed military hero, a dictator yet a charismatic figure who fought in the name of liberty. The chief literary influence on *The Corsair* is the *Sturm und Drang* German dramas which featured rebellious young men immured in moribund societies and who turn to crime or anti-social acts. J. C. F. Schiller's *The Robbers* or *Fiesco* are the prime examples. The name of Conrad was taken from Byron's reading of J. C. L. Sismondi's history of the Italian republics, for it alludes to a thirteenth-century Ghibelline aristocrat who continued to support republicanism though history seemed to be consigning it to oblivion. Adherence to the republican Ghibelline party had been superseded by support for their enemies, the Guelph grouping. For Byron, this meant the rule of despots (*CPW* III, 445), especially as the Guelphs were ancestors of the House of Hanover, now ruling Britain.

Byron announced in his preface that he was abandoning 'the fatal facility of the octosyllabic verse' in order to return to the more traditional metre of the heroic couplet. Susan Wolfson has pointed out the paradox of choosing this greater poetic discipline when writing of an outlaw: 'Byron's poetry shimmers with a complex interplay of formal commitments in which the energies of freedom and eruption are set against the demands of constraint and conservatism' (Wolfson 1997: 134).

> Let him who crawls enamoured of decay,
> Cling to his couch, and sicken years away;
> Heave his thick breath; and shake his palsied head;
> Ours- the fresh turf, and not the feverish bed.
>
> (*The Corsair* I, 27–30)

The hero of the poem, Conrad, is a stern and villainous pirate chief (I, 203–26), whose only redeeming quality is his uxorious devotion to the fragile and vulnerable Medora who patiently awaits his return at home. In Canto II he leads a daring raid on his enemy the Pacha Seyd, gaining entry disguised as a dervish or holy man. The palace is torched and all would be well but for Conrad's chivalrous instruction that the women of the harem must be saved. He himself rescues the beautiful odalisque, Gulnare. Losing the advantage of speed and surprise, Conrad becomes separated from his men, most of whom escape, and he is captured. He is doomed to an agonising death by impalement (a sort of symbolic rape), for Seyd is 'thirsting for revenge' (III, 161). However, Gulnare visits him and promises to try and set him free. Conrad is reluctant to be saved by a woman. When she returns, declaring her love for Conrad, and with a plan to murder Seyd in his sleep, Conrad is horrified, but she is resolved to 'try the firmness of a female hand' (III, 381) to revenge herself for the sexual slavery she has endured. The conventional gender roles now seem reversed with Gulnare murdering the Pasha and arranging the escape and Conrad the reluctant follower.

In Gulnare, the heroine, for the first time, plays a more active and resourceful part than the male hero. He is reluctant to act, rendered impotent and passive by his adherence to an unrealistic code of masculine honour. Gulnare is masculinised by her actions, and Conrad is unmanned by the sight of her with a spot of blood on her forehead, the image of revolutionary passion. When, after their escape, she shows signs of feminine distress, however, Conrad rewards her return to normality with a kiss. But after they have met up with the pirates and Conrad returns to Medora's isle, he finds the love of his life has died in his absence.

The alarming transformation of Gulnare from feminine maiden in distress to blood-freezing homicide symbolised for Byron's wealthy readership their widespread fear of the revolutionary passions of the lower classes gaining the upper hand, as in the French Revolution. A female assassin epitomised the unnaturalness of overturning the social order. This is underlined when the Byronic heroine's revolt against the sexual oppression of women coincides with the death of the conventionally angelic and feminine 'wife' figure in the home (see Criticism, p. 116).

Other verse tales

Byron would go on experimenting with the ambivalent figure of the warrior maiden in the character of Kaled in *Lara*, a tale set in Europe concerning a mysterious nobleman and his devoted young squire, which can be seen as a sort of sequel to *The Corsair*. Only when being tended for wounds on the battlefield is it discovered that Kaled is a woman. As with the character of Matilda in *The Monk*, this device allows for a gay reading of the Lara–Kaled relationship (see Criticism, p. 115). Byron had *Lara* published with Rogers' verse tale *Jacqueline*: 'Larry and Jackie' as he called the volume. He thought *Lara* rather slight to stand alone, but another reason, perhaps, might have been that he was aware of the piquant contrast between his cross-dressed warrior woman and Rogers' heroine, who embodies the conventionally feminine ideal of domesticity. (Byron's interest in questioning the gender boundaries would later be evident in the creation of another warrior woman: Myrrha, a passionate Greek odalisque in the Orientalist play, *Sardanapalus*, ironically in love with her effeminate master.)

In the last tale set in the Ottoman Empire, *The Siege of Corinth*, Byron returned to a definite historical setting for a strongly Philhellenist story, when the Venetians fought against the incursion of the Turks, to retain possession of the city of Corinth in Greece in 1715. There is a bleak dualism in the way that Western and Ottoman imperialism are depicted as equally predatory and militaristic and equally driven by fanatical religious faiths. As in *The Giaour*, possession of Greece is symbolised by the struggle between two men for possession of a woman, a woman who has died unbeknown to the renegade protagonist, Alp. This tale is strongly Gothic: Byron uses the supernatural as well as graphically realistic description of the horrors of war to rouse the emotions of the reader.

Further reading

Gleckner (1967: 91–202) gives a detailed account of all the tales, relating them to imagery of the fall and to the poet's philosophical pessimism. For the context of contemporary politics, essential to understanding the mood that produced *The Corsair*, see Byron's journal in *BLJ* III, 204–58. On this political context, see Peter Manning, 'Tales and Politics: *The Corsair, Lara, The White Doe of Rylstone*' (1981). Politics is also the main preoccupation of Daniel P. Watkins's Marxist study, *Social Relations in Byron's Eastern Tales* (1987). Nigel Leask's *British Romantic Writers and the East: Anxieties of Empire* (1993) deals extensively with the tales in a fine study of Byron's ambivalent relationship with imperialism and literary Orientalism. Marilyn Butler's historicist essay 'The Orientalism of Byron's *The Giaour*' (1988) is also essential reading. On gender politics, see Franklin (1992: 38–98). On the relationship of form to ideology and gender see Susan Wolfson's 'Heroic form: Couplets, "Self", and Byron's *Corsair*', in *Formal Charges: The Shaping of Poetry in British Romanticism* (1997: 133–163).

Manfred

Byron began writing *Manfred* in the summer of 1816 in Switzerland; the first two acts were probably composed as he was touring the Alps. The first draft was completed in Venice by February 1817, but when Murray's adviser, William Gifford found the third act weak, the poet agreed to provide a new version. The play was published on 16 June 1817, and, though this was a large edition of 6,000 copies, it was so popular that a second was called for the same year (*CPW* IV, 465). Byron wrote of the central character who dominated the poem: '[H]e is one of the best of my misbegotten – say what they will' (*BLJ* V, 249).

The protagonist, a Byronic hero, was similar to a Gothic villain, in that he nursed a dark secret which, it is hinted, was incest with his twin sister, Astarte. More than that, the deed had led to her death, perhaps by suicide (II, ii, 104–21). The biographical context of Byron's remorse and self-disgust, his preoccupation with the concept of damnation following his incestuous relationship with his half-sister, Augusta, and the breakdown of his marriage, is obvious (see Life and Contexts, **p. 12**). On the other hand, many Gothic and Romantic writers wrote about incest without personal experience. McGann suggests that Astarte should be seen not as representing Augusta, but as Manfred's star or epipsyche, for the theme is self-destruction rather than sexual guilt (*CPW* V, 467). The play certainly should be regarded not merely as therapeutic self-expression but, in literary terms, as a bold generic experiment.

The poet had been strongly influenced by M. G. Lewis's oral translation of parts of the German poet Goethe's play, *Faust* (see Life and Contexts, **pp. 15–16**). However, Goethe approved of *Manfred*, for he felt that Byron had transformed the Faustian theme of the Promethean rebel who stands up to the gods, and made it his own. Byron had also evoked the atmosphere of Lewis's own Gothic novel, *The Monk* (1796), and Beckford's *Vathek* (*BLJ* V, 268; *CPW* V, 465–6). Manfred is an experimental poem: a modified monodrama, or short lyrical play, concentrating on one protagonist's psyche, which included songs and could be accompanied by music. Byron's play was not intended for the stage, but to be read as a poem (see Criticism, **pp. 117–19**). It dramatises the struggle within the mind of one man, and we could see the supernatural spirits as representing aspects of that mind.

The play opens melodramatically in a Gothic gallery at midnight, and the Magus figure, Manfred, a Faustian seeker after knowledge, conjures up seven spirits of earth and air. But he asks them not for more life, wealth or powers, but for forgetfulness. They can only offer 'Kingdom and sway, and strength, and length of days' (I, i, 168). The Satanic Manfred commands the most powerful of them to manifest itself in 'such aspect' which 'may seem most fitting' (I, i, 187). Now the seventh – that which once ruled Manfred's star of destiny – takes on a beautiful female shape and Manfred, in trying and failing to embrace it, falls senseless to the ground. We take it that the spirit took on the appearance of Astarte, from whom Manfred is separated by death. A voice, perhaps that of the same spirit, pronounces an incantation or curse over his recumbent body, that his tormented mind will be his own hell. In fact, Byron had originally written this curse about his wife! In the play, it is the evil Manfred who has brought this punishment on himself. He is compelled to go on living after all joy in life has gone, like Cain, the eternal wanderer, or Coleridge's ancient mariner.

The next scene finds Manfred tottering on a crag, high on the Alps, intent on suicide. The setting is reminiscent of Prometheus on the rock of the Caucasus in Aeschylus's *Prometheus Bound* (*CPW* IV, 472). Just as he seems about to throw himself down, he is saved by an agile chamois hunter. He realises he must accept his fate. His name suggests that in some ways Manfred is representative of mankind in general. He epitomises the strange combination of nobility and the despicable that condemns humanity to be pulled in two directions, earthward and heavenward:

> But we, . . .
> Half dust, half deity, alike unfit
> To sink or soar, with our mix'd essence make
> A conflict of its elements.
> (*Manfred* I, ii, 39–42)

The kindly hunter's sturdy independence and pastoral life in tune with nature make him a representative of Wordsworthian values. Though Manfred respects these, he would not exchange his lot with the older man's, he wants intensity of experience. To go to the limits he is willing to endure 'what others could not brook to dream' (II, i, 78).

This theme is developed further in Act II Scene ii, when Manfred conjures up the Witch of the Alps, the spirit of the sunbow produced from sun on the cataract. She represents the spirit of Nature itself, and Manfred tells his story to her. The imagery of mountains, of the solitary wanderer, emphasises that this aristocratic intellectual is a solitary Promethean rebel who has turned away from society: 'I had no sympathy with breathing flesh' (II, ii, 56). He epitomises Romantic individualism. He breathes 'The difficult air of the iced mountain's top' (II, ii, 62). He dives 'In my lone wanderings, to the caves of death' (II, ii, 80). We could make comparisons with Mary Shelley's *Frankenstein*, or Percy Shelley's *Alastor*, which both portray the aspiring and solitary seeker after philosophical truth or forbidden knowledge (see Life and Contexts, **p. 15**).

Manfred describes his sister as his counterpart or twin: the only person he could confide in (II, ii, 104–17). He confesses that he destroyed her, not literally by shedding her blood, but by breaking her heart (II, ii, 118–21). He wants either to raise Astarte from the dead, to speak to her, or to die and thus join her. The Witch is willing to help, but Manfred refuses to swear obedience to her. We begin to see that the pattern of the play is that Manfred is on a quest for oblivion but that each time he proudly rejects the spirits he consults, by refusing to grant them authority over his mind. Each supernatural being is of a higher order than the last, as Manfred penetrates deeper into the secrets of nature.

Act II Scene iii, on the summit of the Jungfrau, shows the three Destinies who are joined by Nemesis, symbolising Fate. They remind us of the weird sisters in *Macbeth*. Their songs show them to be more powerful spirits of nature than the seven elemental spirits of the opening scene. Though they are also aspects of Nature, they are destructive forces of negation and have been at work spreading storms, plague and destroying political freedom in human society. They are on their way to the Hall of Arimanes, whom we meet in Scene iv, seated on a globe of fire. The setting is reminiscent of the domain of Eblis in *Vathek*. The name 'Arimanes' derives from Ahriman, the evil principle in the dualistic ancient Persian religion of Zoroastrianism. He is a more powerful version of Satan. Manfred's quest has brought him to some form of Hades, but he will show that he has free will.

The elemental spirits and Destinies and Nemesis all bow down and worship the terrible Prince of Earth and Air (II, iv, 21). Manfred has knelt to his own desolation (II, iv, 40), and is willing to kneel to the Creator of the universe (II, iv, 48), but – as by now we would expect – he proudly refuses to worship Arimanes. Nevertheless, Manfred is acclaimed by the spirits, for:

> his sufferings
> Have been of an immortal nature, like
> Our own.
>
> (*Manfred* II, iv, 53–5)

He has gained a power unique amongst the spirits (II, iv, 69–72). Because of this, Arimanes grants his wish to raise the phantom of Astarte from the dead. However, she refuses to speak to Manfred when commanded. Nemesis concludes: 'She is not of our order, but belongs / To the other powers' (II, iv, 115–16). This indicates that she is perhaps in Heaven or at least in Purgatory. Manfred makes an agonised speech begging her again and again to speak to him, to say she 'loath'st [him] not', that he may bear the punishment for both, that she will be 'one of the blessed' but that he shall die (II, iv, 125–7). Finally she tells him that his earthly ills will be ended on the morrow, but only bids farewell in answer to questions as to whether he will be forgiven, whether they will meet again or whether she loves him. The phantom then disappears, not to be recalled, and this seems to mean that their bond is broken and that she will remain with the powers of good and Manfred will be released to die.

The third act shows the abbot of St Maurice attempting to save Manfred's soul, but he refuses a mediator between himself and any deity (III, i, 55). He respects the priest but he has never accommodated his mind to the judgement of others, even to gain sway in order to benefit humankind with his great gifts. He won't begin now. Then Manfred makes his orisons to the setting sun (III, ii) and later, from his tower, to the moon and stars. The Abbot returns to pray for him and thus witnesses the dreadful evil spirits that come to claim Manfred, presumably to take him to Hell. However, he repudiates these also and dies as fiercely independent as he had lived.

Commentators differ over their interpretations of the play's precise philosophical meaning, and some judge it muddled (see Criticism, p. 89). But what is clear is that it dramatised one man's sceptical refusal to conform to Christian doctrine, to pay homage to a pantheistical god of nature or to accept the idea of judgement and punishment in the hereafter. Only an exceptional individual can stand alone from all philosophical systems, relying entirely on his own value judgements. Not only does he risk damnation but also the charges modern readers may make of solipsism and Romantic egoism. Such an individual may perform a service to society by challenging the limits on human behaviour, but will become an alienated outcast. Incest represents a social taboo that such a hero is willing to break in the name of antinomianism (the repudiation of moral law). If we take Astarte to represent Manfred's epipsyche, the best part of himself, then he has destroyed the feminine or humanitarian side of his nature to achieve his iron will.

Further reading

For the biographical context and the effect of the scenery on the poem, see Byron's journal which he kept for his sister: *BLJ* V, 96–105. On Manfred as a Byronic hero, see Thorslev (1962: 165–76). For the relationship between *Manfred* and Byron's œuvre, see Joseph (1964: 103–7), and on the philosophical dimensions, see Gleckner (1967: 250–65). For a feminist reading, see Franklin (1992: 222–32). As a closet play, see Simpson (1998: 129–96). On allusions to the Bible, see Travis Looper, *Byron and the Bible: A Compendium of biblical Usage in the Poetry of Lord Byron* (1978: 234–7).

Don Juan

Although modern critics discuss the poem as if it were one entity, we should remember that it was a serial publication: with John Murray bringing out the first two volumes (Cantos I–V) and the radical publisher John Hunt the next four (Cantos VI–XVI). It was unfinished at Byron's death in 1824, so it is a fragment poem as well as a satire which functions as a mock epic. Byron began the poem on 3 July 1818, and Cantos I and II were finally published anonymously on 15 July 1819 (see Life and Contexts, **pp. 18–21**). This first edition was minus the satiric Dedication Byron had written to his foe the Tory Poet Laureate, Robert Southey, and had been somewhat Bowdlerized by Murray and Gifford. Byron's London friends, such as Hobhouse, and Murray's advisers had been opposed to publication altogether, because they feared the poem might be prosecuted for obscenity, blasphemy and defamation, that it would reignite the separation scandal and that it would complete the ruin of Byron's reputation. The first two cantos met with almost universal moral outrage and critical condemnation of its supposed nihilism (see Criticism, **p. 87**). Byron had to struggle to continue with the poem and have the second installment published by the reluctant Murray on 8 August 1821 (see Life and Contexts, **pp. 21–2**). Byron began a new section of the poem in January 1822 (*CPW* V, 715), but Murray was alarmed at both the sexual frankness and Byron's increasing radicalism and would publish no more of *Don Juan*. Eventually, his alliance with Shelley and Leigh Hunt led to the break-up of Byron and Murray's business partnership altogether. Byron had already lost his quarto-buying upper-class readership, but, by the 1820s, lower-class reformers were championing the noble poet, and cheap editions of his poetry sold well to the public at large. John Hunt published Cantos VI–VIII on 15 July 1823; and Byron composed a preface in which he rededicated himself to the fight for liberty (see Life and Contexts, **p. 26**). Cantos IX–XI were published on 29 August 1823, XII–XIV on 1 December 1823, and XV–XVI on 26 March 1824. The beginning of Canto XVII was found amongst Byron's papers after his death.

The models for the poem were the same as for *Beppo*: principally the Italian tradition of *ottava rima* burlesques by Luigi Pulci and Giambattista Casti. This burlesque tradition travestied the exalted chivalric values of romance, exemplified by the sprawling verse narratives of Francesco Berni and Ludovico Ariosto, often incorporating anti-clerical or political satire (Vassallo 1984: 94). Like *Childe Harold's Pilgrimage*, *Don Juan* is a quest narrative, but one with an innocent idealistic hero brought face to face with grotesque instances of vice and corruption in the manner of Voltaire's *Candide*. The verse form had been seldom used in English literature, but its abbreviated sonnet form ABABABCC was so flexible it could be adapted to description (II, 77), speech (I, 153), dialogue (V, 84), lyrical introspection (I, 214), narrative action (VIII, 71), but particularly allowed a swelling lyricism deflated by a comic couplet.

> And she bent o'er him, and he lay beneath,
> Hush'd as the babe upon its mother's breast,
> Droop'd as the willow when no winds can breathe,
> Lull'd like the depth of ocean when at rest,
> Fair as the crowning rose of the whole wreath,
> Soft as the callow cygnet in its nest;
> In short he was a very pretty fellow,
> Although his woes had turn'd him rather yellow.
>   (*Don Juan* II, 148)

Byron turned the main disadvantage of the stanza, the lack of sufficient rhymes in English, to comic effect ('mathematical'/'Attic all'/'what I call' in I,12), with polysyllabic rhymes:

> But—Oh! ye lords of ladies intellectual,
> Inform us truly, have they not hen-peck'd you all?
>   (*Don Juan* I, 22)

The influence of the satiric tradition of the Roman poets Horace, Juvenal and Persius may often be seen in the rhetoric of individual passages (e.g., Canto V; see Beatty 1985: 138–46). However, as a Romantic writer, Byron was unable to appeal to a moral and literary consensus, as the Augustan or classical satirists did. A piece of defiantly libertine writing, *Don Juan* was definitively Romantic – an individual's protest against social conformity. The poem was experimental in adapting a conversational, apparently improvisatory voice to narrate a medley of material, and Byron cited Chaucer, Ariosto and Prior as forebears having developed such a colloquial style (*BLJ* VI, 76–7, 91). His epigraph from Horace, *Ars Poetica*, 128, he translated ' 'Tis no slight task to write on common things', which indicated his intention to write on the power relations underlying the personal sexual life.

The autobiographical impulse was central to the poem, which was written coterminously with the composition of his *Memoirs* (burned after his death by his literary executors). The narrator uses the past sense and a specific late eighteenth-century setting for Don Juan's story: 'There was an end of Ismail—hapless town! / Far flashed her burning towers o'er Danube's stream' (VIII, 127). But a diary-like present tense and contemporary time scheme conveys the immediacy of his own thoughts: 'But now at thirty years my hair is grey' (I, 213). A particular feature is that he constantly comments on the compositional process:

> I feel this tediousness will never do –
> 'Tis being *too* epic . . .
> (*Don Juan* III, 111)

Don Juan has sometimes been compared with eighteenth-century fiction (England 1975). For example, Henry Fielding's *Tom Jones* and Laurence Sterne's *Tristram Shandy* both incorporated ironic questioning of the nature of fiction itself. Rousseau and Richardson's novels of sentiment were epistolary, thus introducing first-person confessional material into prose fiction. Byron was one of Britain's most brilliant writers of informal letters, especially when describing his experiences as a libertine in Venice in missives designed to amuse Murray's circle (e.g., *BLJ* V, 164–7). It was these which had made the publisher suggest he try his hand at sexual comedy in the first place, and the style of the poem owes much to these letters.

Both the *Memoirs* and *Don Juan* were self-justificatory ripostes to the London Establishment which had cast the poet beyond the Pale. British hypocrisy and religious cant were in his sights:

> Happy the nations of the moral north!
> Where all is virtue, and the winter season
> Sends sin, without a rag on, shivering forth;
> (*Don Juan* I, 64)

Much of the poem's sharpest satire was aimed at individuals, such as the stanzas on Wellington:

> You are 'the best of cut-throats:'—do not start;
> The phrase is Shakespeare's, and not misapplied:—
> War's a brain-spattering, windpipe-slitting art,
> Unless her cause by Right be sanctified.
> If you have acted *once* a generous part,
> The World, not the World's masters, will decide,
> And I shall be delighted to learn who,
> Save you and yours, have gained by Waterloo?
> (*Don Juan* IX, 4)

Dedication

Satire traditionally contained such *ad hominem* attacks on individuals, and the Dedication to the poem is another example. Byron had intended to instigate a literary feud with Robert Southey, on the personal grounds that he believed the Poet Laureate had spread slanderous gossip about him and Shelley, as well as his contempt for Southey's metamorphosis from revolutionary idealist in the 1790s to Tory sycophant by 1813. Byron omitted the Dedication when the poem was published anonymously 'I won't attack the dog in the dark' (*CPW* V, 670–1). However, Southey doubtless got wind of its existence through literary gossip. The Dedication constructs an opposition between its young, radical, cosmopolitan author and the older-generation conservatives whose poetry mythologised the British countryside. Byron attacked Southey and his fellow lake poet Wordsworth as placemen, who have accepted sinecures from the Tory government and Prince Regent for whom they 'sing' (Dedication, 1–2, 6, 17). As in *English Bards and Scotch Reviewers* and the later disputation with the minor poet Revd Bowles, Byron took a somewhat quixotic position in defending Pope and attacking the Romantic movement he himself was popularly thought to symbolize, and he resented the rising critical reputation of Wordsworth, which challenged his own supremacy. The pomposity of Southey (3), long-windedness of Wordsworth (4), philosophical obscurity of Coleridge (2), insularity and conceit of all three (5) lead the narrator to declare that Scott, Rogers, Campbell, Moore and Crabbe (7) will be judged greater by posterity (the middle three were Whigs). Byron adversely compares the would-be epic poet Southey to the blind bard John Milton (10–11), republican author of *Paradise Lost*. Milton also experienced the overthrow of a revolution and the restoration of the monarchy, 'But closed the tyrant-hater he begun'. Byron was influenced by 'On the Sublime' by the classical writer known as the pseudo-Longinus who equated real poetic sublimity with dedication to liberty (*CPW* V, 669).

A traditional aspect of satiric vituperation was to attack one's victim's sexual potency, and Byron, in a poem vindicating libertinism, now targets 'The intellectual eunuch Castlereagh' (11) as 'emasculated to the marrow' (15), perhaps implying that the statesman was homosexual. Byron loads the foreign secretary with abuse for his part in aiding the British government and its allies in imperial tyranny over Ireland, Italy and all the subject nations of Europe (12–16).

Cantos I–IV

This dedication would have made plain the political purpose of the poem, which the Tory Murray obscured by his 'cutting and slashing'. The first five stanzas of Canto I were also extremely provocative: complaining of the want of true heroism just a few years after the battle of Waterloo and implying that French warriors such as Bonaparte were on a par with Wellesley, the Duke of Wellington. The narrator asserts the overwhelming power of poetry. It is poets who choose to confer immortality on some soldiers rather than others, says the Byronic narrator, implying that he could do for Wellington what Homer did for Agamemnon if he chose (I, 5). Instead, he chooses a famous lover not a fighter. This is in tune with the function of the poem as an anti-epic, and one of the most powerful anti-war poems in English literature (see Cantos VII–IX, and further execration of Wellington: IX, 1–5).

The Don Juan myth also enables Byron, who had thrown himself into libertinism whilst living in Venice, to use his protagonist as an alter ego, to project aspects of himself for moral scrutiny, as he had with Childe Harold. The story of Don Juan first surfaced, probably from folklore, in a 1630 morality play, *El*

Burlador de Sevilla, y Comidada de Piedra (*The Joker of Seville and the Stone Guest*) by a Spanish monk known as Tirso de Molina (see Criticism, **p. 106**). It told the story of an aristocratic libertine endlessly seducing vulnerable women, who killed the father of one of his victims in a duel. One day, the stone statue of the father spoke to foretell the libertine's damnation, but Don Juan merely mockingly invited him to join him for dinner that evening. The statue of the father, the Commandant of Seville, took the insouciant seducer at his word and appeared at the appointed time. Taking Don Juan by the hand, he pulled him down to face retribution in Hell.

Byron may have seen the original play performed in Spain in 1809, though it is unlikely. The story was adapted as a comedy by Molière in 1665, but as a tragedy by Thomas Shadwell (1676). The moral of the latter was praised by Coleridge in *Biographia Literaria* (1817), who suggested that someone should write an up-to-date version of the myth. Byron may well have been inspired by this suggestion, though not by its didacticism. His version has more in common with Goldoni's comedy, *Don Giovanni Tenorio*, which he is likely to have seen in Venice, as well as the brilliant opera, *Don Giovanni* (1787), by Mozart and Da Ponte. In the wake of the latter's first performance in Britain in 1817, the Don Juan myth had become the subject of many comic pantomimes and musicals in London. It is to the most famous of these that Byron's poem alludes (I, 1). Byron's poem was the first major adaptation of the Don Juan myth to portray the protagonist not as a villain but as the good-natured recipient of women's libidinous advances. As well as self-justification, such a twist enabled a masculinist aristocratic attack on the bourgeois Evangelicalism sweeping Britain, and the enhanced role of women as custodians of moral virtue (Franklin 1992: 101). But, however benign the young seducer seems as a seeker for ideal love, and however subversive of marriage, the myth itself may be seen as inherently conservative. Don Juan's seductions challenge the ethos of masculine honour, which, some critics think, only provides an opportunity for the reaffirmation of the social and cultural hegemony of patriarchy (Mandrell 1992: 273). Psychoanalysts have pointed out the Oedipal nature of the myth and suggest that the many women seduced by the great lover represent the one and unobtainable mother (Rank 1975: 20).

Because Byron's protagonist is young, passive and speaks little, he is something of an empty centre of the narrative, in contrast to the confident, loquacious, older and experienced man who tells his story. The narrator often freezes the action while stepping forward to the front of the stage to speak to the reader in confidence:

> For my part I say nothing—nothing—but
> *This* I will say—my reasons are my own—
> (*Don Juan* I, 52)

The narrator and the hero have been seen as age-related versions of the same man. To some extent they split sensibility between them: one is all spontaneous bodily sensation and the other meditative human consciousness. The act of narration has been described as a process of 'simultaneous self-dramatisation and self-detachment' (Joseph 1964: 196). After a few gestures towards characterising the narrator as a gossipy Spanish bachelor (I, 23–4), Byron makes him a multi-faceted and ever-changing poetic voice with many recognisably Byronic characteristics, especially his feeling that he can no longer experience the intense feelings of youth (I, 214–16), his 'mobility' and his intense interest in the process of composition. The narrator's frequent digressions perpetually destroy the illusion of fiction: 'The coast—I think it was the coast that I / Was just describing—' (II, 181). He is not omniscient but likes to drop hints: 'Julia was—yet I never could see why— / With Donna Inez quite a favourite friend' (I, 66), and he puzzles over the characters' motivations (I, 68). He is sexually suggestive rather than overt:

> And then—God knows what next—I can't go on;
> I'm almost sorry that I e'er begun.
> (*Don Juan* I, 115)

Sometimes the narrator seems to take an orthodox Christian stance, suggesting Juan and his second lover, Haidée, will suffer eternal damnation because they are lovers but unmarried (II, 192–3) and promising the reader outright: 'A panorama view of hell's in training' (I, 200). Yet he minutely and empathetically enters into the thoughts and feelings of the lovers (I, 75–85; II, 190–1, 195–7), though occasionally cooling down the most emotional passages with a hint of man-of-the-world cynical deflation (IV, 24–5, 51). The poet mockingly anticipates the condemnation of the censorious reader of the subject matter (III, 12), yet at other times allows the ironic mask to slip, confessing:

> And if I laugh at any mortal thing,
> 'Tis that I may not weep,
> (*Don Juan* IV, 4)

He often claims the poem is moral (I, 207–8; V, 2) and asserts 'this story's actually true' (I, 202) in the manner of naïve didacticism. Byron's contemporaries would have more readily excused the subject matter if the narrator had straightforwardly guided the reader's moral judgement and the poem had concluded with the conventional punishment of Juan with damnation. Byron's narrator's apparent aimlessness and frequent digressions (about a third of the poem) foreground and question such assumptions about the purpose of fiction and, indeed, the morality of punitive religion (III, 96; IX 41–2; XII, 39). The poet had written on 12 August 1819: 'I *have* no plan – I *had* no plan – but I had or have materials' (*BLJ* VI, 207–8). In the same letter he replied to a reader who had complained that reading the poem was like being scorched and drenched at the same time: 'Why man the Soul of such writing is it's [*sic*] licence?—at least the *liberty* of that *licence* if one likes'. The longer Juan's story was extended, the more it defied the effect of closure and approached moral relativity. Yet the poem always asserts a common humanity (Joseph 1964: 209) even while epic allusions implicitly set human weakness against the high aristocratic ideals of honour and chivalry.

Byron uses the traditional Spanish setting of the Don Juan myth, but adopts the psychological stance of a *Bildungsroman* by, for the first time in the history of the myth, filling in details of Juan's repressive childhood, unhappily married parents and strict religious education. The portrait of his widowed mother Donna Inez is a composite of Byron's mother and wife, but also a stock misogynist type of the female pedant (I, 10–22). Her friend Julia, who seduces the sixteen-year-old, is another comic type, the self-deceiving sentimentalist (I, 79–81). Such a contrast between two female characters representing sense and sensibility was a stock device of the moralistic feminocentric novel, though here the formula is undermined as both characters are eventually shown to be hypocrites (I, 66, 146–57).

The fabliau-like plot of Juan's seduction by the married woman, Julia, was modelled on the *Novelle Galanti* of Casti, which usually pit innocence against the guile of experience and particularly feature the resourceful trickery of unfaithful wives (Vassallo 1984: 67–81). After the broad comedy of the discovery of Juan in the bedroom by Julia's husband, the canto concludes with a return to the novelistic in Julia's farewell letter to Juan before she is shut away in a nunnery for her sins (I, 192–7). This letter echoed similar complaints to those expressed by the heroines of Madame de Staël's *Corinne* and Jane Austen's *Persuasion*, foregrounding an awareness that, because of the sexual double standard, women rather than men risked everything in illicit love. Byron's mimicry of the female-authored novel surfaces again in the English cantos (Cantos X–XVII), which could be seen as rewriting Canto I in subtler terms.

Canto II is an extraordinary poem, which seems provocatively to contrast mankind at its very worst and very best. The account of the shipwreck and the ordeal in the longboat of the starving survivors amongst whom eventually 'the longings of the cannibal arise' (II, 72), alludes to the notorious wreck of the French vessel *Medusa* in 1816. As with Géricault's famous painting, Byron was daring in depicting this taboo subject: treating the conservative myth that cannibals (especially French republicans) went mad and died with ironic overstatement in Stanza 79 (Martin 1982: 209–13). The device of having Julia's exquisitely penned letter ripped up to draw lots for 'who should die to be his fellow's food' (II, 73) darkens the theme of the demonic possession of the spirit by the body, which had already provided the broad comedy of the sea-sickness scene (II, 18–23).

> Sooner shall heaven kiss earth'—(here he fell sicker)
> 'Oh Julia! what is every other woe?—
> (For God's sake let me have a glass of liquor,
> Pedro, Battista, help me down below.)
> Julia, my love!—(you rascal, Pedro, quicker)—
> Oh Julia!—(this curst vessel pitches so)—
> Beloved Julia, hear me still beseeching!'
> (Here he grew inarticulate with reaching.)
> (*Don Juan* II, 20)

This is very typical of the carnivalesque subversion of the life of the spirit by the drives of the body, in grotesque images comparable to those the literary critic Mikhail Bakhtin has identified in the work of Rabelais, where the lower body gains the ascendancy over the upper (Wood 1993: 113). In a ghastly parody of the Mass, the sailors partake of the body and blood 'from the fast-flowing veins' (II, 77) of one of their number, Juan's tutor. The poet emphasised: ' 'Twas nature gnaw'd them to this resolution' (II, 75), as if nature herself was preying on humanity.

Yet on the wild Greek isle where Juan is washed up, it is a divine nature which presides over his sacramental union with his beloved Haidée:

> Ocean their witness, and the cave their bed,
> By their own feelings hallow'd and united,
> Their priest was Solitude, and they were wed:
> And they were happy, for to their young eyes
> Each was an angel, and earth paradise.
>
> (*Don Juan* II, 204)

It is a commonplace of criticism that Byron's imagery obsessively evokes the biblical theme of the lost Eden (see, for example, in this episode II, 117, 189, 193, 204). That imagery hints at the temporary nature of their happiness and even of their love, but – while it does exist – romantic love is described in the highest terms. Haidée saves Juan's life, risking her piratical father's wrath secretly to shelter, feed, clothe and nurse him back to life. Selfless human love is beautifully evoked in stanzas on her watching him sleeping (II, 195–8):

> For there it lies so tranquil, so beloved,
> All that it hath of life with us is living;
> So gentle, stirless, helpless, and unmoved,
> And all unconscious of the joy 'tis giving;
> All it hath felt, inflicted, pass'd, and proved,
> Hush'd into depths beyond the watcher's diving;
> There lies the thing we love with all its errors
> And all its charms, like death without its terrors.
>
> (*Don Juan* II, 197)

Byron revisits the Orientalist subject matter of his earlier verse in the Greek and Turkish episodes (see Life and Contexts, **p. 5** and Criticism, **p. 113**). Cantos II–IV strongly evoke Homer's *Odyssey*, Books V–VIII and XXI–XXIV (*CPW* V, 669), which Byron would expect his readers to realise. Most obviously, Haidée reminds us of Nausicaa when she discovers a naked man washed up on the beach (II, 129). Her corsair father's return to the island after his long absence had made everyone think he was dead, evokes the return of Odysseus to Ithaca (III, 23–43). The luxurious splendour of Juan and Haidée's feast, after which they are entertained by the singing of a Philhellenist song by a Southeyan turncoat poet, is therefore framed by our ironic awareness of modernity's loss of classical heroic values. The young lovers are not shown as inspired by the call to arms in the song: they take a siesta. They will be rudely awakened by the return of Haidée's absent father, Lambro. His name alludes to the Greek patriot Lambros Katsones, who was a rebel against Turkish rule during the Turkish-Russian war of 1787–91, the precise period during which the poem is set (Boyd 1958: 76). At the time this section of the poem was published, in 1821, the Greek War of Independence had just broken out. So the narrator's digression on the power of poetry shows that 'The Isles of Greece', his pastiche of Greek patriot songs of the 1790s inspired by the real

Lambro, may draw on the past, holding latent power to persuade when the time is right:

> But words are things, and a small drop of ink,
> Falling like dew, upon a thought, produces
> That which makes thousands, perhaps millions think
> (*Don Juan* III, 88)

Anne Barton has commented on the sheer length of the Haidée episode, with the protracted homecoming of Lambro, hanging fire like an interminable Nemesis (Cantos III–IV had originally been written as one canto). Its idealised love yet tragic conclusion 'threatens not only the balance [but] the characteristically mixed tone of *Don Juan*' (Stabler 1998: 198). She points out that Byron solves the problem by employing the Hamletian device of bringing on a troupe of players to break the mood. They are chained together with Juan on the slave ship taking them all away to be sold in Turkey. As in the Shakespearian mixing of modes which Byron's contemporaries deplored, tragedy is interrupted by the comic dialogue of the Italian opera troupe whose real experience of being enslaved outdoes their own melodramatic plots. We remember now the operatic theatricality of the descent into madness and death of Haidée:

> And they who watch'd her nearest could not know
> The very instant, till the change that cast
> Her sweet face into shadow, dull and slow,
> Glazed o'er her eyes—the beautiful, the black—
> Oh! to possess such lustre—and then lack!
> (*Don Juan* IV, 6)

The Turkish and Russian cantos

The central episode of *Don Juan*, around which the timescale of the whole poem was centred, was the protagonist's participation in the Siege of Ismail in the Turkish–Russian war which had taken place in November–December 1790 (Cantos VII–VIII). This section was to be a denunciation of wars of conquest, all the more savage for being incorporated into a sexual satire. The war cantos are sandwiched between the most salacious episodes of the poem, which take place in the palaces of both warring monarchs. Juan is first smuggled into the Turkish Sultan's harem and later, after escaping and fighting on the Russian side, joins the Russian Empress's court. In both episodes, the character loses all his dignity. In the former he is bought in the slave market as a sex slave for the Sultana: ordered to perform under the threat of castration and death (V, 139). In the second he becomes Catherine of Russia's favourite, exchanging sex for money, position and flattery (IX, 68; X, 23). It is significant that the humiliation then prostitution of Juan and the loss of his innocence happens in these courts which both epitomise despotism (Franklin 1992: 149–56). Byron diagnoses the grandiose imperial ambitions of both despotic monarchs – one a man, one a woman – as a perversion of the sexual instinct, a lust for power (IX, 59). If Catherine and the Sultan had understood their own true interests, they should have called off the war and met one to one for a grand copulation:

> She to dismiss her guards and he his harem,
> And for their other matters, meet and share 'em.
> (*Don Juan* VI, 95)

The whole poem links sex and power relations, but the Turkish and Russian episodes are particularly interesting for Byron's carnivalesque inversion of normative sexual roles. Juan is dressed as a woman to hide him in the harem, and with the clothes comes 'feminine' behaviour such as flirting (V, 84) and weeping (V, 117). Similar role reversal occurs in the Russian court when the boy soldier Juan dazzles all with his beauty in his gorgeous uniform (IX, 43–4). When he catches Catherine's eye, he is ogled at by the female courtiers, while the men frown and cry with vexation (IX, 78). Susan Wolfson suggests that this impulse to transgress gender norms may be connected with the poem's transgression of generic constraints and poetic conventions (Stabler 1998: 94–109). The confrontation between the masculinised sultana, Gulbeyaz, attired with a phallic poignard, and Juan triply effeminised by the assumption of inferior race, gender and class unsettles any essentialist notions about identity, even if only temporally. Caroline Franklin has related this sexual masquerade to the overall political themes of the poem (1993: 56–89).

Preface to Cantos VI, VII and VIII

As this section of the poem was to be published by John Hunt, Byron no longer had to make concessions to a pusillanimous publisher. He therefore made clear his radical politics in a new preface, in which he took up the cudgels against Castlereagh even more fiercely than he had done in the suppressed Dedication (see Life and Contexts, p. 26). Byron was undeterred by the fact that Castlereagh was now dead (he had committed suicide) and pronounced him 'the most despotic in intention and the weakest in intellect that ever tyrannized over a country' (*CPW* V, 295). Indeed, he attacked the sentimental cant of the Tory newspapers over the manner of death, pointing out that suicidal radicals would have been treated very differently for committing what was still a mortal sin and a crime. Byron, representative of high art, here makes common cause with the lower-class freethinkers such as Richard Carlile who had been imprisoned for circulating radical texts, and who were often the same people who pirated his poems (see Criticism, p. 110). A libertine text such as *Don Juan* was also participating in a challenge to the laws against blasphemy, obscenity and libel, deployed by the government in a heavy-handed way at this time of political unrest. The aristocratic libertarian poem was at one with the radicals' broadsheets and satires in calling for freedom of speech (Franklin 1993: 122–51).

Canto VII

The account of the siege of Ismail, as Byron admits in this preface, was indebted to his reading of Marquis Gabriel de Castelnau's *Essai sur l'histoire ancienne et moderne de la Nouvelle Russie* (1820). Castelnau drew his information from journals and memoirs of participants, and Byron, who reverenced facts, followed the details very closely. However, Byron's purpose was to write an anti-*Iliad*, and he often took an ironic slant to his materials if they were blatantly ideological. Castelnau assumed war is glorious and that the assault on Ismail was an example of the greatest heroism. The material details of the carnage of the eye-witness accounts he used jostled uncomfortably with this rhetoric and were an invitation to Byron's irony (Boyd 1945: 149). At this time, the poet was reading Voltaire, and the Voltairean Italian poet Casti's *Il Poema Tartaro*, whose hero also visits Catherine's court, is another likely influence (Vassallo 1984: 100).

So Byron inverts Spenser's values in his account of 'Fierce loves and faithless wars' (VII, 8) and sarcastically calls upon the aid of 'eternal Homer' (VII, 79–80). For his satire of Russia's imperialism in 1790–1 was spurred by the fact that Catherine had encouraged the Greeks to rise against the Turks and then deserted them. In the poem's present-time, the Tsar was again deploying the concept of a 'crusade' in the Holy Alliance, as a front for dynastic aggrandisement. The poet debunks the military hero Prince Potemkin ('His glory might equal half his estate', VII, 37), who had brutally ordered that the city of Ismail was to be taken at any price:

> 'Let there be light! said God, and there was light!'
> 'Let there be blood!' said man, and there's a sea!
> (*Don Juan* VII, 41)

General Suwarrow takes a professional pride in accomplishing this gory task: 'Surveying, drilling, ordering, jesting, pondering' (VII, 55). The bluff Englishman, Johnson, who had befriended Juan in Constantinople, is down another notch on the moral scale: a mercenary who has no patriotic motive at all to be involved in the 'work of Glory' (VII, 78).

Yet Juan, symbolising the ordinary individual soldier, is shown committing foolhardy acts of bravery (VIII, 27–33) and impractical yet humanitarian deeds such as saving a Turkish child still alive in a heap of bodies, whom the Cossacks are about to dispatch (VIII 91–9). Even the Russians respect the Tartar Khan who threw himself on enemy spears after all his sons had been killed in the defence of the city. Such flashes of heroism, enough to remind us of epic values of old, are intercut with such graphic imagery of war as the purging of the body politic: as Martin comments, the verbal equivalent of a cartoon by James Gillray (Martin 1982: 201).

> Three hundred cannon threw up their emetic,
> And thirty thousand musquets flung their pills
> Like hail, to make a bloody diuretic
> (*Don Juan* VIII, 12)

The quicksilver narrator gives a kaleidoscope of realistic details of war in all its energy and physicality, ready on one hand to see its black humour and on the other to point out war is never justified unless to defend one's liberty from an invader.

The English cantos

After his sojourn at Catherine's court, Juan is sent on diplomatic business to England (X, 65–XVII, 14). The pace of the poem slows markedly, and the narrator teases the reader that the first twelve cantos are only the introduction (XII, 87). This episode is novelistic in scale, with settings in town and country and a gallery of contrasting characters (see Criticism, **p. 97**). The use of the innocent foreigner, Juan, visiting Britain for the first time is a stock satiric device. Idealistic Juan believes Britain, with its constitutional monarchy and habeas corpus, to be 'Freedom's chosen station' (XI, 9), but his thoughts are interrupted when he is held up by a highwayman. The social satire of England in 1791–2 (when the French Revolution was going through its most idealistic phase) as a materialistic, hypocritical and vulgar oligarchy is finely balanced by the nostalgic digressions of the narrator, remembering 'that microcosm on stilts / Yclept the Great World' (XII, 56) of his youth in 1812–16 when Britain was fighting against Napoleon (XI, 82–5) and the momentous historical changes that have occurred in his lifetime. Though he lived abroad, Byron had plenty of letters, newspapers, periodicals and British visitors to keep him up to date with the news, and he also incorporated topical allusions to current events, for example 'Peterloo', when peaceful working-class reformers were cut down by the yeomanry in Manchester in 1819 (XI, 84–5).

Canto XII satirises the marriage market, implying that women are bought and sold in England as much as in Turkey. The political economist, Thomas Malthus, who had argued that the poor should delay marriage and procreation, was a particular satiric target here (XII, 14). In Canto XIII Juan is befriended by Lady Adeline and the politician Lord Henry Amundeville whose passionless arranged marriage symbolises English sexual mores (XIV, 55–7, 69–74, 85–7). It was probably based on that of Caroline and William Lamb (he later became Queen Victoria's prime minister, Lord Melbourne). But the character of Adeline is a composite, the most complex of the poem. The poet hints that the pure friendship of Juan and Adeline may eventually turn adulterous (XV, 6), but meanwhile the well-meaning Adeline tries to save Juan's soul by advising him to get married (XV, 28–9). At this point, the character of Juan and that of the narrator begin to converge. Marriage has been treated ironically throughout the poem with most marriages portrayed as unhappy, and the narrator muses ruefully on his own experience:

> I think I should have made a decent spouse,
> If I had never proved the soft condition;
> *(Don Juan* XV, 24)

When Juan is invited to their house party in the country, the poet creates a portrait of a country mansion, Norman Abbey, which he imagines as Newstead Abbey would have been if his forebears had not frittered away their money and let it deteriorate (XIII, 55–72). Though critics who view Byron as a Whig have even suggested the Amundevilles represent a qualified Whig ideal (Beaty 1985: 163; Kelsall 1987: 179), the satire seems to me deliberately to conflate the Whig and Tory *bon ton*: sarcastically implying that they are politically indistinguishable. For, by the 1820s, any hope of reform lay with the Radicals. We see the influence of Thomas Love Peacock's *Melincourt* (Boyd 1958: 155–7), a comic novel of ideas, in the cast of characters whose names caricature them: Countess Crabbey (XIII, 79), the Duke of Dash (XIII, 85), General Fireface (XIII, 88). An elaborate banquet is held (XV, 62–74). The pastimes of the bored and blasé upper classes – shooting, conversation, electioneering, lounging, billiards, cards and music – are described ironically, especially fox-hunting as seen through the eyes of a puzzled and overenthusiastic foreigner (XIII 95–111; XIV, 32–5).

Adultery is another dangerous game Juan is tempted to play. While Adeline introduces him to suitable brides, and Juan is intrigued and unsettled by the grave and virginal Aurora Raby (partly a sympathetic portrait of Annabella), he is targeted by the married but flirtatious blonde, Duchess Fitz-Fulke. Then Byron tries his hand at the parody of a Gothic novel, as Juan sees the ghost of a monk stalking the passages of the mansion at midnight. Like Peacock, Byron has Adeline singing a ballad telling of the Black Friar who haunts the Abbey when there are deaths, births or marriages in the Amundeville family, to avenge the family having taken over the abbey when the monasteries were dissolved (XV, 40). The second time Juan meets the midnight monk, he is brave enough to stretch out his arm and finds it 'pressed upon a hard but glowing bust' – that of 'her frolic Grace—Fitz-Fulke' (XVI, 123), who seems to have adopted the costume to change bedrooms undetected. The last stanza we have tells us she looked 'rebuked' the next morning, but we are not sure whether or not she had her way with Juan.

We can only speculate how the poem would have gone on. Byron had written on 16 February 1821,

> I mean to take him [Juan] the tour of Europe—with a proper mixture of siege—battle—and adventure—and to make him finish as *Anacharchis Cloots* in the French Revolution.—To how many cantos this may extend—I know not—nor whether (even if I live) I shall complete it— but this was my notion.—I meant to have made him a Cavalier Servente in Italy and a cause for a divorce in England—and a sentimental 'Werther-faced man' in Germany—so as to show the different ridicules of the society in each of those countries—and to have displayed him as gradually gate and blasé as he grew older—as is natural.—But I had not quite fixed whether to make him end in Hell—or in an unhappy marriage,—not knowing which would be the severest . . .
>
> (*BLJ* VIII, 78)

He told Medwin: 'He shall get into all sorts of scrapes, and at length end his career in France. Poor Juan shall be guillotined in the French Revolution!' (Medwin 1969: 165).

It certainly seems, from the narrator's hints, that Juan was destined to be the cause of the divorce of the Amundevilles. It is also possible that the Don would have turned from adultery to be reformed by marriage to the staunchly Catholic Aurora, whom many critics see as representative of orthodox morality. Had Juan subsequently travelled to revolutionary France, then he would probably have been guillotined during the Terror of 1793–4, when idealists, such as the proponent of universal liberty, Anacharsis Clootz, found themselves targeted by Robespierre as much as aristocrats. The symbolic association of aristocratic sexual libertarianism with political radicalism would be a daring yet at the same time deeply ironic stroke with which to cut off the poem. But the lack of closure Byron's death imposed is certainly the most appropriate of all possibilities for the style of the poem.

Style

The poem has no single style for it is continually turning from one mode to the other – a sentimental idiom followed by the farcical, the heroic by the grotesque. Contemporary readers sometimes complained that this procedure constitutes a misanthropic mockery of humanity's highest feelings (see Criticism, **p. 87**), but it can be argued that the poem does not allow cynicism to outweigh idealism but gives each equal weight. Some critics have found it difficult to deal with a poem that seems to lack consistency or a coherent philosophical stance. However, it might be argued that scepticism towards all systems of belief is itself a form of consistency productive of Romantic irony. This is irony not just as a rhetorical device, but as a way of looking at the world. The view of human nature in *Don Juan* is comparable with its representation of external nature: it is in eternal flux.

> The heart is like the sky, a part of heaven,
> But changes night and day too, like the sky;
> Now o'er it clouds and thunder must be driven,
> And darkness and destruction as on high:
> But when it hath been scorch'd, and pierced, and riven,
> Its storms expire in water-drops; the eye
> Pours forth at last the heart's blood turn'd to tears,
> Which makes the English climate of our years.
> (*Don Juan* II, 214)

The form of the poem expresses this by its episodic repetitive nature, mirroring the endless rise and fall of desire. The poet revels in displaying his own creativity – making and unmaking stories, highlighting the artistic process itself by commenting on it:

> I therefore do denounce all amorous writing.
> (*Don Juan* V, 2)

> I won't describe; description is my forte,
> But every fool describes in these bright days.
> (*Don Juan* V, 52)

> Remember, or (if you can not) imagine,
> Ye! who have kept your chastity when young
> (*Don Juan* V, 13)

The reader is seduced, lectured, challenged, teased, confided in – for the relationship with the narrator is dynamic and changeable too. Just because language is protean and the acts of reading and writing cannot ever put a grid of meaning over life, does not mean that art is irrelevant. The attempt to mirror its eternal changeability and to communicate its heartbreaking absurdity is an act of faith in humanity.

The imagery of the verse is as expansive as its storytelling. Byron declares:

> My similes are gathered in a heap,
> So pick and chuse . . .
> (*Don Juan* VI, 68)

The effect is often cumulative and relative, with each image in the list contributing something to the montage and modifying the effect of another:

> An infant when it gazes on a light,
> A child the moment when it drains the breast,
> A devotee when soars the Host in sight,
> An Arab with a stranger for a guest,
> A miser filling his most hoarded chest,
> Feels rapture; but not such true joy are reaping
> As they who watch o'er what they love while sleeping.
> (*Don Juan* II, 196)

Byron lets us see him at work in the process of selection (Joseph 1964: 216). He comments as he goes along '(*Now* for a commonplace!)' or 'I hate to hunt down a tired metaphor' (XIII, 36); or promising 'I'll have another figure in a trice' (XIII, 37).

There is a polyphonic diversity of language and poetic registers in *Don Juan*. The poet mimics his earlier self in the Philhellenist lyric 'the Isles of Greece' in Canto III, sings a hymn of praise to the Virgin Mary (III, 102–3) and incorporates the Gothic ballad of the black Friar into the English house party (XVI, 40). The narrator loftily drops unexplained Latin tags (XIV, 21), yet enjoys schoolboy scatological humour with foreign names:

> There was Strongenoff, and Strokonoff,
> Meknop, Serge Lwow, Arseniew of modern Greece,
> And Tschitsshakoff, and Roguenoff, and Chokenoff
> (*Don Juan* VII, 15)

Verbal tricks abound: he enjoys using 'engineering slang' (VII, 11) in describing military defences, incorporates the jargon of menus into the Amundevilles' dinner (XV, 66) and makes a stanza out of a prescription to revive the flagging Juan in Russia:

> But here is one prescription out of many:
> Sodae-Sulphat.3 vi.3.s. Mannae optim.
> Aq. frevent. F3. ifs 3ij. tinct. Sennae
> Haustus.' (And here the surgeon came and cupped him)
> 'R. Pulv. Com. gr. iii. Ipecacuanhae'
> (With more besides, if Juan had not stopped 'em.)
> 'Bolus Potassae Sulphuret. sumendus,
> Et Haustus ter in die capiendus.'
>
> *(Don Juan* X, 41)

The aristocratic narrator often assumes his reader will understand classical allusions and foreign phrases (XIII, 47). But he also relishes demonstrating his command of Regency thieves' slang in the episode when Juan shoots a highwayman in England:

> Poor Tom was once a kiddy upon town,
> A thorough varmint, and a *real swell*,
> Full flash, all fancy, until fair diddled,
> His pockets first, and then his body riddled.
>
> *(Don Juan* XI, 17)

In fact, in his war against the cant of Evangelical Tory Britain, Byron had written a poem which, through mimicry, parody and allusions to all sorts of cant, alerts the reader through his humour and satire to the linguistic codes in which ideology is passed on.

Further reading

On the composition and publication of the poem, as well as *CPW* V, also see *Byron's 'Don Juan'*. Vol. I: *The Making of a Masterpiece* by Truman Guy Steffan. Vols II–III: *A Variorum Edition*, ed. Truman Guy Steffan and Willis W. Pratt (1971). On the publication and piracies of the poem, see Hugh J. Luke Jr., 'The Publishing of Byron's *Don Juan*' (1965); and on the poem's reception, see E. D. H. Johnson, '*Don Juan* in England' (1944). For a study of the literary sources of the poem, see Elizabeth French Boyd, *Byron's Don Juan: A Critical Study* (1945), and on the poem's specific relationship with the Italian *ottava rima* tradition, see Peter Vassallo, *Byron: The Italian Literary Influence* (1984). McGann relates the poem to classical satiric and epic tradition in his sophisticated study, *Don Juan in Context* (1976). A. B. England's *Byron's Don Juan and Eighteenth-Century Literature* (1975) considers the poem's novelistic attributes.

Anne Barton's *Byron: Don Juan* (1992) is the best general introduction to the poem. Bostetter's collection of critical essays, *Twentieth Century Views of Don Juan* (1969) is outdated, as is Jump's in the Macmillan Casebook series (1973). However, Nigel Wood (ed.), *Don Juan* (1993) offers four challenging but important essays which each take a different theoretical perspective: Bahktinian, Lacanian, socialist-feminist, psychoanalytical. McGann's piece 'Lord Byron's Twin Opposites of Truth [*Don Juan*]' in Stabler (1998: 27–51) offers a wide-ranging discussion of current critical issues, comparing Byron with the other canonical Romantic poets in relation to Romantic ideology.

Byron's adoption of Romantic irony is central to modern critical interest in *Don Juan* as a work linking the poet and his age with contemporary decon-structionist theory. This is discussed by Frederick Garber in *Self, Text and Romantic Irony: The Example of Byron* (1988); Anne Mellor's *English Romantic Irony* (1980); Terence Hoagwood, *Byron's Dialectic: Scepticism and the Critique of Culture* (1993). On Byron's poem and satiric form, see Alvin B. Kernan, *The Plot of Satire* (1965: 171–222); and Frederick L. Beaty, *Byron the Satirist* (1985: 104–64). For the relationship of the poem to the epic tradition, see Brian Wilkie, *Romantic Poets and Epic Tradition* (1965), and Hermione de Almeida's *Byron and Joyce through Homer: Don Juan and Ulysses* (1981).

For approaches focusing on gender in the poem, see Caroline Franklin's *Byron's Heroines* (1992), chapters 4 and 5, and Susan Wolfson, ' "Their She-Condition": Cross-Dressing and the Politics of Gender in *Don Juan*', in Stabler (1998: 94–109). The argument that the poem should be read in the context of the Don Juan myth is explored by Moyra Haslett, *Byron's Don Juan and the Don Juan Legend* (1997); while Bernard Beatty's *Byron's Don Juan* (1985) also relates the poem to the originating myth by examining the spiritual aspects of the poem. Peter Graham's *Don Juan and Regency England* (1990) considers the Englishness of the poem, and relates the English cantos to the literary context of Byron's experiences in Regency London. See Jerome McGann on the narrative time-scheme of the poem, on 'mobility' and 'The Isles of Greece' (1985: 264–93).

For a vindication of Byron's linguistic subtlety and a rejection of the scathing view of his poetic abilities by T. S. Eliot, see Peter Manning's '*Don Juan* and Byron's imperceptiveness to the English word', *Studies in Romanticism* 18 (1979), 207–33. See also Stabler (1998: 204–16) for Drummond Bone's essay 'The Art of *Don Juan*: Byron's Metrics'. Mark Storey's *Byron and the Eye of Appetite* (1986) traces recurrent imagery of the predatory gaze. For a study that adopts a very broad definition of the trope of digression as a frame for a close formalist reading, see chapters 4 and 5 of Jane Stabler, *Byron, Poetics and History* (2002).

DRAMAS

As well as *Manfred*, Byron went on to publish three historical five-act plays: *Marino Faliero, Doge of Venice*, written in 1820; then *Sardanapalus* and *The Two Foscari*, written in 1821 (see Life and Contexts, p. 22 and Criticism, p. 89). In these he attempted a modified neo-classicism in style, with compressed dialogue and regard for the unities. All had strongly political themes, and *Marino Faliero* and *The Two Foscari* fictionalised events from Venetian history. Each of the plays portrays a moribund society in which the hero finds himself trapped by the forces of history, leading him to debate the rights and wrongs of revolutionary action and to meditate on the meaning of patriotism. It can be seen that Byron's own involvement with the Carbonari and his ardent desire for a successful uprising against the Austrians in Italy was the context for this outpouring. The poet prin-cipally wanted to influence British public opinion, but also probably hoped the plays would be translated into Italian and encourage the nationalist movement there.

Byron also wrote a Gothic drama, *Werner*, at this time, in the style of a popular stage play. Another Romantic drama, *The Deformed Transformed*, remained unfinished but is a fascinating and experimental fragment. He always denied that any of his dramas were written for the stage. However, *Marino Faliero* was performed, against his wishes, but was only a moderate success. *Werner*, however, became a popular stage play in the time of Queen Victoria.

In 1821 Byron would also write two controversial plays on biblical themes, which expressed his revulsion against religious authoritarianism: *Cain* and *Heaven and Earth*. Both were fictionalised episodes from the Old Testament: the first told the story of Adam and Eve's son who became the first murderer and was doomed to wander the earth, tainted with sin; the second dramatised the story of the flood which drowns most of humanity, except those who accompany Noah in the Ark (see Life and Contexts, p. 26). Both plays questioned the theological concepts of original sin, predestination and damnation and depicted human intellectual bravery, capacity for love and endurance as more admirable than the righteousness of the stern god depicted in the Old Testament. Space does not permit discussion of all these dramas, so *Cain* is taken as an example.

Cain

Byron began work on this controversial drama in Ravenna on 16 July 1821, and by 10 September he was sending it off to Murray, wryly describing it as 'in my gay metaphysical style & in the *Manfred* line' (*BLJ* VIII, 206) (see Life and Contexts, p. 23 and Criticism, p. 89). Though Murray was reluctant to publish and Hobhouse violently disapproved of it, Sir Walter Scott was pleased that the new poem was to be dedicated to him, declaring 'I do not know that his Muse has ever taken so lofty a flight amid her former soarings. He has certainly matched Milton on his own ground' (*CPW* VI, 648). It appeared in December 1821 and was immediately denounced by religious reviewers and pamphleteers (Steffan 1968: 330–422). The Lord Chancellor refused Murray an injunction against pirates on the grounds of the play's 'blasphemy'. On 8 February 1822, Byron wrote to Murray protesting that *Cain* was a drama, not an argument, and therefore could hardly be deemed blasphemous. However, he offered to come to England to take the consequences of publication in person, to save Murray from the risk of imprisonment (*BLJ* IX, 103–4). The lower-class radical publisher Richard Carlile managed to obtain a copy of this letter and printed it together with a pirated edition of the play at sixpence, in order to challenge the authorities to prosecute such an establishment figure as Murray, whose author was a lord of the realm (Franklin 2000: 141). Of course they did not do so, but the point about the class differential applied to censorship of controversial publications was well taken. Carlile was soon imprisoned for selling the republican thinker Thomas Paine's *Age of Reason*. Murray later obtained an injunction against pirated editions of *Cain* through a jury trial (*CPW* VI, 649).

Byron took Cain's story from Genesis, and boasted that he dramatised it literally, as in the medieval mystery plays (Preface, *CPW* VI, 228). But his purpose was to defamiliarise and thus bring out the sinister patriarchal ideology which underpinned orthodox religion. He used Pierre Bayle's *Dictionnaire historique et critique* (1695–7), a work of Enlightenment scepticism, to help him subject the biblical materials to a rationalist critique of their theology. He also cited modern science, such as the geological research of Baron Cuvier, which challenged the biblical account of the history of the world, as would Darwin's later in the century (Preface, *CPW* VI, 229). Rather than imagining evolution as a progression, Byron and his contemporaries were fascinated by the speculation that 'the pre-adamite world was also peopled by rational beings much more intelligent than man' (Preface, *CPW* VI, 229). They imagined history as a decline from former greatness.

Cain was a closet play: a three-act drama in blank verse for the reader's imagination, not the theatre (see Criticism, **pp. 117–19**). It was too philosophical in subject matter and avant-garde in form for a bourgeois theatre audience, and its attack on orthodox theology was too 'blasphemous' for the censor to have permitted a performance anyway. Byron was determined to resist imitating Shakespeare, the idol of the Romantics. He attempted to modify his Romanticism by adopting a classically simple unified plot, and a time scheme of twenty-four hours. His chief literary model was Milton's *Paradise Lost*. Milton had daringly made his Satan magnificent – an opponent worthy of God. Dante's *Inferno* influenced the compressed dialogue and Cain's visit to Hades. Byron also remembered Salomon Gessner's Rousseauistic *Death of Abel* (1761) in touches of sentimental pastoralism. This play and *Heaven and Earth*, on Noah's flood, were steeped in the apocalyptic passages of the Bible and also inspired by the apocryphal Book of Enoch which was translated in 1821.

Byron used the basic shape of a morality play, such as that of Faust, where a man is tempted by the Devil and loses his immortal soul. However, he gave the Devil the best intellectual arguments and did not explicitly refute them in the play. Byron claimed he did not know Christopher Marlowe's *Doctor Faustus*, but he had heard M. G. Lewis translate portions of part one of Goethe's *Faust*, which had already influenced *Manfred*. Manfred was portrayed as a Promethean rebel, admirable even though unequivocally a sinner. However, Cain, though also too proud to bow down, is less Satanic (leaving that to Lucifer), being a simple child of Eve: a naïve but intellectually curious representative of humanity.

The play is another example of Byron's preoccupation with the Fall. The setting is outside the locked gates of Paradise. Cain will repeat the trajectory his parents have already followed, from innocence to sin, as will his son Enoch (III, i, 20–34), and all the generations to come are doomed to redouble their wretchedness (II, ii, 220–7). The opening scene of morning prayers shows the patriarchal and theocratic nature of the 'politics of Paradise' (*BLJ* V, 368). All the rest of the family accept that God is the eternal parent who must be worshipped and whose authority must not be questioned. Only Adam's rebellious son, Cain, refuses to pray, and his resentful thoughts about being punished for his parents' sins call forth Lucifer to materialise and tempt him further. Cain's crime cannot be understood in merely psychological terms, but is the product of frustration at an unjust society – he is expected to submit cheerfully to punishment he has not deserved, to endorse and praise a tyrannical authority (Watkins 1993: 146).

The climax of the play happens when Cain kills his own brother, a far worse sin than Adam's disobedience. He will commit the first murder and humanity will experience death for the first time. Cain will therefore be exiled yet further away from the garden: cursed by his family and destined to wander 'Eastward from Eden'. Only Cain's wife, Adah, who projects her own love of humanity onto her idea of the Almighty, accompanies him. Adah, who represents the human emotions, is the counterpart to rational Lucifer: he is intellectual and solitary; she embodies human love and the social bond (I, i, 466–76). Cain is poised between the bad angel and the good woman (I, i, 345–8) (Franklin 1992: 232–46).

Lucifer's rebelliousness encourages Cain's. He describes them both as:

> Souls who dare look the Omnipotent tyrant in
> His everlasting face, and tell him, that
> His evil is not good!
>
> (*Cain* I, i, 137–9)

Lucifer promises to teach Cain all he wishes to know if he will fall down and worship him (I, i, 303). Like Manfred, Cain will bow down neither to God or his opponent (I, i, 318). Nevertheless, Lucifer interprets any refusal to worship God as equivalent to worshipping him and rewards Cain with a cosmic flight through space, which owes something to Edward Young's *Night Thoughts* as well as Shelley's *Queen Mab* (Joseph 1964: 120).

This is the poetic heart of the play: a vision of the spatial dimensions spanning the minuteness and the immensity of creation, 'both worms and worlds' (II, i, 126). At first, Cain naïvely thinks that:

> The little shining fire-fly in its flight,
> And the immortal star in its great course,
> Must both be guided.
>
> (*Cain* II, i, 130–1)

But the insignificance of man and his world to the creator is brought home to Cain and the reader when he views an ever-changing universe where beauty is endlessly born only to be destroyed. Byron's is a very modern concept of nature as an amoral power. Lucifer tells Cain that:

> many things will have
> No end; and some, which would pretend to have
> Had no beginning, have had one as mean
> As thou; and mightier things have been extinct
> To make way for much meaner than we can
> Surmise; for *moments* only and the *space*
> Have been and must be all *unchangeable*.
>
> (*Cain* II, i, 156–62)

Then they enter Hades, and Cain sees the spirit forms of beings superior to man, whose whole world, with all its enormous creatures, was reduced to chaos before Adam was even made. With regard to both the spatial and temporal immensity of creation, man is reduced to the level of a lower life form, at the mercy of a remote, terrifying God. Byron had commented on these scenes to a friend:

I have gone on the notion of Cuvier, that the world has been destroyed three or four times, and was inhabited by mammoths, behemoths, and what not; but *not* by man till the Mosaic period, as indeed, is proved by the strata of bones found;—those of all unknown animals, and known, being dug out, but none of mankind. I have therefore supposed Cain to be shown, in the *rational* Preadamites, beings endowed with a higher intelligence than man, but totally unlike him in form, and with much greater strength of mind and person. You may suppose the small talk which takes place between him and Lucifer upon these matters is not quite canonical.

The consequence is, that Cain comes back and kills Abel in a fit of dissatisfaction, partly with the politics of Paradise, which had driven them all out of it, and partly because (as it is written in Genesis) Abel's sacrifice was the more acceptable to the Deity.

(*BLJ* VIII, 215–16)

One could compare Lucifer's portrait of a lonely, power-hungry, tyrannical God to William Blake's remote Jehovah figure, which he named Urizen:

> But let him
> Sit on his vast and solitary throne,
> Creating worlds, to make eternity
> Less burthensome to his immense existence
> And unparticipated solitude!
> (*Cain* I, i, 147–51)

Cain now struggles between the self-disgust produced by this knowledge – Alas! I seem / Nothing' (II, ii, 420–1) – and his natural love of Adah which links him with humanity (II, ii, 255–69). Lucifer is incapable of such love. So is Jehovah. We the audience realise this irony, but Cain does not grasp its implications – that humanity is the source of all goodness. It is a shocking measure of just how far Cain has metaphorically travelled from Adah and her life-affirming values during their separation, that he imagines dashing their baby, Enoch, against the rocks, and wishes that he had never been born, rather than perpetuate a race born only to suffer (III, i, 124–36). This anticipates the violent rage that will cause him to deflect his anger against God's callousness into an attack on his innocent brother Abel.

The climax of the play is precipitated when the family put pressure on him to join in their new religious ritual. Byron commented wickedly on the biblical account: '[I]t is singular that the first form of religious worship should have induced the first murder' (Medwin 1969: 126). Cain finds the blood sacrifice of a lamb to God's power repugnant (II, ii, 290–304; III, i, 255–8):

> His!
> His *pleasure!* what was his high pleasure in
> The fumes of scorching flesh and smoking blood,
> To the pain of the bleating mothers . . .
> (*Cain* III, i, 297–300)

We sympathise intellectually also with Cain's repugnance for the idea of atonement (III, i, 86–92), a concept based the sacrifice of a scapegoat. This will be central to the development of Christianity in the future. But the terrible irony now unfolds that he who found a lamb's sacrifice unacceptable now unintentionally makes a human sacrifice of his brother Abel on the same altar (III, i, 316).

Some, such as the Christ-like Abel, who passively obey undervalue themselves: 'I love God far more / Than life' (III, i, 315). But those, like the stubborn Cain, who oppose unjust power become tainted with the egoism of Romantic individualism: 'That which I am, I am' (III, i, 509). This constitutes the contrarieties of Blake's clay and the pebble, whose dialectic matches the endless dualism in heaven.

Further reading

As well as the notes in *CPW* VII and McGann's commentary, see: Truman Guy Steffan, *Lord Byron's 'Cain': Twelve Essays and a Text with Variants and Annotations* (1968). As well as critical material, this edition includes a bibliography of scholarship on *Cain* up till 1966. Three essays on the play may be found in Robert Gleckner and Bernard Beatty (eds), *The Plays of Lord Byron: Critical Essays* (1997), which also contains a useful bibliography of work on the play up the mid-1990s. On the literary relationship between Byron and Goethe, see E. M. Butler, *Byron and Goethe* (1956). On *Cain* and the radicals, see Stephen L. Goldstein, 'Byron's Cain and the Paineites' (1975). On the ideology of the play, see Edward E. Bostetter, 'Byron and the Politics of Paradise' (1960). On *Cain* and Byron's religious scepticism, see Hoagwood (1993: 90–151). On *Cain* as closet drama, see Alan Richardson, *A Mental Theater: Poetic Drama and Consciousness in the Romantic Age* (1988: 59–83); and Michael Simpson, *Closet Performances: Political Exhibition and Prohibition in the Dramas of Byron and Shelley* (1998: 264–80). For the performance history of the play, see Boleslaw Taborski's 'Byron's Theatre: Private Spleen or Cosmic Revolt. Theatrical solutions – Stanislavsky to Grotowski' 1981).

3

Criticism

This section provides a brief history of Byron criticism from the nineteenth century to the present day, divided into sub-sections entitled: 'Byron's Contemporaries'; 'The Victorians'; and 'The Twentieth Century' and 'Contemporary Criticism'. The main preoccupations and disagreements between critics will be indicated. The last section will be further sub-divided into those critical approaches that have been particularly relevant to contemporary interest in Byron and have produced the most illuminating studies of the poetry: Post-structuralism, Psychoanalytical Approaches, New Historicism, Post-colonialism, Gender, and Genre and Literary Form.

Byron's contemporaries

The literary world of the first quarter of the nineteenth century was intensely ideological, and reviews of Byron's poetry must be read in the light of this context. From 1812 to 1816, critics' doubts about whether the verse was sufficiently moral were seemingly stilled by three factors: its unprecedented popularity, the author's rank and the commanding influence and good marketing of his impeccably respectable publisher, John Murray. From 1816 to 1822, Byron's poetry set reviewers a dilemma, for during the separation scandal he had been execrated in the newspapers for his treatment of his wife and the radicalism of his politics, yet it was after this, in exile in Italy, that he produced his greatest masterpieces. Controversial works such as *Don Juan* and *Cain* gave the government a particular headache by inadvertently highlighting the issue of the liberty of the press, for if the author had not been a nobleman and his publisher an influential Tory with links to the government itself, the latter would surely have been prosecuted and even perhaps imprisoned under the 'Six Acts' of 1819, harsh laws passed to stem the flood of publications calling for parliamentary and constitutional reform. After Byron broke with Murray in 1822, his poetry was published by the radical Hunt brothers and this unleashed a storm of vituperation on his head in the respectable literary journals. Byron's death in Greece endowed him with an heroic aura as a martyr for liberty which softened this a little. By the time of his death, Byron's poetry was finding a new working-class popular audience, even whilst critical opinion in the periodicals was turning against it.

Byron's literary debut had been intimately bound up with the two rival magisterial monthly periodicals, the main arbiters of literary quality in the first half of the century: the *Edinburgh Review*, which had been founded in 1802, and which was Whig in politics, and the *Quarterly Review*, founded in 1809 to oppose it by supporting the Tory government. Byron's first book, *Hours of Idleness* (1807), was exceptionally personal in tone: its 'occasional' lyrics arranged to sketch the childhood memories, public-school and university friendships, stately home and aristocratic heritage of the teenage author (see Life and Contexts, **p. 5** and Works, **p. 31**). Though well received by a majority of reviews, it was mercilessly mocked in the *Edinburgh Review* (anonymously) by the radical lawyer, Henry Brougham, as the egoistic posturing of an aristocratic dilettante who expected his rank alone to command a hearing: 'Besides a poem above cited on the family seat of the Byrons, we have another of eleven pages on the self-same subject . . . It concludes with five stanzas on himself' (Rutherford 1970: 31).

Byron retaliated by ridiculing the *Edinburgh Review* in his Popeian satire *English Bards and Scotch Reviewers* (1809) and hailing as his mentor the satirist William Gifford, who was just about to be made the editor of the newly founded *Quarterly Review* (see Works, **p. 33**). Despite his own Whig politics, Byron followed this up by having his poetry henceforth printed by the publisher of the *Quarterly Review*, John Murray. Literary criticism during this period of the Napoleonic wars was fiercely partisan and sometimes quite brutal. The flood of poetry which was produced in the first quarter of the century was regarded with suspicion and intensely scrutinised to ascertain whether it was sufficiently patriotic and religious. Young liberal poets such as Leigh Hunt, Percy Shelley and John Keats would be regularly savaged by the *Quarterly Review*. Yet Byron managed to get his sceptical verse published and enjoyed special treatment in the journal, as long as his professional connection with Murray lasted.

The first two cantos of *Childe Harold's Pilgrimage* (1812) became a literary sensation, and the various Oriental tales which followed, often set in the Ottoman Empire, sold in unprecedented numbers as soon as they were published (see Life and Contexts, **pp. 5–9** and Works, **p. 34**). Reviewers found themselves trailing behind. All they could do from the outset was to try and account for Byron's extraordinary popularity. They highlighted the exceptionally personal quality of the verse. In his review of *Childe Harold's Pilgrimage*, Francis Jeffrey, editor of the *Edinburgh Review*, noted that, though the poet cautioned his readers against identifying him with his melancholic protagonist, Harold:

> [T]he mind of the noble author has been so far tinged by his strong conception of this satanic personage, that the sentiments and reflections which he delivers in his own name, have all received a shade of the same gloomy and misanthropic colouring which invests those of his imaginary hero.
>
> (Rutherford 1970: 39)

George Ellis went further in the *Quarterly Review*, regretting that some sceptical, irreligious, meditations on death and decay were voiced by the poet-narrator and not Harold (Rutherford 1970: 50). So, even during the height of Byron's phenomenal popularity from 1812 to 1816, when the journals hardly dared utter a breath of censure, critics did worry whether satanic protagonists such as Harold or the pirates and renegades of the tales were presented too sympathetically for the moral good of the reader. This was because – despite Byron's prefatory disclaimers – they seemed to have elements of the self-portrait about them. They reflected the charisma of the handsome young author himself, which, Lady Caroline Lamb confided to her journal, consisted in appearing 'Mad, bad and dangerous to know'.

Byron's acknowledged inability to keep the protagonist separate from the narrator in the further cantos of *Childe Harold's Pilgrimage* seemed to confirm the moralistic critics' fears. The poet's later anti-heroes, Manfred and Cain, would often be condemned as self-indulgent self-projections rather than read as the fictional protagonists of dramatic poems. This view would last well into the twentieth century, though Peter Thorslev's study of the so-called 'Byronic hero' has shown that this personage did not in fact originate in the poet's personality, for Byron had merely developed existing literary trends by combining characteristics from protagonists featured in Gothic and *Sturm und Drang* literature.

After the separation scandal in 1816, the critical climate cooled. Even his rank failed to overawe reviewers, as it had done in the past, and Byron began to be severely condemned by religious and conservative critics on moral and political grounds. His poetry was also censured as metrically irregular and occasionally careless and ungrammatical. However, he had some passionate supporters, even in the Tory press, who recognised that Byron was now extending his poetic range: experimenting in genre, form and subject matter. For example, John Wilson, writing anonymously in the vituperative new journal, *Blackwood's Magazine*, hailed the third canto of *Childe Harold's Pilgrimage* as evidence that Byron was as great a nature poet as the best of the 'Lake poets':

> He came into competition with Wordsworth upon his own ground, and with his own weapons; and in the first encounter he vanquished and overthrew him. His descriptions of the stormy night among the Alps . . . shews that he might enlarge the limits of human consciousness regarding the operations of matter upon mind, as widely as he has enlarged them regarding the operations of mind upon itself.
>
> (Rutherford 1970: 113)

Wordsworth himself complained bitterly of 'Byron's plagiarisms from him' to Thomas Moore, feeling that the younger poet had been inspired by his own 'Lines Composed a Few Miles above Tintern Abbey' rather than directly by nature herself (Chew 1924: 123).

The melancholy of Byron's verse was frequently mocked by his contemporaries, such as the novelist Thomas Love Peacock, who satirised him as Mr Cypress in the comic novel *Nightmare Abbey* (1818). However, Sir Walter Scott, in anonymously reviewing the fourth canto of *Childe Harold's Pilgrimage* for the *Quarterly Review*, argued that Byronic melancholy was the outcome of a search for philosophical truth rather than merely a fashionable pose (see Works, **p. 44**). The exceptionally confessional nature of the poem and its gloomy contempt for worldly values were but 'the point or sharp edge of the wedge by which the work was enabled to insinuate its way into that venerable block, the British public' (Rutherford 1970: 140). For the 'frozen shrine' of Byronic scepticism was belied by the idealism at its core, 'the heart ardent at the call of freedom or of generous feeling', perceptibly 'glowing like the intense and concentrated alcohol, which remains one single but burning drop in the centre of the ice' (Rutherford 1970: 140). However, Scott asserted that rather than dwelling on the despair produced by an individual turning inward in contemplative introspection, an artist ought to feed the flame of his humanity by looking outward at man as a social being.

The poet's friend and fellow liberal, Percy Shelley, in the preface to his poem *The Revolt of Islam* (1818) perceptively pronounced that gloom and misanthropy predominated in contemporary art, because this reflected the spirit of an age that had seen the blasting of its political ideals in the failure of the French Revolution. Shelley also believed that Byron should struggle against pessimism, but in order to use his poetry to inspire a visionary belief in the eventual progress of liberty, even though monarchies and dynastic empires had been restored throughout Europe. The Tory Scott, meanwhile, castigated Byron for failing to celebrate Wellington's victory over Napoleon in the passages on the battle of Waterloo in the third canto of *Childe Harold's Pilgrimage* (see Works, **p. 39**). But, ironically, the Bonapartist critic and essayist, William Hazlitt, was equally disgusted with the stanzas expressing the poet's disillusion with Napoleon (Rutherford 1970: 133).

When Byron turned from the melancholic and 'romantic' to digressive sexual satires in *ottava rima* verse form, with the anonymous publication of *Beppo* (1817) and the serial publication of *Don Juan* (1819–24), critics in journals with a religious affiliation became vociferous in their condemnation (see Works, **p. 62**). William Roberts, in an unsigned review of *Beppo* (which had been published anonymously) for *The British Review*, wrote sarcastically:

> Put feeling, and virtue, and the interests of human happiness, out of the question; assume the hypothesis of a world without souls; level man to the consideration of brutes; take him out of his moral state; set him at large the vagrant son of nature in full physical freedom to indulge his temperament; suppose all the enclosures of civilised life laid open, and family ties, and 'relations dear', and 'all the charities—of father, son and brother' fairly out of the way, and then this little poem of Beppo, which it is said, but which we are slow to believe, Lord Byron, an English nobleman, an English husband, and an English father, hath sent reeking from the stews of Venice, is a production of great humour and unquestionable excellence.
>
> (Redpath 1973: 226)

The reviewer of *the British Critic* wrote of the first two cantos of *Don Juan*:

> Upon the indecency, and the blasphemy which this volume contains, a very few words will suffice. The adventures which it recounts are of such a nature, and described in such language as to forbid its entrance within the doors of any modest woman, or decent man. Nor is it a history only, but a manual of profligacy. Its tendency is not only to excite the passions, but to point to the readiest means and method of their indulgence.

Vice is here represented not merely in that grosser form which carries with it its own shame, and almost its own destruction, but in that alluring and sentimental shape, which at once captivates and corrupts.

(Redpath 1973: 253)

Blackwood's Edinburgh Magazine published an article entitled 'Remarks on *Don Juan*' which proclaimed that 'the exalted intellect' of the poet was linked to his 'depraved heart', and contained an attack on his character and treatment of his wife (Redpath 1973: 44). Byron was stung into writing a lengthy reply but it was not published in his lifetime.

The radical journalist and poet Leigh Hunt was the exception in defending *Don Juan* in his newspaper *The Examiner*, on the grounds that it was not an immoral work but merely realistic in depicting the attractiveness of sexual 'vice', and no more than properly satiric in showing society's 'folly and wickedness' in allowing arranged marriages that went against nature in pairing elderly rich men with young girls for mercenary reasons (Rutherford 1970: 177). The *Edinburgh Review* and the *Quarterly Review* remained silent on the poem. This may have triggered the ire of the Tory Poet Laureate, Robert Southey. In 1821, Southey, whom Byron regarded as his chief literary foe, devoted part of the preface of his poem *The Vision of Judgement* (a eulogy on the late King George III) to a moralistic denunciation of *Don Juan*, though he refrained from naming it or its author. Southey was particularly worried that because the poem was being pirated and countless cheap copies hawked upon the streets, it would corrupt young, female, lower-class or uneducated readers and he implied that Byron had committed a mortal sin in writing it:

The publication of a lascivious book is one of the worst offences which can be committed against the well-being of society. It is a sin, to the consequences of which no limits can be assigned, and those consequences no after repentance in the writer can counteract.

(Rutherford 1970: 180)

Even Francis Jeffrey, who had previously reviewed Byron's verse favourably, wrote anonymously in the *Edinburgh Review* in 1822 'more in sorrow than in anger' of the pernicious tendency of the poem (see Works, **p. 68**). He declared himself no bigot and thought the poem no more obscene than some canonical literature of earlier eras. But the morally earnest Jeffrey charged Byron with destroying 'all belief in the reality of virtue' because the poem juxtaposed touching evocations of mankind's deepest feelings with sceptical passages which made 'all enthusiasm and constancy of affection ridiculous' (Rutherford 1970: 201).

Many anonymous pamphlets appeared, usually denouncing the poem, and there were several parodies and spurious 'continuations' of it (Chew 1924: 27–75). Byron himself enjoyed reading the anonymous *ad hominem* pamphlet *Letter to the Right Hon. Lord Byron. By John Bull* (1821), which we now know was written by John Gibson Lockhart, at the time a regular contributor to the brash Tory periodical, *Blackwood's Magazine*. Writing in a colloquial man-of-the-world manner, Lockhart mocked the hypocrisy of the *Quarterly Review* which had given Byron conspicuously special treatment by remaining silent on the controversial poem. He also considered the melancholy of Byron's earlier verse had been 'humbug'. But instead of joining in the chorus of critical condemnation, 'John Bull' spoke on behalf of the poem's popularity with the ordinary reader, and robustly advised the poet 'Stick to *Don Juan*: it is the only sincere thing you have ever written' and 'out of all sight the best of your works; it is by far the most spirited, the most straightforward, the most interesting, and the most poetical' (Rutherford 1970: 184). When Cantos III–V appeared, the reviewers were largely hostile, denouncing the poem on moral grounds, with only the *Monthly Magazine* and *The Examiner* willing to defend it (Redpath 1973: 189). The same pattern may be observed in reviews of later cantos as they appeared.

Byron's dramas received a lukewarm critical reception in his own lifetime (see Works, **pp. 61, 78**). *Manfred* (1817) was so avant-garde that it baffled even supporters such as John Wilson; while Jeffrey declared uncertainly: 'This is a very strange – not a very pleasing – but unquestionably a very powerful and most poetical production' (Rutherford 1970: 115). Jeffrey argued against another critic who had felt that the drama borrowed something from Christopher Marlowe's Renaissance tragedy, *Doctor Faustus*. The poet himself had declared he did not know Marlowe's play, though he admitted having heard a recitation of parts of Goethe's *Faust*. Goethe, in his review of the play (which he greatly admired), felt Byron had been inspired by his own drama, but had nevertheless made the theme his own:

> Byron's tragedy, *Manfred*, was to me a wonderful phenomenon, and one that closely touched me. This singular intellectual poet has taken my *Faustus* to himself, and extracted from it the strangest nourishment for his hypochondriac humour. He has made use of the impelling principles in his own way, for his own purposes, so that no one of them remains the same; and it is particularly on this account that I cannot enough admire his genius.
>
> (Rutherford 1970: 119)

Byron's historical tragedies, *Marino Faliero*, *The Two Foscari* and *Sardanapalus* were politely but unenthusiastically received. Jeffrey in the *Edinburgh Review* (1822) was typical in finding such 'closet' plays fundamentally undramatic and questioning why the author prided himself on obeying the conventional unities of place, time and action, when he paid no other heed to what would work best in a performance (Rutherford 1970: 231). Byron's sceptical biblical play, *Cain*, was, however, very harshly denounced by religious critics in several periodicals because it challenged orthodox theology (see Works, **pp. 79–83**). Even the judicious Francis Jeffrey protested that its 'whole argument' was 'directed against the goodness or the power of the deity', though he conceded that the play's denouement also showed the tragic relationship between Cain's spiritual rebellion and his descent into murder (Rutherford 1970: 233–4).

As with *Don Juan*, so controversial was this dramatic poem that many pamphlets and rewritings of the play appeared, mainly adverse and some quite hysterical. They continued to be published for twenty years (Chew 1924: 76–104). One remonstrated with Byron's publisher for daring to print a poem which 'rebels against that providence which guides and governs all things'. This was the anonymous *A Remonstrance addressed to Mr. John Murray, respecting a Recent Publication* (1822) signed 'Oxoniensis', whom we now know was the Revd. H. J. Todd (Rutherford 1970: 219–20). The play was defended in another pamphlet by 'Harroviensis' who compared *Cain* with Milton, and argued that since all the unorthodox theology is put into the mouth of Lucifer, Byron himself cannot be charged with blasphemy. Despite such arguments, *Cain* was pronounced blasphemous by the authorities. The paradoxical outcome of this was that Murray was not allowed to prosecute pirates to defend his copyright, so cheap copies could be widely disseminated on the streets by radical propagandists.

The *Quarterly Review* now broke its conspicuous silence, when its anonymous reviewer (Bishop Reginald Heber) weighed in. He declared that all Byron's plays showed that the poet lacked dramatic talent. But his main concern was to give orthodox answers to Cain's theological doubts and to argue against this drama-tisation of a Manichean universe, which seemed to show the powers of evil and good at war with each other. Heber declared himself particularly anxious that pirated copies would enable 'the young, the ignorant, and the poor' to read a work which would lead them to question religious teaching (Rutherford 1970: 238). Byron's friend, the radical politician John Cam Hobhouse, who had previously opposed the publication of *Don Juan*, was equally frightened by the boldness of *Cain* which he pronounced in his diary 'a complete failure'; but the writers Thomas Moore, Percy Shelley, Sir Walter Scott (in their private letters) and Goethe (in a review) thought very highly indeed of its poetical power, the former three declaring it had a sublime grandeur comparable even with the biblical epics of the great seventeenth-century poet, John Milton (Rutherford 1970: 214–18).

The increasing radicalism of Byron's poetry had put such a strain on the rela-tionship with his Tory publisher, John Murray, that a break was inevitable. In 1822, Byron founded his own journal, *The Liberal*, together with poet Percy Shelley and journalist and poet Leigh Hunt (see Life and Contexts, **p. 25**). In this he published various works anonymously, some of which Murray had been unwilling to be associated with (for example, the satire *The Vision of Judgment* – a parody of Southey's poem which denounced the rule of George III – and *Heaven and Earth*, a drama in the spirit of *Cain*, based on the biblical story of Noah's flood). Now, without the protection of Murray's influence in literary London, the full fury of the religious and right-wing press was unleashed on Byron and his journal (Marshall 1960). Byron now suffered for the first time the indignity of being classed with the 'Cockney school' of Hunt, Shelley and Keats. Tory journals such as *Blackwood's Magazine* and the *Quarterly Review* were conducting an ideological war against this radical literary circle and berated the poetry produced by it in elitist class terms as vulgar, showy trash, the product of uneducated suburban hacks. They now portrayed Byron as lowering himself and besmirching his rank by consorting with such social inferiors, and, unable to believe a lord could also be a radical, they felt he was merely putting on an act to court pub-licity. If Byron had but realised it, the extent of the outcry was an indirect com-pliment to the sparkling quality of *The Liberal*, but it frightened the poet so much that he withdrew his support for the journal after only four numbers and it foundered.

None but radicals would now dare to publish Byron's poetry. He chose the most respectable of them, John and Leigh Hunt, to put out the rest of *Don Juan*. John Hunt did this, despite being indicted in 1822 for publishing *The Vision of Judgment*, considered as libelling the late king, for which he would be fined 100 pounds in 1824. Seemingly, Byron thought his literary career was over when he chose direct action over print in his campaign against tyranny, and set sail in 1823 for Greece and the war of independence.

The Victorians

Although the critical establishment had turned against Byron before his death, the cult of Byronism continued unabated amongst the British public until at least the middle of the century and until much later than this in America and Europe, with new editions of his poetry continually demanded. Victorian criticism of Byron was dominated by the biographical approach to literature. The poet himself, in alliance with John Murray, had forged an image of the passionate Romantic poet, forever associated with the Phillips portrait of the curly-haired writer in his open-necked shirt. Byron's verse, prefaces and notes often contained confessional or personal passages, and these helped to encourage a biographical critical approach which saw the main interest of the verse as the expression of the author's psyche. Because of this personality cult, and because fame had come so early, all the letters, manuscripts and items connected with the poet were carefully collected throughout his lifetime. After his death, acquaintances hurried to put their detailed recollections of his conversations into print. Byron was undoubtedly the first writer whose personal life was so familiar to his readers, and perhaps none since has been quite so intimately known.

In 1830 was published Thomas Moore's magisterial biography of his friend: *Letters and Journals of Lord Byron: With Notices of his Life*. The details given here about Byron's marriage and separation reignited the controversy over the poet's character. This flared up for a third time in 1869 when Harriet Beecher Stowe made public that Lady Byron, before her death, had confided to the American novelist that the cause of the marriage breakdown had been the poet's incest with his half-sister. The scandal over Byron's sex life, at a time of religious evangelicalism and Victorian moralism, made the poet a figure of controversy for the whole period. Victorian critics found it difficult to analyse the verse without becoming moralistic. There is no doubt that attacks in print on Byron's character and sexual behaviour were often politically motivated, for his radicalism and his libertinism alienated alike the middle-class Establishment and campaigners for women's rights such as Stowe.

Those critics who disliked the personality cult of Byronism, such as William Hazlitt in *The Spirit of the Age* (1825), charged Byron's verse with egotism: '(I)n reading Lord Byron's works, he himself is never absent from our minds' (Rutherford 1970: 271). The man of letters, Thomas Carlyle, saw the hero-worshipping of Byron as a symptom of a spiritual malaise afflicting the age which should now be cast off as a youthful aberration. In his *Sartor Resartus* (1836) he counselled: 'Close the *Byron*; open thy *Goethe*' (Rutherford 1970: 294). How-ever, the essayist Thomas Babington Macaulay, favourably reviewing Moore's biography in the *Edinburgh Review* in 1831, charged the British public with hypocrisy and prurience in its obsession with the separation scandal and the question of Byron's immorality. He acknowledged that it was impossible for his contemporaries to separate the poetry from the personality of such an influential figure: 'A generation must pass away before it will be possible to form a fair judgment of his books, considered merely as books. At present they are not only books, but relics' (Rutherford 1970: 302).

Macaulay tried to take a more historical perspective and argued that Byron's verse was shaped by the age in which he wrote: he saw it as straddling the old school of poetry (Augustanism) and the new (Romanticism) (Rutherford 1970: 308). He was the first critic to make this important point (see Life and Contexts, p. 29). Macaulay thought Byron's self-centred art was fundamentally undramatic: stating that even his plays tended towards soliloquy. Likewise, he judged that his narrative poems lacked structure and careful plotting. But Byron excelled in impressionistic description and personal meditation, and his 'rapid, sketchy' concentrated manner was more effective than the detailed minutiae of William Wordsworth (Rutherford 1970: 312–13).

At just the time Byron's critical fortunes were waning amongst British critics, his poetry was being discovered and praised throughout the rest of Europe. His verse represented the voice of liberty to patriots of countries seeking to throw off the yoke of dynastic imperialism and form nationalist movements. The Italian patriot and writer Giuseppe Mazzini, in his important 1839 essay on 'Byron and Goethe', considered that the works of these two writers summed up their age, which had been one of revolutionary individualism. According to Mazzini, Byron represented the subjective form of this spirit of the age: the aspiration of the individual human will to control the world around it. The present epoch was turning away from such poetry for it wanted action not contemplation, useful activity not negation. The inadequacy of mere individualism to reform society in the areas of economics, politics and philosophy was by now evident. Yet Mazzini pays a tribute to Byron's greatness, for the poet had pointed the way to the 'new social poetry' of the democratic future through his actions as well as his words: 'never did he desert the cause of the peoples; never was he false to human sympathies' (Rutherford 1970: 338).

Mazzini's historical approach to Byron, seeing him as the European poet of revolution, was much later taken up and developed by John Morley in a seminal essay for the *Fortnightly Review* of 1870 (Rutherford 1970: 384–409). Morley argued that literary criticism should stand clear of the sort of biographical issues which are merely driven by prurient moralism. Byronic melancholy was seen by Morley, not as a character trait of the author, but as a reaction to the age of stagnation and repression, which had been setting in at the close of the revolutionary period, when Byron was writing. He judged Byron to be a particularly modern writer, in that he tended to subordinate aesthetic to social concerns in his verse, which was primarily political and infused with 'a passionate feeling for mankind'. This explained his predilection for historical drama, which Morley saw as anticipating Victorian positivism (a scientific way of viewing the development of society):

> Partly, no doubt, the attraction which dramatic form had for Byron is to
> be explained by that revolutionary thirst for action . . . but partly also it

may well have been due to Byron's rudimentary and unsuspected affinity with the more constructive and scientific side of the modern spirit.

(Rutherford 1970: 403)

From the middle of the century, much more of the poetry of lesser-known fellow Romantics such as John Keats, Percy Shelley and William Blake had become available, as their collected works were assembled and assessed. William Wordsworth's reputation was also much enhanced by his posthumously published philosophical poem, *The Prelude*. This was also the period when English literature became a subject of study in most universities and schools. Literary criticism was becoming professionalised, at just the time when Victorian men and women of letters were sifting and comparing the poetry of the Romantics and thus converting it into a canon of acknowledged great works. Byron was still so popular with the reading public that his poetry could not be ignored, yet in the journals he was often compared unfavourably with Wordsworth, whose nature poetry was felt to be spiritually consolatory in an age experiencing religious doubt. Shelley was frequently judged a more mellifluent versifier than Byron, and his political poetry – though equally obnoxious to the Victorians – could be more easily pruned from his corpus, to produce 'family' editions. Byron was destined to become excluded from this canon: he had not been buried in Westminster Abbey, and would not be commemorated in poets' corner until the 1960s. Nevertheless, as we have seen, perceptive critics such as Morley did champion Byron. Chew comments that the reviving revolutionary spirit on the continent contributed to the beginnings of a new critical interest in the poet which grew until 1870s (Chew 1924: 263).

In 1853, the Christian novelist Charles Kingsley in *Fraser's Magazine*, courted controversy at the time of Byron's decline in critical estimation by contemptuously declaring that his own age was an effeminate one: for it preferred the mysticism and 'pompous sentimentalism' of the sensitive vegetarian, Shelley, to the hatred of cant and greater intelligibility of his more 'masculine' friend, Byron. More importantly, according to Kingsley, while the atheist Shelley substituted internal sentiment for external law, Byron's verse – however Satanic – showed 'the most intense and awful sense of moral law – of law external to himself' (Rutherford 1970: 355). Kingsley singled out *Cain* and *Manfred* to exemplify this aspect of Byronic scepticism:

[I]n *Cain*, as in *Manfred*, the awful problem which, perhaps had better not have been put at all, is nevertheless fairly put, and the solution, as far as it is seen, fairly confessed; namely, that there is an absolute and eternal law in the heart of man, which sophistries of his own, or of other beings, may make him forget, deny, blaspheme; but which exists externally, and will assert itself. If this be not the meaning of *Manfred*, especially of that great scene in the chamois hunter's cottage, what is? – If this be not the meaning of Cain, and his awful awakening after the murder, not to any mere dread of external punishment, but to an overwhelming, instinctive, inarticulate sense of having done wrong, what is?

(Rutherford 1970: 356)

The poet Algernon Swinburne was the most eloquent spokesman to argue that the quality of Byron's verse was insufficiently recognised, in the introduction to his *Selections from the Works of Lord Byron* (1866). He did point out that, in comparison with the more technically proficient Shelley, Byron possessed 'a feeble and faulty sense of metre': 'No poet of equal or inferior rank ever had so bad an ear. His smoother cadences are often vulgar and facile; his fresher notes are often incomplete and inharmonious' (Rutherford 1970: 376).

But he felt that as far as the *ottava rima* metre was concerned, Byron had 'conquered' and wrested it from its native Italian tradition. Swinburne was perceptive enough to realise that Byron's *Vision of Judgment*, snobbishly damned by most critics because of its association with Leigh Hunt, actually showed the perfection of the poet's satiric powers:

> Satire in earlier times had changed her rags for robes, Juvenal had clothed with fire, and Dryden with majesty, that wandering and bastard muse. Byron gave her wings to fly with, above even the reach of these. . . . Above all, the balance of thought and passion is admirable; human indignation and divine irony are alike understood and expressed.
>
> (Rutherford 1970: 380)

Despite Swinburne's praise, Margaret Oliphant, in her survey of the poets of the past 100 years for *Blackwood's Edinburgh Magazine* in July 1872, still spoke for the critical consensus when she argued that whereas Wordsworth had been insufficiently valued, Byron was at present overpraised. For though undeniably a great poet, his poetry had a strain of the commonplace and vulgar: 'He had pre-eminently that power of tricking out the poorest and most threadbare conceptions in glittering, sentimental and heroic garments, which the multitude loves' (Franklin 1998: II, 773).

This was the view of many late-Victorian readers, who cynically regarded Byron's rhetoric as merely a means of courting easy popularity and censured his passionate style as insufficiently mellifluous. However, by 1880 the time had arrived when some leading men and women of letters began to take Byron's poetry seriously and presented reassessments of it. Matthew Arnold, probably the most important Victorian literary critic, wrote in *Macmillan's Magazine* in 1881 that he considered Byron, though not so great as Wordsworth, a better poet than Shelley, because the latter, with all his musical diction, suffered from the 'insubstantiality' of visionary subject matter (Franklin 1998: II, 781). This was a charge that would be levelled once more against Shelley in the twentieth century by F. R. Leavis. Arnold, like Oliphant, argued that Wordsworth's greatness had still not been sufficiently recognised, and that by contrast Byron had been over-praised. Yet Arnold also believed that the reaction against Byron now being felt in critical circles was in danger of going too far in the other direction. The French critic H. A. Taine, for example, had charged Byron with being incapable of the true impersonality and disinterestedness of art, writing only about himself. Not only this, Taine accused him of being a shallow human being, a poseur. Arnold, however, argued that a distinction should be made between the man and the writer. However changeable or silly Byron the man could sometimes be, as a writer Byron was sincere. But he conceded that Byron was not enough of an artist to perfect his poetry, which was hurriedly written and uneven in quality. It would thus benefit from being published as an anthology of the best passages. But this was true of Wordsworth's poetry too: 'With a poetical gift and a poetical performance of the very highest order, the slovenliness and tunelessness of much of Byron's production, the pompousness and ponderousness of much of Wordsworth's, are incompatible' (Franklin 1998: II, 785).

Arnold's dictum as a critic was that 'the end and aim of all literature . . . was *a criticism of life*' (Franklin 1998: II, 788). It was in these terms that he argued that both Wordsworth and Byron were superior to their contemporary the Italian poet Giacomo Leopardi, even though the latter was a better artist in stylistic terms than either of them. Wordsworth's tremendous power lay in communicating his joyful response to nature and the 'primary human affections and duties'; whereas Byron's great sincerity and strength were demonstrated in his attack on English Philistinism and cant. And Byron was more than a mere rhetorician:

> Along with his astounding power and passion, he had a strong and deep sense for what is beautiful in nature, and for what is beautiful in human action and suffering. When he warms to his work, when he is inspired, Nature herself seems to take the pen from him, as she took it from Wordsworth.
>
> (Franklin 1998: II, 792)

Indeed, Arnold concluded his essay with the surprising observation that

> in spite of his prodigious vogue, Byron has never yet, perhaps, had the serious admiration which he deserves. . . . His own aristocratic class, whose cynical make-believe drove him to fury; the great middle-class, on whose impregnable Philistinism he shattered himself to pieces, – how little have either of these felt Byron's vital influence!
>
> (Franklin 1998: II, 792)

The essayist John Addington Symonds also edited a selection of Byron's poems for *The English Poets* (1880) and drew attention to the sheer quantity of verse as well as the variety of forms attempted by the poet in his short life (Rutherford 1970: 410–20). He conceded that Byron had not been that influential on those who followed him. The great Victorian poets Tennyson and Browning had taken a different direction from the poetry of Byron, and taste in British poetry now preferred 'the production of studied perfection on a small scale' to the grand sweep of Byron's uneven oeuvre. Nevertheless, Symonds declares Byron to be 'the only British poet of the nineteenth century who is also European' (Rutherford 1970: 410–20). Symonds, like many of his contemporaries, was aware of the irony that Byron's poetry was now more highly estimated abroad than in his native country, and gives the credit for this to the humanitarianism and universality of the verse:

> Such power, sincerity, and radiance, such directness of generous enthu-siasm and disengagement from local or patriotic prepossessions, such

sympathy with the forces of humanity in movement after freedom, such play of humour and passion, as Byron pours into the common stock, are no slight contributions. Europe does not need to make the discount upon Byron's claims to greatness that are made by his own country.

(Rutherford 1970: 410–20)

The art critic John Ruskin at this time wrote a series of articles for the *Nineteenth Century* (1880) devoted mainly to the verse of Scott and Byron, in which he made the important further point on Byron's humanitarianism that he 'was the first great Englishman who felt the cruelty of war, and, in its cruelty, the shame' (Chew 1924: 299).

As the nineteenth century came to a close, this revaluation of Byron ebbed and the poet's critical standing largely reverted to the negative view which had predominated for the Victorian era. Swinburne, who had formerly championed the poet's satiric gift, now savagely denounced his lack of artistry in the *Nineteenth Century* (1884) and sneered that only European readers who read Byron in translation thought his verse impressive (Franklin 1998: 794–816). Eminent men of letters such as George Saintsbury in 1896 maintained that Byron was second rate (Rutherford 1970: 477). But from 1898 to 1904 appeared E. H. Coleridge and R. E. Prothero's magisterial edition, *The Works of Lord Byron*, which provided a wealth of new editorial and textual material. This great work of scholarship provided the sound base on which further serious study of Byron's œuvre could be built.

Further reading

The contemporary reviews of Byron's poetry are reprinted in full in Donald H. Reiman (ed.), *The Romantics Reviewed, Part B: Byron and Regency Society Poets*, 5 vols (1972). A detailed survey and an anthology of contemporary critical opinion can be found in Theodore Redpath, *The Young Romantics and Critical Opinion 1807–1824* (1973: 179–303). A broader anthology of nineteenth-century criticism of Byron's poetry 1807–1909 is provided in Andrew Rutherford (ed), *Byron: The Critical Heritage* (1970). See also a selection of Victorian views using the *Wellesley Index to Victorian Periodicals 1824–1900*, Caroline Franklin (ed.), *British Romantic Poets*, 5 vols, (1998: II, 653–828). For a scholarly monograph surveying of Byron's reputation in the nineteenth century, consult S. C. Chew, *Byron in England: His Fame and After-Fame* (1924).

The twentieth century

Modernism and the 'New Criticism'

The school of 'New Criticism' that dominated twentieth-century literary criticism until the 1960s was characterised by an emphasis on the actual experience of practical criticism, the here and now of reading. Knowledge about the author, his psychology, intentions regarding his work, and the historical context of his own day were put to one side when discussing the meaning of a poem. The literary criticism of the eminent modernist poet T. S. Eliot inspired a group of British critics at Cambridge: I. A. Richards, William Empson and F. R. Leavis were the most predominant in the 1930s and 1940s. Their American counterparts and successors, such as Cleanth Brooks, Allen Tate and W. K. Wimsatt, laid even more emphasis on the formal patterning of a poem as an entity in itself and even less on its ideological or political content. The sort of poem that best repaid the new critical approach was a short but intense lyric, perhaps by Keats or Donne. How was the poetry of Byron regarded?

T. S. Eliot took issue with his great Victorian predecessor, Matthew Arnold, in his attitude to Romantic poetry because he thought the latter's views were too much influenced by his religious doubts (Eliot 1933: 110). Eliot felt that because of the waning of Arnold's Christian faith, he placed an exaggerated emphasis on morals in literature, using Wordsworth's joy in the solace of nature to give him a quasi-religious uplift rather than seeing the poetry in its own terms. Eliot said he wanted criticism to get away from judging literature moralistically and to avoid the Victorian emphasis on personality. For Eliot and his avant-garde contemporaries, poetry should only be judged against artistic criteria. This boded well for a less judgemental and prurient view of Byron's verse. However, Byron also represented the Romantic excess of egoism in art against which the modernists wanted to react. They strove for impersonality in literature and objectivity in criticism.

In 1937 Eliot published one of the most blistering attacks the poet has ever received. Eliot's method was to subject Byron's verse to supposedly disinterested aesthetic appreciation. He and the New Critics expected poetry 'to be something very concentrated, something distilled', but Eliot complained that 'if Byron had distilled his verse, there would have been nothing whatever left' (Eliot 1957: 194). Of course, this was partly a matter of genre: Byron is not primarily known for his lyric poetry, but for long narrative and dramatic works which are bound to be uneven in quality. Eliot conceded that Byron was an entertaining storyteller in his Oriental tales, and that his adoption of the Berni tradition of digressive narrative verse in *ottava rima* displayed his talent, such as it was, to the full. Eliot particularly admired the English cantos of *Don Juan* (see Works, **pp. 73–5**). However, he found *Childe Harold's Pilgrimage* inferior to these, and asserted that Byron had no ear for language:

> Of Byron, one can say, as of no other English poet of his eminence, that he added nothing to the language, that he discovered nothing in the sounds, and developed nothing in the meaning, of individual words. I cannot think of any other poet of his distinction who might so easily have been an accomplished foreigner writing English. The ordinary person talks English, but only a few people in every generation can write it; and upon this undeliberate collaboration between a great many people talking a living language and a very few people writing it, the continuance and maintenance of a language depends. Just as an artisan who can talk English beautifully while about his work or in a public bar, may compose a letter painfully written in a dead language bearing some resemblance to a newspaper leader, and decorated with words like

'maelstrom' and 'pandemonium': so does Byron write a dead or dying language.

(Eliot 1957: 201)

Note the elitism evident in Eliot's belief that 'only a few' great artists continue and maintain the cultural tradition on which true civilisation depends. The masses follow their lead. Though his analogy comparing the aristocratic poet's rhetoric with an artisan's journalese may seem a perverse paradox in class terms, it reveals that it is the worryingly *vulgar* appeal of Byronism (literally to the masses) which underlies the apparently objective attack on Byron's political verse as bad English. For Eliot himself was a right-wing practising Christian and out of sympathy with the philosophical scepticism that set Byron apart from the other canonical Romantic poets, and hostile to his revolutionary politics. One suspects that his supposedly objective critical analysis was unconsciously influenced by ideology.

Another modernist poet and critic, W. H. Auden, took comedy as a mode more seriously than Eliot and analysed how Byron produced his comic effects in *Don Juan* (see Life and Contexts, **p. 18** and Works, **pp. 74–7**). Auden characterised the humour as typically produced by 'a situation . . . in which the profane intrudes upon the sacred but without annulling it' (Auden 1962: 389). The conflict between the desire to laugh and the feeling that laughter is inappropriate pro-duces an uncomfortable desire to giggle. Auden defined this as comedy rather than satire (though the poem does contain satire too) because it was not the product of outright atheism. The poet and his reader have to have a genuine sense of the spiritual for true incongruity to be produced and to be released through laughing. Auden commented that the protagonist, Don Juan, is in no way the usual atheist and sexual predator of the traditional story: indeed, 'his most con-spicuous trait is his gift for social conformity' (Auden 1962: 392–3). This was because Byron, as part of his defensive strategy against those who accused him of libertinism, was deliberately puncturing the myth and bringing it down to mundane reality.

In his 1936 *ottava rima* poem 'Letter to Lord Byron', Auden had identified with the Romantic poet as a fellow exile, addressed him in the second person and updated him on the progress of democracy and, in his partly parodic tribute, explored the exigencies of the formal properties of *Don Juan* for himself. He was therefore an excellent commentator on the poem's style. He pronounced: 'Byron's poetry is the most striking example I know in literary history of the creative role which poetic form can play' (Auden 1962: 394). Auden gave an incisive analysis of the rhyming problem in converting *ottava rima* to English. In Italian the stanza was usually hendecasyllabic (consisting of eleven syllables) with feminine rhymes, whether the verse was comic or serious. But in English, feminine rhymes are traditionally thought weak or comic. Because of the paucity of rhyme words, English poets therefore either shortened the lines and used masculine rhymes, or resorted to half rhymes if they were using *ottava rima* for serious or heroic pur-poses. But 'the very qualities of English ottava-rima which force a serious poet to resort to banal rhymes and padding are a stimulus to the comic imagination' (Auden 1962: 399); and, Auden pointed out, that it is often forgotten that the Romantic period was actually also still an age of comic verse, where Byron was among many who experimented with using the stanza for satiric purposes. Auden argues:

> What had been Byron's defect as a serious poet, his lack of reverence for words, was a virtue for the comic poet. Serious poetry requires that the poet treat words as if they were persons, but comic poetry demands that he treat them as things and few, if any English Poets have rivalled Byron's ability to put words through the hoops.
>
> (Auden 1962: 399)

Auden also corrected the common misconception that Byron dashed off his poetry effortlessly, referring in a later edition of his essay to the 1957 Variorum edition edited by Steffan and Pratt, which gave detailed information on the amount of revision, especially in the manuscripts of the early cantos. He did, however, insist that the verse must be *read* rapidly 'as if the words were single frames in a movie film', because he thought Byron's particular forte was to evoke movement and the mind in motion.

Attention was also paid to Byron by the eminent Shakespearean critic G. Wilson Knight, whose essay on the poet appeared in *The Burning Oracle* (1939). Wilson Knight was exceptional in seeing Byron as possessing the Shakespearian power of dramatising opposing forces, for example the characteristically Byronic antithesis between 'pagan fire and Christian gentleness' in the Oriental tales. Also Shakespearian was Byron's feeling for humanity combined with the 'impersonal historical interest of *Childe Harold*': 'Byron is the only poet since Shakespeare to possess one of Shakespeare's rarest gifts: that of pure artistic joy in the annals . . . of human action; in close association, moreover, with places' (West 1963:22).

Wilson Knight's innovative defence of Byron's dramatic power would be followed up later in the century by Anne Barton and Jonathan Bate, eminent Renaissance scholars interested in the connections between Shakespeare and Romantic drama (see Criticism, **pp. 117–18**). Another critic who took the play of binary oppositions as the key to exploring the seeming contradictions of Byron's verse was W. J. Calvert in *Byron: Romantic Paradox* (1935), while E. W. Marjarum brought out a study of Byron's philosophical scepticism, *Byron as Sceptic and Believer* (1938), which for the first time paid serious attention to the poet's romantic irony. European critics, however, still tended to be more interested in the 'Romantic' Byron of *Childe Harold's Pilgrimage* and the tales than the satires, and Mario Praz, in *The Romantic Agony* (1933) identified the poet with the dark side of Romanticism, its Gothic fascination with perversity, melancholy and extremes of passion. This aspect of Romanticism was routinely minimised by insular British critics concentrating on Wordsworthian desexualised nature poetry, but Praz took a broader and more inclusive view of Romanticism, in which the connections between Byron and his German and French contemporaries were readily apparent.

The popular identification of Byron with the Satanic was reinforced when connections were made between Byronism and the rise of fascism, for in the 1930s and 1940s scholars were analysing the origins of the Nazi ideology. In 1945 the philosopher Bertrand Russell devoted an entire chapter to the poet in his *A History of Western Philosophy*. He pointed out the influence of the poet, who had hero-worshipped Napoleon, on the philosopher Nietzsche, who went even further in envisaging a godlike hero or superman than had Byron with his titanic *magus* figure, Manfred. Russell asserted that through such cultural interconnections 'nationalism, Satanism, and hero worship, the legacy of Byron, became part of the complex soul of Germany' (West 1963: 156).

Generally speaking, however, in the first half of the century, Byron received considerably less attention from literary critics than the other male Romantic poets of the canon. Wordsworth was now considered far and away the superior and was classed with Shakespeare and Milton. Coleridge's critical writing had been extremely influential on the whole direction which the discipline and study of English Literature had taken. Keats was generally extremely highly regarded though his poetic œuvre, like that of Coleridge, was admittedly relatively small. Blake's critical reputation was growing all the time, as the patronising impression that he was a mad recluse was re-examined. Shelley's eminence was disputed by some who found his imagery insufficiently concrete, such as the influential critic F. R. Leavis, who was fond of making authoritative league tables which ranked major and minor authors in rank order. In his *Revaluation: Tradition and Development in English Poetry* (1936), F. R. Leavis allots merely five pages to Byron's satire, implying its minor status by asserting it has less affinity with Pope than with Burns. Leavis takes up the notion of Byron as a Regency hybrid straddling Augustanism and Romanticism, by characterising Byron's satire as appealing to a generous common humanity though adopting a lamentable 'recklessness' towards forms and conventions inconceivable in the neo-classical period.

Because he was seen primarily as a satirist, because he was not thought of as a 'nature poet' and because Byron had himself mocked the high seriousness of Romanticism, he was not easily grouped with the other British Romantic poets (see Life and Contexts, **p. 29** and Criticism, **pp. 91–2, 107**). In 1953, M. H. Abrams produced a magisterial study, *The Mirror and the Lamp: Romantic Theory and the Critical Tradition* (1953) which pointed out that modern literary theory had developed out of the critical thought of the Romantics themselves, especially Coleridge. Yet Abrams was content to continue to define Romanticism in Coleridgean terms. For Byron was left out of Abrams' *Natural Supernaturalism: Tradition and Revolution in Romantic Literature*: 'Byron I omit altogether; not because I think him a lesser poet than the others but because in his greatest work he speaks with an ironic counter-voice and deliberately opens a satirical perspective on the vatic stance of his Romantic contemporaries' (1971: 13).

For Abrams, it was only the poetry that secularized inherited theological ideas which constituted Romanticism, and expressed, in Shelley's words, 'the spirit of the age'. More sceptical voices were out of tune.

From the 1950s to 2000

The 'New Criticism' produced a steady stream of critical studies that analysed the verse dispassionately, determined to resist reading it merely as illustrative of Byron's personality and biography. In fact, repudiating Byron's heroic status and cutting his reputation down to size seemed a challenge particularly relished by some 1960s critics. An austere monograph by Rutherford (1962) concentrated on the post-1816 poetry, especially Cantos III and IV of *Childe Harold's Pilgrimage* and *Don Juan*. He neglected the dramas, dismissed the Byronic heroes of the Oriental tales as adolescent fantasy and described *Manfred* as muddled and pretentious. A similarly debunking stance towards the charisma surrounding Byron was adopted by Paul West's witty and influential *Byron and the Spoiler's Art* (1960), which portrayed Byron as disaffected, escapist and a literary poseur: 'Byron had no philosophy, was no great social wit, and was not even essentially a writer' (West 1960: 12). Later studies such as the sharply intelligent *Byron: A Poet before his Public* (1982) by Philip W. Martin would also represent Byron as a flashy showman who played to his audience rather than perfecting his art. This emphasis can be seen to demonstrate the continuing influence of a modernist aesthetic, inclined to associate popularity with insincerity and both with bad art.

The modern biographer of the poet and editor of his letters, Leslie Marchand, provided in 1965 a straightforward brief introduction to the major poems, which sought to counter this emphasis on Byron's cynicism by arguing that, though modern readers found the realistic and satiric in Byron more conducive to their tastes, romantic aspiration was the core and basis of all his poetry. More innovative was the structuralist critic William H. Marshall (1962), who was influenced by a critical movement away from the search for meaning of New Criticism, in favour of an objective, almost architectural analysis of the underlying structures of genres or types of poems. Rather than relating the verse to the author's psyche, Marshall concentrated on the recurrence of literary devices and tropes, such as the interaction of characters representing the elementary themes of Love or Death. He did not see his critical role as judgmental, so took seriously even the earliest verse. Marshall discerned an organic patterning in the apparently aimless Canto III of *Child Harold's Pilgrimage*, which he represented by a diagram with the Rhine journey as the apex of the poem. He highlighted Byron's use of dramatic irony in many poems, where speakers such as the various Byronic heroes of the Oriental tales, or the subjects of dramatic monologues such as 'The Prophecy of Dante' or characters in *Don Juan* unconsciously reveal a discrepancy between the intended effect of their rhetoric and the affect on the reader. Like the important studies which followed, Gleckner (1967) and McGann (1968), Marshall was more interested in tracing a line of development leading from the earlier 'Romantic' verse to the *ottava rima* satires than he was with actually analysing *Don Juan* itself.

M. K. Joseph (1964) successfully evaded this focus on the poet's 'development', for his ambitious study asserted that Byron had been trying to reconcile his warring Romantic and Augustan impulses right from the beginning of his career. This holistic approach enabled Joseph to devote half of his well-researched and extensive monograph to *Don Juan*, which was or would be relatively neglected by other studies of the poet in the 1960s. Throughout the book, Joseph concentrates on multiple examples of the poet's 'search for form': his methods of composition, his choices of genres and metres and adaptations of literary tradition, his imagery and the frequency and deployment of his stylistic devices and his use of narratorial personae. For Joseph, Byron's Romantic irony in *Don Juan* constitutes a type of reconciliation of opposites: 'for it enables him to maintain a consistent attitude towards a world whose inconsistencies make all systems unreal' (Joseph 1964: 318).

Robert Gleckner (1967) followed an earlier and influential critic George Ridenour (1960) in attempting to impose coherence on Byron's œuvre by viewing it through its obsessive concern with the myth of the Fall in themes, style and metaphors. What made Gleckner's impressive study particularly significant was that he related his observation and analysis of this recurrent imagery to the view that it expressed a vision of the darkest philosophical despair, approaching nihilism:

> As a true Romantic, Byron envisions an Edenic past from which man has fallen, a past he endows with two basic sets of values and thus two basic image patterns. On the one hand, it is the heroic past of Greece and Grecian heroes, vigorous, brave, loyal, martial, and fundamentally simple . . . The other past is that of love, associated in Byron's mind not only with Adam and Eve but, as we have seen, with the garden of unspoiled nature and with childhood . . .
>
> (Gleckner 1967: 150–1)

Byronic guilt is not a pose but 'the heartfelt lament of man for what he is not' and can never attain. Gleckner wanted Byron's non-satiric poetry to be given its due, and he produced fine readings of *Childe Harold's Pilgrimage* and especially the Oriental tales, though at the cost of paying scant attention to the comedy and drama. Some critics (including McGann) felt Gleckner exaggerated Byron's pessimism. He certainly unsettled any complacent assumptions still remaining of the poet's essential frivolity, setting the tone for a new recognition of the depth of thought in Byron's poetry, but undoubtedly overstated his case.

The most important monograph of the 1960s and perhaps of the twentieth century was that of McGann (1968), which covered the same ground as Gleckner in re-evaluating the non-satiric poetry, especially by meticulously analysing the whole composition process of *Childe Harold's Pilgrimage* and by taking the drama and the Oriental tales seriously (see Life and Contexts, pp. 7–9, 14, 16–17). Perhaps the most impressive aspect of this book was that it began by taking the bull of the cult of personality by the horns. McGann focused on what was exceptional in Byron's poetry from the very beginning of his career: its self-dramatisation. Nether seduced nor embarrassed by Byron's persona, McGann examined the way narratorial strategies produced it. He made a comparison with Wordsworth, explaining that the experience described in Wordsworth's *The Prelude* is primarily cognitive.

> But because *Childe Harold's Pilgrimage* is fixed within a realistic environment; and second, because the act of narration and the narrated events occur simultaneously in a virtual present; and finally, because the poem tells the story of the psychological modifications that the narrating poet undergoes during the four cantos, the poem demands that the narrating poet be considered a participant in an action whose future progress he cannot know and whose ultimate issue he is, at all points prior to the climax, only partially aware of. Like a character in a novel or a

play, he has neither the author's prevision not the audience's objectivity, but is immersed in the immediacy of the events he himself recounts.

(McGann 1968: 35)

McGann saw the world of *The Giaour* and indeed of all the poetry as 'deeply religious: human life cuts athwart two opposed spiritual planes of reality and thus constantly plays out the war in heaven fought between deathless angels and devils' (McGann 1968: 157). He endorsed Shelley and Goethe's extreme admiration for *Cain* which, together with *Heaven and Earth*, illustrated Byron's theory of history as 'a blind series of cycles, totally without morality as such' (McGann 1968: 249). Byron's philosophy was dark: he could not accept the progressive meliorism of Shelley or the eighteenth-century theologian Joseph Priestley. The theories of Georges Cuvier, that geology showed traces of the cataclysms marking the descent of the earth from her golden age into a degraded present, appealed to Byron's sceptical mind. According to McGann, this is why Byron's poetry abounds in repeated 'falls'. Yet McGann did not see the *ottava rima* verse merely as the hollow laughter of existential despair, as had Gleckner. In his brilliant analysis of *Beppo*, he asserted that Byron, like the other Romantic poets, fused the divine and the natural, but by his own idiosyncratic reinterpretation of Platonic aesthetics:

> Because all spiritual values are momentary and physical they are both irretrievably lost and necessarily found again. . . . What we find after loss is not the same as what we have lost – all loss is irrevocable – but it is equivalent to it in value, or perhaps even more valuable. Each particular is absolute to itself, and human life is a succession of such absolute moments.
>
> (McGann 1968: 293)

The 'fiery dust' of the title is Byron's way of expressing the inseparability and equality of value between flesh and spirit in human nature.

McGann's view of *Don Juan* was equally affirmative in his sophisticated study, *Don Juan in Context* (1976), which specified the poem's relation to literary tradition – its reactions to and adaptations of Homer, Horace, Juvenal and Milton. McGann then devoted himself to editing *Lord Byron: The Complete Poetical Works* (1980–93). Throughout this time, he continued to produce a series of brilliant essays on Byron: sometimes written in the form of dialogues or experimental variations on the scholarly essay. These have been collected together and published as *Byron and Romanticism* (2002). McGann is a particularly subtle critic of Byron as a lyric poet and teases out the 'mobility' of the poet's voice, for example, in the setting of 'The Isles of Greece' in the lavish court of Haidée and Juan, which produced multiple ironies (McGann 2002: 36–52). He explored the significance of the context(s) of original publication of 'occasional' verse, for example, in a reading of Byron's much-pirated poem to his wife after their separation, 'Fare thee well!' (McGann 2002, 80–92). He was fascinated with the way the poet created yet questioned 'sincerity' in lyrical verse and explored Byron's equivocal literary relationship with popular women poets of the day, such as the Della Cruscan 'Rosa Matilda' or Charlotte Dacre (McGann 2002: 53–76, 160–72) and his rivalry with William Wordsworth (2002: 173–201). For an introduction to these preoccupations, see McGann's chapter on 'Byron's lyric poetry' in the *Cambridge Companion to Byron* (Bone 2004: 209–23).

Further reading

Jane Stabler gives a brief but stimulating overview of each decade in the introduction to the Longman Critical Reader (Stabler 1998: 1–26). Paul West edited an anthology of Byron criticism of the first sixty years of the century for the Twentieth Century Views series (West 1963). Likewise John Jump's Macmillan Casebook offered a selection of Byron criticism from 1905 to 1968 (Jump 1973). Both these collections are representative of the critical preoccupations of the earlier twentieth century. A comprehensive listing of criticism is offered in Oscar José Santucho's and Clement Tyson Goode's *George Gordon, Lord Byron, Lord Byron: A Comprehensive Bibliography of Secondary Materials in English, 1807–1977*, updated to 1990 (1997).

Contemporary criticism

Post-structuralism

In the 1970s, post-structuralist critical approaches came to the fore. Influenced by the ideas of the French philosopher, Jacques Derrida, deconstructionists emphasised the relational nature of the way language works. They took even further the emphasis of the New Critics on the way that textual meaning is not inherent or fixed by authorial intention, but produced by the act of reading. There were obvious comparisons to be made between this late-twentieth-century relativism, with its vision of the endless play of language and deferral of meaning, and Romantic irony: defined in his notebooks by Byron's contemporary, the German Romantic theorist Friedrich Schlegel, as 'a feeling of the insoluble opposition of the absolute and the relative' (quoted in Garber 1988: 169). Romantic irony was best exemplified in English literature by Byron's *Don Juan*, which represented both nature and human creativity as an endless cycle of construction and decomposition. Therefore, deconstruction stimulated new critical interest in Byron and his philosophical modernity. Major studies appeared which took Byron's philosophical scepticism seriously for the first time (Mellor 1980; Garber 1988; Hoagwood 1993).

In his seminal study of Byron's irony, poststructuralist critic Frederick Garber produced a sophisticated analysis of the way selves are made and unmade in relation to their settings in Byron's poems. Though Garber's approach was formalist rather than historicist, he was careful to place the poetry in its literary context – for example, by distinguishing the poet's Orientalism from that of his contemporaries, the Gothic novelist William Beckford and artist Eugène Delacroix. Garber also compared Byron's Romantic irony with that of his German contemporaries, the Gothic writer E. T. A. Hoffman and poet Heinrich Heine. Garber illustrated the way Byron's dualistic irony produced gaps, contradictions and open-endedness in his texts, in contrast with the organic structure and closure associated with Wordsworth's poetry. On the other hand, Garber pointed out that, unlike the irony of a contemporary poststructuralist critic such as Paul de Man in *The Allegories of Reading: Figural Language in Rousseau, Nietzsche, Rilke, and Proust* (1979), which always results in aporia and signifies 'the void of signification', Romantic irony 'is not a dead end but a very lively one, a dialectic of break-up and renewal' (Garber 1988: 258).

The points of discussion between Garber and other writers on Byron's philosophical irony concerned the extent to which Byron's Romantic irony in *Don Juan* is more ambivalent about selfhood and darker generally than in Schlegel, and, second, whether the style of the poem constitutes a refusal of the Romantic aesthetic, defined by Abrams as affirming organic wholeness. Mellor (1980) was criticised by McGann (McGann 1983a: 12) as being too eager to equate Romantic irony such as Byron's with a Coleridgean reconciliation of opposites. Garber (1988) emphasised that Byron's stanzas are made out of the clashing rhetoric of self-contradiction which does not constitute an attempt at a Coleridgean synthesis, but he continued to use Schlegel's definitions as a yardstick with which to measure Byron's Romantic irony (Garber 1988: 244). Hoagwood (1993), however, took the larger context of philosophical scepticism as his frame of reference and pointed out that Schlegel's irony was 'a singularly individualistic mode of thought', which was conservative in comparison with the political dimension of Byron's scepticism which performed an iconoclastic attack on systems and institutions (Hoagwood 1993: 25).

Frederick L. Beaty in *Byron the Satirist* (1985), in contrast to these studies, took a more traditional approach by reasserting the 'Augustan' rather than 'Romantic' aspect of the verse: treating Byron as a satiric poet rather than as a philosophical ironist and denying that Byron's satires were nihilistic or despairing. He set each of the satires, from *English Bards and Scotch Reviewers* to *Don Juan* and *The Vision of Judgment*, in its historical context in order to investigate its genesis and to view the aims of the poet positively, as attempts to puncture illusions and thus to reform society. Many links and correspondences were traced between early and later works, and the reader was also made aware of Byron's place in the satiric tradition of literature and the influence on the poet of earlier satirists from classical times to his own day.

Another critic inspired by post-structuralism, William H. Galperin, devoted a section to Byron in a book focusing on the visible in Romanticism rather than the traditional concern with the visionary, comparing Byron's self-conscious foregrounding of the act of fictionalising with contemporary postmodernism. Galperin suggested that even the early poem *Childe Harold's Pilgrimage* Cantos I and II may be described as a 'postmodern' impression of the visible and chaotic world, whose 'tensions have been subsumed and virtually synthesized' in Canto III, though in Canto IV there was something of a return to a fragmentary and unstable narrative (Galperin 1993: 257–70). In Canto III, in a more Wordsworthian 'Romantic' fashion, the visible was repressed in favour of the thoughts of a more coherent and authoritative narrator whose presence 'furnishes the reader with direct access to poetic authority' (Galperin 1993: 258).

In her recent essay 'Byron, Postmodernism and Intertextuality', Jane Stabler persuasively argued that Byron's own acknowledgement that *Don Juan* was following in the tradition of Laurence Sterne's eighteenth-century novel *Tristram*

Shandy is evidence that self-reflexive delight in fictionality, usually now termed 'postmodernism', but which is also found in *Don Juan*, 'is a genre co-existent with the rise of print culture' rather than a merely contemporary phenomenon (Bone 2004: 266).

Psychoanalytical approaches

In 1993 a collection of four specially commissioned essays on *Don Juan* appeared, taking post-structuralist theoretical approaches to *Don Juan* (Wood 1993). Two of the contributors adopted psychoanalytical approaches to the poem. Laura Claridge used the theories of the French theorist Jacques Lacan, who had adapted Freud's account of subject formation to take account of Ferdinand de Saussure's structural linguistics. Claridge explains this as follows:

> The demands of symbolization upon a needy, biological creature institute desire – the continuous force at the centre of Lacanian psychoanalytical theory. . . . Language works as a surrogate for the satisfaction of needs, and if we consider the conundrum of signification – of the inability of language ever to complete a circuit of meaning without referring to yet another signifier – we readily grasp how desire generated from this substitution is infinite in nature.
>
> (Wood 1993: 34)

Such a theory fitted well with the myth of Don Juan which had itself evolved to represent the insatiability of desire, and with a Romantic poem that endlessly makes and unmakes itself (see Works, **p. 65**). Claridge read the narrative structure of the poem in terms of Juan's ego-development as he 'figures himself through the image of a desired other' in the various love episodes (Wood 1993: 37). Though suggestive, such applications of Lacanian theory to literary texts are sometimes criticised as predictable or mechanical, as similar paradigms tend to be illustrated over and over again.

David Punter, in the same volume, squarely confronted the course the post-structuralist psychoanalytical critic attempts to steer 'between the rebarbitive workings of the Lacanian machine on the one hand and the siren-song of reconstructive biography on the other' (Wood 1993: 127). He cited, as an example of the latter, Peter Manning's 1970s psychobiography, which found repeated images in Byron's poetry of woman as mother-substitute: transgressively desired yet also feared as possessive and engulfing (Manning 1978). Though he acknowledged Manning's book to be excellent of its kind, Punter felt the Freudian critic should deal with the text's unconscious rather than ascribe causes of such patterning to the author's psyche. In his witty and wide-ranging essay, Punter began by considering Otto Rank's psychoanalytical interpretation of the Don Juan legend itself as a fantasy of power over women, which had originated in refutations of memories of infantile dependence on the mother (Rank 1975). The libertine killed in a duel the father of one of the women he had seduced. Furthermore, he dared to invite to dinner the dead man's statue. But in shaking hands, the ghostly statue pulled him down to Hell. This symbolised the Oedipal fear of vengeance exacted on one who sinned against patriarchal exchange of women. Building on an interesting reading by Bernard Beatty of the importance of the character Aurora Raby (Beatty 1985: 88–90), Punter suggested that this pious virgin is 'a displaced representation of the Stone Guest' (Wood 1993: 135) who, had the poem been finished, would have proved the hero's Nemesis. The 'question of individual coherence – and particularly the coherence of the "armed" phallic male – was at stake throughout the poem', and, according to Punter, led towards 'the castration motif embodied in the long destiny of decapitation', which Byron had projected would be the protagonist's fate in the French revolution (Wood 1993: 147).

New Historicism

In the 1970s and 1980s a wholesale cultural revaluation, including a re-examination of the special status previously accorded to texts deemed 'Romantic', was spearheaded by feminist scholars, whose rediscovery of the leading role played by women writers of the time had made it necessary to tear up the map of the old route between the Enlightenment and Victorianism. Feminists led the way and New Historicists inspired by deconstruction followed. They endorsed the opening up of the 1750–1850 archives to scrutiny: breaking down the barriers between 'literary' texts and other genres, and ignoring the hierarchy of 'major' and 'minor' writers set up by critics inspired by modernist aesthetics. This was enabled by the democratisation of conventional bibliographical and editorial scholarship through IT – a development which New Historicists such as Jerome McGann and Alan Liu have made the centre of both their critical practice and theory.

In part, the new movement was a critical reaction to the ahistoricism of both formalism and deconstruction. On the other hand, New Historicists took on board the criticism made by formalism and deconstruction of nineteenth-century teleological historiography and the doubt cast on a diachronic understanding of texts. New Historicism sought to combine deconstruction's insights into the reader's role in producing meaning with a recognition that texts are not produced simply by individuals but also by society. Genres, literary styles and language itself are collectively formed, deployed and understood. Knowing something of the historical moment of the text's production and reception and its relationship with precursor texts helps modern readers appreciate the otherness of that moment. Good New Historicist criticism is always, on the other hand, self-consciously aware of the concerns of the present which inevitably influence and frame studies of past literature. The label 'new' supposedly distinguished a more sophisticated concept of 'context' from that of traditional historicist critics. New Historicists don't make clear-cut divisions between fictional texts and those classified as factual: histories, travels, diaries and other documentary evidence. They find many affinities between different sorts of writing in terms of rhetoric, literary techniques and language and see history itself as a process of textual production which relates as much to its own present as to the past it seeks to represent.

Jerome McGann was a leading theorist in developing the ideas of New Historicism in Romantic-period studies, and it was no coincidence that he was the leading critic and editor of Byron. Byron epitomised the sort of anomaly that could develop when insufficient attention is paid to history: that the most popular and influential poet of his century, who epitomised Romanticism for his contemporaries, had come to seem irrelevant to Romanticism for modern critics (see Life and Contexts, **p. 29**). In his controversial polemic, *The Romantic Ideology: A Critical Investigation* (1983), McGann pointed out that the thought and practice of both editorial scholarship and criticism in contemporary Romantic studies was itself saturated in Romantic preconceptions, derived often from Samuel Taylor Coleridge's theories of the imagination which had been influenced by the German philosopher Emmanuel Kant. McGann adopted a demythologising sceptical stance of self-scrutiny which unmasked as false consciousness the uncritical endorsement by critics such as Meyer Abrams and Northrop Frye of 'romanticism's own self-representations' (McGann 1983: 1). Other New Historicists, such as Marilyn Butler, pointed out the central importance to the development of the discipline of English Literature of the construction of the Romantic canon with Wordsworth's *The Prelude* at its centre, whose turning away from revolution to solace in nature inculcated quietism and endorsed political conservatism (Levinson 1989).

Byron studies were therefore central to McGann's frequent and important interventions in the theoretical debates within New Historicism (McGann 1983, 1985a, 1985b, 1988, 2001), as he negotiated between the Scylla and Charybdis of Marxist and post-structuralist theory. His most important contribution to the debate was to question the idealism behind rigid abstractions such as 'the text', which ignored the indeterminacy inevitably built in to editorial practice, no less subjective or impervious to historical change than interpretation. McGann argued that editorial, bibliographic and interpretative scholarship should not be discrete areas but be brought to bear on each other, in order to fully acknowledge the social nature of the textual transmission of meaning. In answer to the charge that New Historicism limits the generation of meaning to the originating moment of the text's production, McGann has called for a 'renovated' dialogical diachronic historicist criticism which he defines as necessarily comparative. This should take account not only of the circumstances of production of a text but also of its subsequent transmissions, in order to compare interpretations with those of the present (McGann 2002: 77, 213, 232).

American New Historicists were inspired by the writings of the French postmodernist philosopher Michel Foucault to paint a somewhat deterministic vision of the inescapability of power. On the other hand, deconstruction made them alert to the nuances of linguistic play. The intricate dialogic essays of McGann on Byron where the critic adopted different personae representing opposed points of view (McGann 2002), the sophisticated work of Jerome Christenson on the poet's ambivalence towards his public image and self-representation (Christensen 1993) and Susan Wolfson's witty deconstruction of the ideology of poetic form (Wolfson 1988) all testified to a postmodernist concern with the play of language in and between texts, but also a sense of this as a closed system in which the individual artist was trapped.

However, in British Romantic-period criticism, Marxist cultural materialism was more prevalent, drawing from Raymond Williams a view of texts as sites of contested ideologies, which enabled less pessimistic takes on cultural production, allowing that literature could be emancipatory. So there was more emphasis on the politics than on the literary form of Byron's poetry. For example, the socialist politician Michael Foot adopted an overtly Marxist approach to Byron, as both a historical figure and a writer, when tracing his contribution to the left-liberal tradition in Britain, to which Foot himself belongs (Foot 1988). Foot took violent exception to Michael Kelsall's revisionist study, which attempted to demythologise the image of Byron as a romantic revolutionary, by portraying him as hopelessly trapped within the binaries of the outworn discourse of aristocratic Foxite Whiggery (Kelsall 1987). Meanwhile, Daniel P. Watkins produced a materialist study devoted entirely to Byron's Oriental tales, poems despised by earlier critics (see Criticism, **p. 101**). Watkins asserted that they offer 'a reflection of human experience as it is lived within specific social frameworks' (Watkins 1987: 138). He saw their pessimism as the product of the poet's burning desire for political change. Watkins viewed poetry and drama 'as a part of the social history of the period' (Watkins 1993: xi). For example, he highlighted the way *The Giaour* offered a powerful critique of authoritarian religion and illustrated the alienation of the protagonist from his society and his relapse into utopian and escapist longings. This type of sociological Marxist approach is sometimes criticised for a relative neglect of the literary qualities of the verse in favour of concentrating on ideology. However, pointing out the political implications of these texts was a useful corrective to the assumptions of older critics, such as Rutherford, that the tales could be dismissed as adolescent self-projections.

A less ideological attempt to illustrate a specific historical context, this time with a particular focus on intertextuality, was Peter Graham's *Don Juan and Regency England* (1990). Earlier scholarly monographs had approached contextualizing the poem by analysing Byron's reading in general, as well as the European sources he cited, in order to trace influences on it (Boyd 1958) or by focusing on Byron's indebtedness to the Italian literature he saturated himself in during his residence in the country, and the Pulcian tradition of burlesque poetry in *ottava rima* in particular (Vassallo 1984). Graham, however, took the unusual angle of illustrating not the poem's overtly cosmopolitan perspective, but the fact that the poet was writing very specifically to a British readership, often responding to British texts and pointedly satirising British insularity. Graham related the style of the poem to the uniquely British tradition of pantomime. He also convincingly argued the influence of Robert Southey's *Letters from England: By Don Manuel Alvarez Espriella, Translated from the Spanish* (1807) and traced the literary battle of the sexes between the poet and Lady Caroline Lamb, whose novel *Glenarvon* had lampooned him as a heartless libertine. In his final chapter, in contrast to Bernard Beatty's assertions of the centrality of Aurora Raby in the English cantos, Graham restored Lady Adeline Amundeville to preeminent significance to these cantos, where her 'mobility' and the narrator's digressions are seen to break down artificial divisions between performance and the real.

Another historicist case study, which took up the theme of the importance of the London pantomimes in even more detail, but this time also engaged with postmodernist and feminist critical theories, was Moyra Haslett's *Byron's* Don Juan *and the Don Juan Legend* (1997). Haslett argued that most critics of Byron's comic epic have too easily dismissed as irrelevant the Don Juan myth and its various manifestations in drama and opera. She pointed out that between 1817 and 1825, when installments of the poem were coming out, theatrical London was undergoing a craze for parodic, burlesque and pantomime versions of the legend (Haslett 1997: 4). Haslett argued that, though Byron's unfinished poem contains no stone guest and hellfire ending and its protagonist is not a predatory villain, even such an aberrant version of the legend relies on knowledge and acceptance of the myth as a fixed point of departure: a precondition for its 'argumentative relationship with the reader' respecting sexual and class politics (Haslett 1997: 9–13).

The very popularity of Byron's verse was a phenomenon in literary history (see Life and Contexts, **p. 10** and Works, **p. 56**): this had been an embarrassment to earlier critics such as Rutherford or had inspired an emphasis on the poet's cynicism and calculated construction of a personality cult (West 1963, Martin 1982, Christensen 1993). But when New Historicism and cultural materialism broke down the barriers between high art and popular culture, the phenomenal sales of Byron's poetry during the nineteenth century became an object of non-judgemental study. This was a major inspiration behind both the magisterial materialist analysis by William St Clair (2004) of book sales and readership in the period, and studies of the appropriation of the poet's image in nineteenth and twentieth-century popular culture (Wilson 1999; Elfenbein 1995). St Clair's work exemplified the extension of cultural materialism in the past ten years into questions of readership, the publishing and dissemination of print culture, copyright, censorship, the part played by periodicals in forming 'taste' and the formation of the canon. St Clair's interest in these issues began with Byron, for in 1990 he had published a ground-breaking article giving a statistical analysis of the marketing and sales of Byron's poetry, which demonstrated that after 1816 Byron began to lose his upper-class readers but found a new audience amongst the middle and lower classes with his *ottava rima* verse (Rutherford 1990).

In his 2004 study, St Clair demonstrated wide gaps between: traditional literary history written by critics and academics, limited to what they thought constituted the 'gold standard' literature of each age, which he dubs the 'parade' model; the more inclusive notion of a textual debate between different sorts of texts, instituted by New Historicism, which he calls the 'parliament' model; and the number and type of texts actually sold and read at the time, different from either. The extent of Byron's popularity was a case in point, and he gave tables detailing the publication of Byron's individual works in his own day and in Victorian times, the phenomenon of Byronism and information on whether Byron's poetry was included or omitted from literary histories, libraries and reading societies in the nineteenth century. Most interesting of all were St Clair's conclusions regarding *Don Juan*, which 'even in its official form, was by far the biggest seller of any contemporary literary work during the romantic period':

> *Don Juan* reached the reading nation unmediated by the normal institutional, publishing, and price conventions. It penetrated more deeply and more widely within the reading nation, although not uniformly, and it continued to be feared, reprinted in large numbers, and widely read as a separate book right through the Victorian period. Few books reveal more vividly the differences between quantified histories of reading and traditional literary and cultural history seen as a parade or parliament of

texts. As an example of literary diffusion, *Don Juan* is unique, an episode in which all the normal activities of authors, publishers, editors, printers, illustrators, reviewers, book buyers, and readers can be seen accelerated and intensified. It repays detailed study not only in its own right, but as a case study from which other more general lessons about the system of texts, books, reading, and cultural formation can be taken. *Don Juan* is the Galapagos Islands of literature.

(St Clair 2004: 333–4)

As St Clair pointed out, the polarisation of the readership of the poem produced a polarisation of official and unofficial supply of books. The question of the censorship and piracy of Byron's poetry and the part it played in working-class radicals' arguments for a free press have also featured in ground-breaking studies of popular culture before the Reform Act of 1832 (Wood 1994; Gilmartin 1996). In a thoughtful essay considering how the poem spoke stylistically to its differently classed and gendered audiences, Philip Martin has made good use of the theories of the Marxist critic Mikhail Bakhtin, who was interested in the folk humour of the grotesque body, in the unofficial culture of the carnivalesque, and polyphonic texts that ventriloquised a range of voices (Wood 1993).

Samuel Chew's classic study of Byron's reputation in the nineteenth century (Chew 1924) has recently been supplemented by Andrew Elfenbein's book on the influence of the cult of the poet on the Victorians (Elfenbein 1995). Elfenbein used the work of theorist Pierre Bourdieu to examine how the idea of celebrity was linked with the idea of transgression and influenced reading practices. His originality lay in showing how Victorian writers Thomas Carlyle, Emily Brontë, Alfred Tennyson and Oscar Wilde reacted with ambivalence to the poet, neither imitating nor entirely rejecting his enormous influence. A more light-hearted approach to 'Byromania' was taken by the contributors to a collection of essays edited by Frances Wilson (1999), which examined the numerous novels, films, plays, forgeries, imitations and art inspired by the Byron myth from the Regency to the present day and also the extent to which the poet was complicit with their manufacture.

Post-colonialism

One of the most revelatory aspects of applying the New Historicist approach in Byron studies was provided by Marilyn Butler (1988, 1992) and Nigel Leask (1992). They were inspired by post-colonial theory, which had taken off from the 1978 polemic of Edward Said, which defined Orientalism in Foucauldian terms as seizing the power of knowledge of the Other: 'by making statements about it, authorizing views of it, describing it, by teaching it, settling it, ruling over it: in short, Orientalism as a Western style for dominating, restructuring and having authority over the orient' (Said 1978: 3). By the late 1980s, this monolithic view was being modified, as many scholars pointed out that the Enlightenment interest in Eastern mores was more relativist and open to Eastern influence than this model implied, and that colonies also played an active part in modifying imperial culture and producing hybridity. Butler and Leask explored the ambivalence of Byron's Orientalist verse, produced at a time when British imperialism was evolving from trade towards rule and missionary activity in India (see Life and Contexts, **pp. 5–6** and Works, **p. 36**).

Marilyn Butler pointed out that when Byron returned from his travels in 1811, he found the Evangelicals mounting a campaign to overturn the policy of the East India Company, which had been to leave Indian social structure undisturbed (Butler 1988: 80). In 1813, when *The Giaour* was published, parliament was debating whether to support missionary activity to India, and Robert Southey's orientalist verse tale, *The Curse of Kehama* (1810), had recently portrayed Hinduism as a cruel and barbaric religion. Butler built up a detailed context from which to view the significance of the attack on orthodox religion, both Christian and Muslim, in *The Giaour*. She brought out the importance of the way the subjectivity of the sceptical protagonist was withheld until the conclusion: 'But nowhere perhaps is there a study of the Byronic humanist so concentrated, intense, and personally felt, so skilfully central and unimpeded, as in the last five hundred lines of *The Giaour*' (Butler 1988, 89). Butler went on to point out the way that the Oriental tales were part of Byron's project to educate the British readership about the campaign for Greek independence within the context of the crumbling Ottoman Empire, and ambivalently portray the Western powers, such as Britain, as ready to make capital out of the situation. But she argued that the political themes were somewhat vitiated by the overlaying of the titillating theme of sexual guilt. Also, they failed to inspire action because the heroes were alienated and doomed to failure, reflecting the poet's own political pessimism. Butler made the interesting point that Byron was castigated more as an anti-clerical writer than as a radical or revolutionary (1988: 94). She went on to develop this theme in a further essay on the orientalist drama *Sardanapalus* (Butler 1992).

In his ground-breaking study of the centrality of Romantic writers' ambivalent attitudes to the East in literature of the period, Nigel Leask followed McGann, Watkins and Butler in the revaluation of the earlier verse, and devoted a third of his substantial book to a detailed and nuanced reading of the Oriental tales. Leask took his cue from McGann's and Watkins' political interpretations of these romances, though he criticised Watkins for reading them as 'didactic fables of an alternative system of social relations' and for underplaying their sexual politics and Orientalism (Leask 1992: 15). In contrast to earlier critics such as Martin, who emphasised Byron's own cynicism about his popular poetry, Leask argued that the poet's defensive remarks testify to his anxiety about imperialism, a discourse in which he found himself implicated. For Leask commented that 'Byron's focus on the Levant in his *Eastern Tales*, and particularly on the predicament of Greece, the "lost source" of European civilisation smothered beneath the blanket of the Ottoman Empire, is to some extent complicit in the jealous gaze of British policy' (Leask 1992: 23). Philhellenism itself might have been, after all, a displaced way of expressing Islamophobia. Like Butler, Leask pointed out the symmetry in *The Giaour* between the Eastern and the Western rivals for Leila's love, but, unlike Butler, he saw the sexual theme as intensifying rather than departing from this structural irony. He emphasised that 'the power relations of gender transcend cultural difference' (Leask 1992: 29). Leask was particularly adept in the illuminating parallels he made between the poetry of Byron and his contemporaries, such as Southey, Rogers and Chateaubriand, and he alerted the reader to Byron's distinctive scepticism and use of satire which qualified his sentimental nationalism.

Leask explicated the contemporary political significance of *The Bride of Abydos*, taking up Malcolm Kelsall's determinist argument that Byron found himself trapped between hidebound aristocratic Whiggery and the unacceptable democracy of the radical artisans. He argued against Kelsall that in his poetry Byron did imagine the breaking of those limits, even if the House of Lords speeches on behalf of the Whigs could not do so. However, he conceded that the poet 'can only contemplate the limits of aristocratic heroism, whilst nurturing a compensatory scepticism about the effects of revolutionary democracy' (Leask 1992: 38–43). In his original and persuasive reading of *The Corsair*, however, Leask suggested that the political dimensions of a 'radicalized hero' are displaced 'into the terms of gender', 'for it is the women who suddenly spring into life' (Leask 1992: 45). Leask suggested that Medora 'exists only as a construct of his [Conrad's] imagination' and represents the ideal, but that Gulnare's murder of the tyrant 'breaks the circuit of signification' though at the cost of Conrad's chivalric code. 'In the figure of Gulnare, the European Self is mimicked and ultimately absorbed by its oriental Other' (Leask 1992: 49–51). Leask's exploration of the gender politics and their significance for Orientalism was continued in his readings of *Lara*, with its cross-dressed androgynous heroine, and the utopian idyll of *The Island*, where female characters continued to represent revolutionary freedom. Leask's emphasis on gender in the Oriental tales may be compared to Franklin's feminist study which appeared in the same year (see Works, **p. 57**).

The mid-1990s saw the publication of three specialist studies devoted to Romantic Orientalism, and of interest to Byronists. A. R. Kidwai's *Orientalism in Lord Byron's 'Turkish Tales'* (1995) investigated Byron's secondary sources and compared his use of them with his Orientalist contemporaries Robert Southey and Thomas Moore. Naji B. Oueijan's *The Progress of an Image: The East in English Literature* (1996) considered a broader canvas of representations of the East in Romantic writing, and argued that Byron's Oriental tales should be seen positively as they express cultural empathy. Mohammed Sharafuddin's *Islam and Romantic Orientalism: Literary Encounters with the Orient* (1994) also challenged Said's sweepingly negative view of Western representations of the Orient, drawing particular attention to the pro-Islamic elements in Romantic writing and giving credit to Byron's realism and the authenticity of many details of local colour in his romances. Though all these studies had useful insights to impart, it could be argued that they dismissed Said's thesis rather too readily and were reluctant to relate a colonialising context to the production of cultural stereotypes of the East.

In *Romanticism and Colonialism 1780–1830*, on the other hand, the 'vexed question of the relationship between culture and imperialism and the complicity of English Literature in the imperialist project' (Fulford and Kitson 1998: 3) was the subject of a substantial and important collection of essays, including one by Leask which included consideration of Byron, and two, by Franklin and Kelsall, entirely on Byron (Fulford and Kitson 1998). Many contributors followed Leask's lead in emphasising the ambivalence, anxiety and guilt of much Romantic writing regarding colonialism and the slave trade. Franklin, in a reading of *The Siege of Corinth* and *Hebrew Melodies* argued that Butler, Leask and Kelsall had overstated the conservatism of Byron's Orientalist poetry, which used its aristocratic sceptical stance to challenge the Evangelical campaign for conversion of pagans and working classes alike (Fulford and Kitson 1998: 221–42). Following the lead of Butler, Franklin highlighted the importance of the poet's sceptical treatment of Christianity and the melancholic presentation of both Philhellenism and proto-Zionism as lost nationalist causes that symbolised and implicitly questioned the parcelling up of Europe into dynastic and monarchical power blocs at the Congress of Vienna in 1815, after the defeat of Napoleon.

Malcolm Kelsall's article on Byron and Venice, in the same volume, made a trenchant critique of the influence of post-colonial critics, such as Edward Said, in promulgating literary critiques of nineteenth-century literature, which tell us more about our own contemporary guilt about European imperialism than they actually illuminate the past (Fulford and Kitson 1998: 243–60). Kelsall argued that, in fact, the Islamic empire had been the originally more significant force in history since medieval times, against which Europe defensively defined its identity. Kelsall also usefully pointed out that classical literature, in which Byron's education had been steeped, was itself deeply divided about the nature of Hellenistic and Roman imperialism. This, in turn, influenced the historians and philosophers of the Romantic period, so that critics of the present should not patronisingly simplify the thinking of the past about colonialism, which was itself contested and nuanced. Kelsall analysed the apostrophe to Venice in *Childe Harold's Pilgrimage*, *Venice, an ode* and *Beppo*, teasing out the way the extinction of the Venetian republic had multiple significance for Byron, as the city, the very gateway to the East, changed from imperial power to colony. Kelsall emphasised the perpetual binaries of Occident and Orient but also pointed to the hybridism of Byron's account of the images which first shaped his image of the city and its cultural diversity:

> But if the poetry is enclosed historically within this arena of perennial, imperial conflict, yet the potent image of Cybele, translated from East to West, received by both cultures, and celebrated as the very signifier of a great commercial city (as well as an imperial power) suggests another kind of historical process by which antagonistic cultures meld and are reconciled.
>
> (Fulford and Kitson 1998: 253)

In a 2000 conference collection devoted to *Byron: East and West*, Michael Franklin presented a view of the poet that stressed his anxieties and ambivalence over the effeminising effect of colonisation even more strongly than Leask. He investigated the poet's questioning of the validity of poetry and even of language's ability to translate an experience into words and compared this Romantic anxiety with the Enlightenment confidence of the premier Orientalist, Sir William Jones (Procházka 2000: 65). Whereas Jones's pioneering work in comparative linguistics and interest in Indian traditions of religious syncretism prized similarities, which unsettled Western preconceptions of cultural superiority, the cosmopolitan Romantic poet revelled in difference and competing voices.

Gender

Pioneering historicist scholarship by Crompton (1985), Franklin (1992) and Wolfson (1987) considered for the first time the representation of gender in Byron's poetry, taking into account, respectively: contemporary attitudes to homosexuality, debate over the role of women and playful Romantic transgression of gender boundaries. Louis Crompton's historical study put Byron's bisexuality at the centre of a full-length study for the first time, though the evidence of his homosexuality was already in print (Marchand 1957: I, 90; Knight 1957: 226–8; Moore 1974: 437–59) (see Life and Contexts, **p. 4** and Works, **p. 37**). He brought to light the rabid climate of homophobia in the early nineteenth century, when sodomy was a capital crime and homosexual behaviour punished by the pillory. Against such a background, Crompton elucidated the cult of male friendships at Harrow and Cambridge, the importance of the homoerotic in classical literature and art and Byron's interest in the Islamic world, whose poetry and culture was also non-judgemental about same-sex love. Especially enlightening was Crompton's explication of the 'Thyrza' poems inspired by the death of the Cambridge chorister, John Edleston, which were appended to *Childe Harold's Pilgrimage* Cantos I and II, and the way that contemporary women readers misread them.

This work stimulated interest in the way Byron's poetry opened itself to secret meanings available to different readerships and sexual orientations. For example, Jonathan Gross studied the relationship between Byron's libertinism and his commitment to political liberty and argued that Byron 'offered a unique literary contribution to liberalism in *Don Juan* . . . by highlighting the double entendres of a "gay" narrator to parody social and sexual mores in Regency England' (Gross 2001, 129–52). Gary Dyer has also published an article on the way the highwayman episode in Canto XI of *Don Juan* exploits the secret linguistic codes linking together the illegal activities of thieving, boxing and sodomy (Dyer 2001).

A pioneering 1987 article by feminist critic Susan Wolfson, expanded the interest in gender in *Don Juan* by focusing on dress as a conventional signifier of gender difference and investigating transvestism as a calling into question of the binaries of masculinity and femininity. Wolfson illustrated both the traditional and even misogynist representations of gender in the poem, but also Byron's critique of 'the sexual politics that underwrite the "she-condition" '. She brought out how 'these inversions and reversals not only erode male privilege, but inhabit plots in which such erosion is associated with images and threats of death', where Juan is at risk from the patriarchal males or the masculinised women whose power he challenges (Stabler 1998: 96). Wolfson carefully combined an ideological gender critique with sensitive attention to literary form here, as she would later in her essay on the couplets in *The Corsair* (Wolfson 1988), by close reading of the rhetoric and imagery which tests out the boundaries of the ego. Wolfson gave Byron credit for a conscious desire to explore through poetry women's experience of sexual submission, as in the episode in the Turkish cantos where Juan is dressed as a woman. However, drawing on Terry Castle's work on the role of the masquerade in eighteenth-century culture, she also stressed that such transgression of gender boundaries were only temporary: 'the sexual politics that inform *Don Juan* at once expose their ideological underpinnings and qualify the potential subversiveness of these exposures with strategies to contain the risks posed to male privilege' (Stabler 1998: 105–6).

Caroline Franklin's feminist monograph took Byron's interest in the oppression of women in his poetry rather more seriously than Wolfson, relating the importance of this theme to Byron's interrogation of the tenets of liberalism generally (Franklin 1992). She saw the powerlessness of women in society as one of those anomalies which, by the nineteenth century, made the concept of Whiggism untenable:

> liberal ideology developed as a dialectic which challenged hierarchical society on the one hand, yet created a series of exceptions and exclusions on the other, in order to minimize the dangers of rampant individualism. Liberal ideology rested on the premise that the basis of power could be extended, yet its limits had to be defined to forestall incipient egalitarianism ... so that some revolutionary ideas could be construed as reasonable and relevant to the development of civilisation (the attack on the church and absolute monarchy), whilst some traditional power relationships (the family, the class system, European world domination) could be portrayed as determined by nature.
>
> (Franklin 1992: 7–8)

So while Byron's young aristocratic protagonists, such as Conrad in *The Corsair*, Japhet in *Heaven and Earth* or Jacopo in *The Two Foscari* found that complicity with male homosocial bonding paralysed their revolutionary potential, marginalised females in patriarchal societies, such as Gulnare, Aholibamah or Marina, were free to voice and sometimes enact transgression. *Don Juan* was seen as a satire on the domestic ideology called for by conservative philosophers in the light of the descent of the French Revolution into terror and endorsed by Evangelical women writers themselves. Though this included misogyny, such as the satire of Inez, it also challenged women to include sexual freedom in their feminist agenda. Byron's anti-imperialist and humanitarian account of the brutal Siege of Ismael, framed by the stories of the Turkish Sultan and Russian Empress's collections of sex slaves, was interpreted by Franklin as expressing Byron's 'pan-sexual sexual diagnosis of both personal and political aggression [which] is biological in emphasis' and which operates alike in men and women (Franklin 1992: 148). In a later essay focusing in detail on the Turkish cantos, Franklin argued that Byronic sexual libertarianism may be seen as part of the radical tradition, forming a dialectic with Wollstonecraftian rationalism and puritanism which was particularly influential on feminists and women writers later in the century (Wood 1993: 69).

Charles Donelan took up Haslett's view that *Don Juan* should be seen in the context of contemporary versions of the myth, especially when focusing on gender (Donelan 2000: 48). He argued that, 'Byron's *Don Juan* abandons the myth's original (exhausted) cultural function of re-enacting the ritual repression that founds monogamy and rejects a commercialized fetishization of monogamy as female chastity' (Donelan 2000: 8). Instead, the poem simultaneously portrays women realistically and also as the objects of male fantasy. Donelan took a Freudian view of the various episodes of the poem which begin as wish-fulfilment fantasy of power over women, only to be interrupted by patriarchal violence and destruction. He went on to investigate the way the poem flouted literary convention and risked censorship, and thus problematised the constricting effect of a narrowly defined bourgeois masculinity.

Genre and literary form

During the past twenty years, whilst New Historicism has undoubtedly revolutionised and revivified Byron studies, it has not been the whole critical story. Studies have continued to be published that focus on genre or traditional New Critical close reading, and there has been a recent call by Susan Wolfson, in a special issue of *Modern Language Quarterly* (2000), to return, not to formalism, but to concern with poetic form, a concern which need not be ahistorical – for form is created by the interface between individual vision and social communication in language. Many formalist critics have been interested in either contesting the modernist view of Byron as a second-rate poet with a cloth ear, or in revaluing unfashionable genres in which he wrote, such as verse romances or closet drama, or combining these aims. Some also have written specifically in opposition to New Historicism, especially by countering the emphasis on ideological readings of the poetry, which pay attention to class, gender and race whilst perhaps neglecting its linguistic texture, patternings and metre.

Genre and Romantic drama

Genre study has played a particularly prominent part in criticism of Byron's plays. Romantic drama has traditionally been regarded as essentially undramatic by theatre historians, as playwrights of this period were chiefly interested in psychological states of mind, and the psyche of an introspective protagonist was often expressed in static soliloquies. Romanticists have been equally dismissive of the literary quality of the pseudo-Shakespearian verse dramas that most poets of the period essayed. The gap between stage and page reflected that between popular theatre and critical taste, while censorship also played its part in producing a climate where poets such as Byron wrote 'closet drama' which was read rather than performed.

In the 1980s, critics began to reconsider the usual pronouncement that Romantic drama was unreadable, realising that it had often been unfairly judged against a Victorian/Edwardian predisposition for naturalism. Several monographs devoted themselves to Byron's plays, building on pioneering work by Chew (1915) and Taborski (1972). Martyn Corbett argued for their centrality in Byron's œuvre, in particular the Ravenna plays of 1820–1, *Marino Faliero*, *Sardanapalus* and *The Two Foscari*, which established him as a tragic poet whose pessimism was balanced 'by a stoical affirmation of human dignity' (Corbett 1988: 1). Corbett argued against those critics who found *Manfred* muddled, seeing the drama as a unified expression of tragic stoicism. For him *Werner* and *The Deformed* were not artistic failures, but experiments in form. He followed the lead of drama critics George Steiner and Anne Barton in calling for stage revivals of Byron's plays, which, he asserted, were considered unsuitable for the theatre of the time largely because they were serious rather than merely entertaining.

Richard Lansdown's study of Byron's historical dramas concentrated a scholarly spotlight exclusively on these three neglected works which were written in Ravenna and researched their political and cultural context in Byron's day (see Life and Contexts, pp. 22–3 and Works, p. 78). He uncovered fascinating background detail of Byron's knowledge of contemporary theatre, when he was involved with the Theatre Royal, Drury Lane in 1815–16, and the attempt at a revival of verse drama there. This set the scene for an examination of the vexed question of Byron's declared hostility to Romantic Shakespearianism and his corresponding and perhaps quixotic attempt to adapt elements of neo-classical dramatic form to create a historical representation of revolution.

Anne Barton has recently given a lively, short and scholarly account of Byron's actual immersion in the works of Shakespeare (Bone 2004: 224–235). However, we can recognise how shrewd he was to refuse to adopt the Bard as a model for his plays. Byron's attempt to discipline his own Romanticism by aspiring towards the austere neo-classicism of Italian dramatist Vittorio Alfieri ensured he would not suffer by comparison with Shakespeare and also provided him with a method of eliminating complex narrative in favour of one sharply focused situation. In these dramas of ideas, we experience with each protagonist the climax of an intense philosophical dilemma.

That is not to say that Shakespeare was irrelevant to Byron's poetry. Shakespeare had been rewritten, trimmed and tidied up in eighteenth-century moralistic productions, which still held the stage in Byron's day. So the rediscovery of his original mixture of tragedy with comedy was immensely inspiring to Byron and his contemporaries and was investigated in Jonathan Bate's *Shakespeare and the English Romantic Imagination* (1986). The debate over whether Shakespeare's plays could ever be performed as they had been written, or whether they should merely be enacted in the imagination of the reader's mind was, of course, very relevant to the development in the Romantic period of the genre of closet drama, that is, plays written to be read rather than performed. For most of the Romantic poets wrote plays, in an attempt to rival or to challenge either the Renaissance or the classical tradition of verse drama.

Some of the paradoxes surrounding the production of closet drama can be illustrated by the example of *Marino Faliero*. Byron himself defined his plays as 'mental theatre' (*BLJ* VIII, 186–7), and when this drama was performed at Drury Lane without his permission the poet attempted to get it stopped. Yet David Erdman (1939) has suggested that, despite his protests, the poet was actually equivocal and may have spoken very differently later, if the production had been a greater success. Thomas Ashton's research showed how very stringently the play had been censored in this production, to avoid prosecution for sedition, yet how the audience nevertheless responded vociferously to its implied political message (Ashton 1974). We may therefore surmise that Byron may well have wished to write for the theatre had not religion and politics been off limits in those days of censorship and had he not also feared and resented the power of the lower-class audience to determine a play's fate by their noisy reception of it. But this does not sufficiently explain the genesis of Byron's 'metaphysical' closet plays such as *Manfred*, *Cain* and *Heaven and Earth*, whose supernatural and extra-terrestrial occurrences would have been difficult to stage. These seem really to have been intended only to be read in the study. Yet Margaret Howell's study shows that in the later nineteenth century, these plays were, in fact, performed on the London stage and were often very successful (Howell 1982).

Modern studies of the genre of closet drama have overturned older lazy assumptions that these were merely failed stage plays by arguing that an experimental 'dramatic poem' such as *Manfred* was a hybrid between lyric and drama and can be compared with other Romantic poetic hybrids, such as Wordsworth and Coleridge's 'lyrical ballads' or Mary Robinson's 'lyrical tales' (Richardson 1988: 59–99). In *Manfred*, *Cain* and *Heaven and Earth*, Byron dramatised the internal debate of the protagonists, expressed through the lyrical voice in dialogue with humans and supernatural beings; he brilliantly revived the chorus, used in classical drama to comment on the action. Purinton (1994) also paid attention to the genre of closet drama, which she saw as bringing together the emphasis on the protagonist's subjectivity with the political necessity of each individual rejecting the shackles of outmoded beliefs in order to attain liberty. She argued that the subject of *Manfred* was the importance of ideological change in mental attitudes which we see enacted when Manfred frees himself from the enslavement of religious cant and accepts responsibility for his own destruction (Purinton 1994: 51–94).

In his sophisticated study of Byron and Shelley's dramas, Michael Simpson also attempted to relate revolutionary politics to the avant-garde form the poetry takes in a historical context of censorship and self-censorship. He argued that the exiled aristocrats Byron and Shelley's post-1815 dramas were attempting to revive the radical agenda of the revolutionary 1790s, but that the uncertain generic status of closet drama was a space separate from artisan radical dissent and which evaded censorship. Simpson sought to demonstrate the way theatricality both repressed yet also shadowed the textual status of these dramas. He argued:

> As dramas they seem to figure an audience palpable enough to be focused, either actually or potentially, in a theatre; as closet dramas they modify this claim by denying themselves the immediate prospect of theatrical realisation and instead imply that their plots, suitably revised by political strategy, might be enacted historically.
>
> (Simpson 1998: 202)

They call for action from the reader in order to complete the full meaning, which is in some way suspended by the generic oscillation between theatre and lyric poetry. This act could be to stage a performance or to enact revolution itself.

Return to form

Three recent monographs all to some degree testify to a recent return to close reading in Byron studies (Rawes 2000, Stabler 2002, Cheeke 2003). As Jane Stabler put it:

> Our experience of reading, teaching, and studying Romantic poetics have been enriched over the last two decades by critical attention to historical context and gender. In the last five years, a resurgence of interest

in form, genre and poetics has enabled us to reflect on how selective some of those early definitions of 'historical context' were. The recovery of socio-political and cultural contexts sometimes tended to overlook the aesthetics of Romantic period works. More recently, however, critics have begun to unite the traditional strengths of close formal analysis with attention to the shaping dynamics of historical contexts.

(Stabler 2002: 1–2)

Rawes' study had a somewhat old-fashioned agenda, however, for – as had the new critics of the 1960s – he set out to champion Byron as an underrated artist who, despite the animadversion of T. S. Eliot, actually had ceaselessly experimented with all the basic poetic forms of narrative, drama and lyric. He saw this experimentation as driven by a search for a form to express a particular philosophical vision. Rawes sought to reverse the thesis of Gleckner (1967) who had overstated Byron's pessimism, especially in his account of *Don Juan*. Rawes, by contrast, saw the chronology of Byron's early works as illustrating a battle between tragic and comic impulses and viewed his eventual development of a comic idiom in the *ottava rima* verse as a success in casting off pessimism. It could be argued that this thesis is as overstated as that of Gleckner, insufficiently engaging with the depiction of Byron's Romantic irony and philosophical scepticism, by such scholars as Garber (1988), Hoagwood (1993) or Reiman (1988). Despite this, the study is valuable for sensitive and detailed readings of the poetry of 1816: the third canto of *Childe Harold's Pilgrimage*, *The Prisoner of Chillon* and *Manfred*.

Both Stabler (2002) and Cheeke (2003) had the word 'history' in their titles and more effectively linked their own methodology with the task of moving on from New Historicism: in Stabler's case by following Wolfson's lead in considering the formal properties of verse in relation to historical context; and in Cheeke's by extending literary criticism's fascination with history to include geography too. Stabler's monograph on Byron's satirical works appeared to be a study of digression, despite the fact that the word was omitted from the title. Instead of defining digression as wandering from the plot, Stabler broadened it to include any strategy for changing the subject or drawing attention to a text's fictionality which disturbs the reading process: such as the use of quotation marks, allusions or parenthetical asides. Rather than ascribing these sudden transitions to Byron's 'mobility' or mercurial personality, Stabler compared them with eighteenth-century satiric techniques, making useful connections between Byron and earlier writers such as Charles Churchill, Laurence Sterne, Matthew Prior and Alexander Pope. She argued that 'while digression offers a poetics of indeterminacy, aesthetic form is always shaped by context', and proceeded to illustrate the way high art interacted with low culture in *Don Juan* by showing how allusions to contemporary newspapers addressed different circles of readership. Stabler's painstaking and intelligent study offered a host of nuanced insights on the details of the satiric verse, but consisted of a microscopic close-up rather than a book with a thesis which offers a particular point of view.

Cheeke's monograph was more historicist in methodology, but just as Rawes' affirmative Byron was slightly Wordsworthian, so there was an implicitly revisionist agenda in Cheeke's portrait of Byron as a Romantic poet of place and of nostalgia rather than of revolutionary politics or scepticism. As had Diego Saglia's earlier study of Byron and Spain (1996), Cheeke attempted to extend the agenda of New Historicism by incorporating notions of cultural geography to illustrate Byron's 'geo-political imagination'. Cheeke investigated precisely the sort of feelings Byron's verse evoked in its tourist readers, through the notion of actually being in a famous place. He pointed out to what an extent history is Byron's subject. Cheeke argued that:

> Byron's engagement with place is not one emptied of the 'something far more deeply interfused'; quite the opposite in fact, as the trope of the *genius loci* is regularly invoked to suggest the mysterious, the super-natural or the ecstatic in Byron's writing. Byron's source of mystery, however, emerges from different sources than Wordsworthian nature, deriving instead partly from an awareness of the strangeness and power of being in places of historical fame, being physically present where history has occurred; partly from the cult of the 'real' which develops in and around Byronism, the desire for accuracy, for re-enactment, and for the material *facts*.
>
> (Cheeke 2003: 9)

Cheeke related his analysis of the verse to biographical and historical context: Byron and Hobhouse's journey as tourists to the East; the poet's visits to Europe's battlefields and to sites associated with literary works. He illustrated his fascination with relics, souvenirs, epitaphs and proofs of authentification. He demonstrated how Byron's work can be seen as always linked to a philosophical exploration of the spirit of place and the meaning of exile, though, unsurprisingly, this thesis is more convincing regarding *Childe Harold's Pilgrimage* than *Don Juan* or the later plays.

Further reading

Frederick Shilstone's theme is the tension between Byron's respect for tradition and desire to establish his individual autonomy in *Byron and the Myth of Tradition* (1989). For an acerbic treatment of Byron's creation of his image, see Philip W. Martin, *Byron: A Poet before his Public* (1982). Christensen's rather recondite study gives a post-structuralist edge to the subject of Byron's awareness of his writing as a commodity, in *Lord Byron's Strength: Romantic Writing and Commercial Society* (1993). On politics see the opposing views of Michael Foot, *The Politics of Paradise: A Vindication of Byron* (1988) and Malcolm Kelsall, *Byron's Politics* (1987). On Byron and gender, consult Louis Crompton, *Byron and Greek Love: Homophobia in Nineteenth-Century England* (1985) and Caroline Franklin, *Byron's Heroines* (1992). Stephen Cheeke's monograph *Byron and Place: History, Translation, Nostalgia* (2003) looks at what 'being there' meant to the poet. For a useful evaluative account of Byron criticism from 1985 to the late 1990s, see Andrew Nicholson, 'Lord Byron' in *Literature of the Romantic Period: A Bibliographical Guide*, ed. Michael O'Neill (1998: 90–117). Useful collections of essays are Bernard Beatty and Vincent Newey (eds), *Byron and the Limits of*

4

Chronology

Bullet points are used to denote events in Byron's life and asterisks to denote historical and literary contexts.

1788
- 22 January, George Gordon Byron born at 16 Holles Street, Cavendish Square, London; son of Captain 'mad Jack' Byron and Catherine (née Gordon); 29 February, christened in Marylebone parish church
* First attack of George III's insanity; impeachment of Warren Hastings; published: Immanuel Kant, *Critique of Practical Reason*

1789
- Mother took lodgings in Aberdeen
* Storming of the Bastille (14 July); Declaration of the Rights of Man; published: William Blake, *The Book of Thel*, *Songs of Innocence*

1790
* Published: Edmund Burke, *Reflections on the Revolution in France*

1791
- 2 August, death of father in France; mother took apartment at 64 Broad Street, Aberdeen
* Published: Thomas Paine, *The Rights of Man*, Part I

1792
* September massacres; abolition of French monarchy; British defeat of Tipu Sultan in Mysore, India; published: Mary Wollstonecraft, *Vindication of the Rights of Woman*; Thomas Paine, *Rights of Man*, Part II (banned)

1793
* Execution of French king and queen and commencement of 'the Terror'; war with France; published: William Godwin, *An Enquiry Concerning Political Justice*; William Blake's *The Marriage of Heaven and Hell*

1794
- Entered Aberdeen Grammar School
* Habeas corpus suspended; treason trials of forty-one radicals; published: W. Blake, *Songs of Innocence and Experience*

1798
- 21 May, on death of the Fifth Lord Byron ('the wicked Lord'), George Gordon Byron became 6th Baron Byron of Rochdale; August, accompanied mother to ancestral mansion, Newstead Abbey, Nottinhamshire
* France conquered Switzerland, northern Italy and Malta; rebellion in Ireland; published: Samuel Taylor Coleridge and William Wordsworth's *Lyrical Ballads*; Jeremy Bentham, *Political Economy*; Malthus's *Essay on the Principle of Population*

1799
- September, entered Dr Glennie's School, Dulwich
* Napoleon became consul; Anti-Combination Laws

1800
- Summer at Newstead and at Nottingham; fell in love with first cousin, Margaret Parker
* First iron-frame printing press built; French conquered Italy; published: second edition *Lyrical Ballads* with Wordsworth's preface

1801
- April, entered Harrow
* Peace of Amiens; Act of Union; George III refused to grant Emancipation to Roman Catholics

1802
- Christmas holiday at Bath
* *Edinburgh Review* and William Cobbett's *Political Register* founded

1803
- July, mother rented Burgage Manor, Southwell; September, fell in love with his cousin Mary Chaworth of Annesley Hall

1804
- March, friendship with the Pigots; performed at Speech Day
* Napoleon crowned Emperor; Britain declared war on Spain

1805
- Performed at Speech Day; 2 August, played in cricket match against Eton; 24 October, commenced studies at Trinity College, Cambridge
* Battle of Trafalgar; death of Nelson; published: Walter Scott, *The Lay of the Last Minstrel*; Robert Southey, *Madoc*; Henry Cary (tr.), Dante's *Inferno*

1806

- September, involved in Southwell amateur theatricals; November, *Fugitive Pieces* privately printed
* Deaths of William Pitt and Charles James Fox; coalition ministry of 'All the Talents'; published: Thomas Moore's *Epistles, Odes and Other Poems*, Mary Robinson, *The Poems* (3 vols)

1807

- January, *Poems on Various Occasions* privately printed; June, *Hours of Idleness* published; became friends with J. C. Hobhouse and C. S. Matthews, and later with S. B. Davies and F. Hodgson; July, reviewed Wordsworth's *Poems* in *Monthly Literary Recreations*; December, left Cambridge
* Abolition of slave trade in British dominions; published: George Crabbe's *Poems*; T. Moore's *Irish Melodies*; Sydney Owenson Morgan, *Lays of an Irish Harp*; Mme de Staël's *Corinne*; W. Wordsworth, *Poems in Two Volumes*

1808

- Received MA from Cambridge; January, Henry Brougham's review of *Hours of Idleness* published in *Edinburgh Review*; March, *Poems Original and Translated* published; October–November, continued satire (to be *English Bards and Scotch Reviewers*) had begun a year previously.
* British campaign in Portugal but Convention of Cintra allowed French withdrawal; Leigh Hunt founded *Examiner* (–1881); published: Felicia Hemans, *Poems*; Walter Scott, *Marmion*; J. W. von Goethe's *Faust*, Part I.

1809

- 13 March, Byron took his seat in House of Lords; *English Bards and Scotch Reviewers* published anonymously; 2 July, departed with Hobhouse on Lisbon packet for Grand Tour; visited Portugal, Spain, Gibraltar, Sicily, Malta, Albania, Greece, Turkey, Asia Minor; October, received by Ali Pasha; began *Childe Harold's Pilgrimage*
* *Quarterly Review* founded; published: W. Blake, *A Descriptive Catalogue*; W. Wordsworth, *Tract on the Convention of Cintra*

1810

- 3 May, swam the Hellespont; 17 July, Hobhouse returned to England.
* French take Holland; London riots in support parliamentary reform; published: W. Scott, *The Lady of the Lake*; Robert Southey, *The Curse of Kehama*; George Crabbe, *The Borough*; Percy Bysshe Shelley, *Original Poetry by Victor and Cazire, Zastrozzi, St Irvine, Posthumous fragments of Margaret Nicholson*

1811

- Byron began *Hints from Horace* and *The Curse of Minerva*; April, travelled back to England on the *Hydra*, the ship carrying the final consignment of the Elgin marbles; 14 July arrived in England; 1 August, mother died; 3 August, friend Charles Skinner Matthews drowned; September, informed that John Edleston had died in May; wrote the 'Thyrza' poems

* Prince of Wales made Regent; Hampden clubs founded to campaign for democracy; insurrection in Colombia and Venezuela against Spanish rule; published: L. Hunt, *The Feast of the Poets*; P. B. Shelley, *The Necessity of Atheism*

1812

• Reviewed Spencer's *Poems*; 27 February, maiden speech in House of Lords against the death penalty for Luddites; 10 March, *Childe Harold's Pilgrimage* I and II published; 21 April, second speech in House of Lords on Roman Catholic civil rights; April, liaison with Lady Caroline Lamb began; October, liaison with Lady Oxford began

* Anti-Luddite act passed and twelve regiments needed to quell unrest and food riots; Napoleon's retreat from Moscow; P. M. Spencer Percival assassinated; USA declares war on Great Britain; published: Anna Barbauld's *1811*; H. Cary (tr.) Dante's *Purgatory*, *Paradise*; George Crabbe's *Tales in Verse*; F. Hemans, *Domestic Affections and other Poems*; P. B. Shelley, *An Address to the Irish People* and *Proposals for an Association*

1813

• February, reviewed William Henry Ireland's *Neglected Genius*; March, *The Waltz* privately printed; May, visited Leigh Hunt in gaol; 1 June, third and last speech in House of Lords in support of Major Cartwright; 5 June, *The Giaour* published; July, liaison with Augusta Leigh, his half-sister began; met Mme de Staël; October, romance with Lady Frances Webster began; 2 December, *The Bride of Abydos* published

* 1813 Wellington victorious in Peninsular war; French expelled from Italy, Holland and Switzerland; Leigh Hunt gaoled for libel; R. Southey appointed Poet Laureate; Wordsworth accepted sinecure as Distributor of Stamps; published: Jane Austen, *Pride and Prejudice*; S. T. Coleridge, *Remorse*; J. C. Hobhouse, *A Journey through Albania and other Provinces of Turkey in Europe and Asia to Constantinople*; T. Moore *Intercepted Letters; or, The Twopenny Postbag*; W. Scott, *Rokeby*; P. B. Shelley, *Queen Mab*

1814

• 1 February, *The Corsair* published; 6 August, *Lara* published anonymously with Samuel Rogers's *Jacqueline*; 9 September, proposed to Annabella Milbanke

* Abdication of Napoleon and exile to Elba; peace with USA; Congress of Vienna; George Stephenson invented first locomotive; development of steam warship and steam printing machine; Edmund Kean's acting debut; published: L. Hunt, *The Feast of the Poets*; W. Scott's *Waverley*; W. Wordsworth, *The Excursion*

1815

• 2 January, married Annabella at Seaham, near Durham; April, *A Selection of Hebrew Melodies* published with musical score by John Braham and

Isaac Nathan; May, *Hebrew Melodies* published by Murray; became a member of the Drury Lane subcommittee; November, bailiffs entered house, 13 Piccadilly Terrace; 10 December daughter, Augusta Ada born

*   Corn Laws; Napoleon escaped to France (March); Battle of Waterloo (18 June); Napoleon exiled to St Helena; 'Holy Alliance' instituted; published: W. Wordsworth, *Poems, The White Doe of Rylstone*; L. Hunt, *The Descent of Liberty, a Mask*

1816

•   15 January, Annabella left, taking Ada; separation proceedings began; 13 February, *The Siege of Corinth* and *Parisina* published; March to April, met Claire Clairmont; April, second number of *A Selection of Hebrew Melodies* published; 5–6 April, library auctioned; 21 April, signed deed of separation; 25 April, sailed for the continent; visited Belgium, Germany and Switzerland; 1–6 May, began *Childe Harold's* Pilgrimage, Canto III; 9 May, Lady Caroline Lamb's novel *Glenarvon* published; 27 May, met P. B. Shelley for first time at Sécheron; 14–18 June, the ghost story competition at the Villa Diodati; 22 June, toured Lake Geneva with P. B. Shelley; July–August, frequently attended the salon of Germaine de Staël at Coppet; 14 August, M. G. Lewis arrived; 26 August, Hobhouse and Scrope Davies visited; 28 August, the Shelley party departed for England; August–September, tour to Chamouni, Mont Blanc and later the Bernese Oberland; 5 October, departed with Hobhouse for Italy; 12 October, arrived in Milan; 10 November arrived in Venice; 18 November, *Childe Harold's Pilgrimage*, Canto III published; November, affair with Marianna Segati; studied Armenian at monastery on island of San Lazzaro; 5 December, *The Prisoner of Chillon and Other Poems* published; Hobhouse left for tour of Italy

*   Post-war depression; Spa Fields riot; march of the blanketeers; exhibition of Elgin Marbles; published: J. Austen, *Emma*; S. T. Coleridge, *Christabel and other Poems*; L. Hunt, *The Story of Rimini*; C. Maturin, *Bertram*; T. Moore, *Sacred Songs*, Vol. I; P. B. Shelley, *Alastor and Other Poems*; R. Southey, *The Poet's Pilgrimage to Waterloo, The Lay of the Laureate*; W. Wordsworth, 'Thanksgiving Ode'; F. Hemans, *The Restoration of the Works of Art to Italy*; W. Cobbett, *Political Register* and 'Twopenny Trash'

1817

•   12 January, birth of Allegra, illegitimate daughter by Claire Clairmont; 17 April, set off for Rome; 29 April, met Hobhouse and toured the antiquities together; 20 May, departed for Venice; 16 June, *Manfred* published; August, met Margarita Cogni, a baker's wife; October, wrote *Beppo*; September, visit of Douglas Kinnaird, Lord Kinnaird, and W. S. Rose, and gift of Frere's *Whistlecraft*; 10 December, received news that Newstead Abbey sold to Thomas Wildman for 94,500 pounds

*   Demonstrations and petitions for parliamentary reform; habeas corpus suspended; Renewal of parts of 1795 Treason Acts to proscribe 'seditious meetings'; death penalty for words inciting disaffection in armed forces; William Cobbett escaped to America; trial of William Hone; Pentridge rebellion; death of Princess Charlotte; published: S. T. Coleridge, *Biographia Literaria*, *Sybilline Leaves*, *Zapolya*; John Hookham Frere, *The Monks and the Giants*; F. Hemans, *Modern Greece*; John Keats, *Poems*; T. Moore, *Lalla Rookh*; P. B. Shelley, *A Proposal for Putting Reform to the Vote*, *Laon and Cythna* (withdrawn); R. Southey, *Wat Tyler* (piracy); William Hone's *Reformists' Register* and *Black Dwarf* founded; *Sherwin's Political Register* founded; *Blackwood's Edinburgh Magazine* founded

1818

- 8 January, Hobhouse returned to England, while Byron, settled in Venice; 28 February, *Beppo* published; 28 April, *Childe Harold's Pilgrimage*, Canto IV published; 3 July, began *Don Juan*; 23 August, rode with P. B. Shelley on the lido (incident in 'Julian and Maddalo'); 24–9, visited by both the Shelleys

* Trial and incarceration of Richard Carlile; strikes of spinners and weavers; Chile declared independence; published: S. T. Coleridge, *The Friend* (3 vols); W. Hazlitt, *Lectures on the English Poets*, *A View of the English Stage*; John Keats, *Endymion*; T. Moore, *National Airs* I (–1827), *The Fudge Family in Paris*; Thomas Love Peacock, *Nightmare Abbey*; Mary Shelley, *Frankenstein*; P. B. Shelley, *The Revolt of Islam*

1819

- February, objections to *Don Juan* Canto I in London; April, fell in love with Countess Teresa Guiccioli; June, visited Ravenna; 18 June, began *Prophecy of Dante*; 28 June, *Mazeppa* and *Ode on Venice* published; 15 July, *Don Juan* Cantos I and II published anonymously; 9 August, followed Guicciolis to Bologna; September, returned to Venice with Teresa; October, visit of Moore and gave him memoirs of life up to 1816; 24 December, followed Teresa to Ravenna and settled there.

* Peterloo Massacre; Six Acts to proscribe radical activity, including Blasphemous and Seditious Libel Act, fourpenny stamp tax imposed on newspapers; British acquisition of Singapore; published: P. B. Shelley, 'Rosalind and Helen'; W. Wordsworth, *Peter Bell, the Waggoner*

1820

- 21 February, finished translation of Pulci's *Morgante Maggiore*; March, finished *Prophecy of Dante*; April, became involved in planned revolt against the Austrians; May, crisis of the Guiccioli marriage; July, finished *Marino Faliero*; Teresa separated from her husband; August, became initiated into secret revolutionary society of the Carbonari; 16 October, began *Don Juan* Canto V; 9 December, commandant shot dead outside house

* Death of George III and accession of George IV; Cato Street conspiracy to assassinate government ministers; trial of Queen Caroline; revolutions in Spain, Portugal, Naples, Piedmont; published: John Clare, *Poems Descriptive of Rural Life and Scenery*; J. Keats, *Lamia, Isabella, The Eve of St. Agnes, and Other Poems*; W. Scott's *Ivanhoe*; P. B. Shelley, *The Cenci*, *Prometheus Unbound*, *Swellfoot the Tyrant*; W. Wordsworth, *The River Duddon, Memorials of a Tour on the Continent*; *London Magazine* founded

1821

- 4 January, began 'Ravenna Journal'; January, began *Sardanapalus*; 10 February, finished first letter on Bowles-Pope controversy; 24 February, plan of Carbonari uprising failed and leaders betrayed; 25 March, wrote second letter on Bowles; 31 March, publication of 'Letter to John Murray Esq.' on Bowles controversy; 21 April, *Marino Faliero* and *Prophecy of Dante* published together; 25 April, *Marino Faliero* staged at Drury Lane; 27 May, finished *Sardanapalus*; 12 June, began *The Two Foscari*. July, promised Teresa he would discontinue *Don Juan*; 10 July, first Pietro Gamba then his father banished from the Romagna; 16 July, began *Cain*; 25 July, Teresa joined her father and brother in Florence; 6 August, Shelley visited Byron in Ravenna; August, wrote *The Blues*; September, wrote *The Vision of Judgment*; 9 October, began *Heaven and Earth*; 15 October, began 'Detached Thoughts'; 29 October, departed Ravenna for Pisa; 1 November, took up residence at Casa Lanfranchi, Pisa; 19 December, publication of *Sardanapalus*, *The Two Foscari* and *Cain*

* Death of Napoleon; death of Queen Caroline; death of John Keats; Greek War of Independence began; suppression of Neapolitan uprising; Simón Bolívar victorious in Venzuelan war of liberation against Spain: Peru, Guatemala, Panama, Santo Domingo declared independence from Spain; published: P. B. Shelley, *Epipsychidion*, *Adonais*; R. Southey, *A Vision of Judgment*

1822

- 28 January, death of Lady Noel, Byron's mother-in-law; Byron took on name of Noel Byron as a condition of sharing the estate; January, resumption of *Don Juan* (Canto VI); February, sent 250 pounds to Hunt for his voyage to Italy; 20 April, death of Allegra; 1 (?) July, Leigh Hunt and his family arrived at Leghorn; 3 July, Leigh Hunt moved into Casa Lanfranchi; July, resumed composition of *Don Juan*; 8 July, P. B. Shelley and Edward Williams drowned in Bay of Spezia; 16 August, cremation of Shelley at Viareggio; 15 September, short visit of Hobhouse; Byron and the Gambas moved to Genoa; 15 October, publication of first issue of *The Liberal*; 23 November, publication of *Werner* by Murray; began *The Age of Bronze*; 14 December, sent *Don Juan* Canto XII to Kinnaird, i.e. seven cantos now unpublished.

* Suicide of Viscount Castlereagh; Liberal Tories Peel and Canning joined Liverpool ministry, Canning became foreign secretary; Brazil achieved independence from Portugal; Simón Bolívar won Ecuador's freedom from Spain; Greeks proclaimed independence; published: P. B. Shelley, *Hellas, A Lyrical Drama*; W. Wordsworth, *Ecclesiatical Sketches*

1823

- 1 January, No. 2 *The Liberal* published; 10 January, finished *The Age of Bronze*; February, finished *The Island*; April–June, friendship with the Blessingtons; 5 April, visited by Edward Blaquiere; 6 May, finished *Don Juan* Canto XVI; May, elected member of London Greek Committee; June, quarrelled with Leigh Hunt and Mary Shelley; 24 July, sailed for Greece on brig *Hercules*, with Pietro Gamba and Edward Trelawny

    3 August, landed at Argostoli, Cephalonia; 13 November, signed agreement for loan on 4,000 pounds to the Greek government; 22 November, arrival of Colonel Leicester Stanhope, agent for London Greek Committee; 29 December, embarked for Missolonghi; chased by Turkish vessels, then driven on the rocks by storms

*   Peel began reform Penal Code; Huskisson initiated reform at Board of Trade; Mechanics' Institute founded; war between France and Spain; published: T. Moore, *The Loves of the Angels*; P. B. Shelley, *Poetical Pieces*

1824

•   5 January, came ashore at Missolonghi to tumultuous reception; January, took 500 Suliotes into his service; 14 January, Stanhope launched Greek newspaper, *Hellenica Chronica*; 22 January, wrote 'On this Day I Complete My Thirty-Sixth Year'; 25 January, commissioned by Mavrocordatos to lead expedition agaonst Lepanto; 5 February, arrival of William Parry, the fire-master; 15 February, Suliotes disbanded; suffered severe convulsive fit; 21 February, departure of Stanhope for Athens; 19 April, Easter Monday, died of fever exacerbated by bleeding

*   1824 Combinations Act repealed; unions permitted; National Gallery opened; Published: James Hogg, *Confessions of a Justified Sinner*; P. B. Shelley, *Posthumous Poems*

Bibliography

The suggestions for further reading following each section should also be consulted.

Abrams, M. H. (1953) *The Mirror and the Lamp: Romantic Theory and the Critical Tradition*, New York and Oxford: Oxford University Press.
—— (1971) *Natural Supernaturalism: Tradition and Revolution in Romantic Literature*, London: Oxford University Press
Almeida, Hermione de (1981) *Byron and Joyce through Homer:* Don Juan *and* Ulysses, New York: Columbia University Press.
Ashton, Thomas L. (1974) '*Marino Faliero*: Byron's "Poetry of Politics" ', *Studies in Romanticism* 13 (winter): 1–13.
Auden, W. H. (1962) *The Dyer's Hand and Other Essays*, London: Faber & Faber, pp. 386–406. First published 1948.
Bainbridge, Simon (1995) *Napoleon and English Romanticism*, Cambridge: Cambridge University Press.
Barton, Anne (1992) *Byron: Don Juan*, Cambridge: Cambridge University Press.
Bate, Jonathan (1986) *Shakespeare and the English Romantic Imagination*, Oxford: Clarendon Press.
Beatty, Bernard (1985) *Byron's Don Juan*, Beckenham: Croom Helm.
—— and Vincent Newey (eds) (1988) *Byron and the Limits of Fiction*, Liverpool: Liverpool University Press.
Beaty, Frederick (1985) *Byron the Satirist*, DeKalb, Ill.: Northern Illinois Press.
Beckett, John (2001) *Byron and Newstead: The Aristocrat and the Abbey*, London: Associated University Presses.
Bone, Drummond (1998) 'The Art of *Don Juan:* Byron's Metrics', in Stabler (1998), pp. 204–16.
—— (ed.) (2004) *The Cambridge Companion to Byron*, Cambridge: Cambridge University Press.
Bostetter, Edward E. (1960) 'Byron and the Politics of Paradise', *PMLA* 75: 571–6.
—— (1969) *Twentieth Century Views of* Don Juan, Englewood Cliffs, NJ: Prentice-Hall.
Boyd, Elizabeth French (1958) *Byron's Don Juan*, New York: The Humanities Press.

Butler, E. M. (1956) *Byron and Goethe*, London: Bowes & Bowes.

Butler, Marilyn (1988) 'The Orientalism of Byron's *The Giaour*', in Beatty and Newey (1988), pp. 78–96.

—— (1992) 'John Bull's Other Kingdom: Byron's Intellectual Comedy', *Studies in Romanticism* 31(3): 281–94.

Buzard, James (1993) *Beaten Track: European Tourism and the Ways to Culture 1800–1918*, Oxford: Oxford University Press.

Calder, Angus (ed.) (1989) *Byron and Scotland: Radical or Dandy?* Edinburgh: Edinburgh University Press.

Cheeke, Stephen (2003) *Byron and Place: History, Translation, Nostalgia*, Basingstoke and New York: Palgrave.

Chew, Samuel (1915) *The Dramas of Lord Byron*, New York: Russell & Russell. Reprinted 1964.

—— (1924) *Byron in England: His Fame and After-Fame*, London: John Murray.

Christensen, Jerome (1993) *Lord Byron's Strength: Romantic Writing and Commercial Society*, Baltimore, Md. and London: Johns Hopkins University Press.

Christie William (1997a) 'Byron and Francis Jeffrey', *The Byron Journal*, 25: 32–43.

—— (1997b) 'Running with the English Hares and Hunting with the Scotch Bloodhounds', *The Byron Journal*, 25: 23–31.

Claridge, Laura (1993) 'Love and Self-Knowledge, Identity in the Cracks: A Lacanian Reading of *Don Juan*', in Wood (1993), pp. 26–55.

Clearman, Mary (1970) 'A Blueprint for *English Bards and Scotch Reviewers*: The First Satire of Juvenal', *Keats-Shelley Journal*, 19: 87–99.

Cline, C. L. (1952) *Byron, Shelley and their Pisan Circle*, London: John Murray.

Colburn Mayne, Ethel (1929) *The Life of Lady Byron*, London: Constable.

Corbett, Martyn (1988) *Byron and Tragedy*, Basingstoke: Macmillan.

Cox, Jeffrey N. (1998) *Poetry and Politics in the Cockney School: Keats, Shelley, Hunt and their Circle*, Cambridge: Cambridge University Press.

Crompton, Louis (1985) *Byron and Greek Love: Homophobia in Nineteenth-Century England*, London: Faber & Faber.

Donelan, Charles (2000) *Romanticism and Male Fantasy in Byron's* Don Juan: *A Marketable Vice*, Basingstoke: Palgrave.

Dyer, Gary (1997) *British Satire and the Politics of Style, 1789–1832*, Cambridge: Cambridge University Press.

—— (2001) 'Thieves, Boxers, Sodomites, Poets: Being Flash to Byron's *Don Juan*', *PMLA* 116(3): 562–78.

Elfenbein, Andrew (1995) *Byron and the Victorians*, Cambridge: Cambridge University Press.

Eliot, T. S. (1933) *The Use of Poetry and the Use of Criticism*, London: Faber & Faber.

—— (1957) *On Poetry and Poets*, London: Faber & Faber.

Elledge, Paul (1998) 'Chasms in Connections: Byron Ending (in) *Childe Harold's Pilgrimage* 1 and 2', in Stabler (1998), pp. 123–37.

—— (2000) *Lord Byron at Harrow School: Speaking Out, Talking Back, Acting Up, Bowing Out*, Baltimore, Md.: Johns Hopkins University Press.

England, A. B. (1975) *Byron's Don Juan and Eighteenth-Century Literature:*

A Study of Some Continuities and Discontinuities, Lewisburg, Pa.: Bucknell University Press.

Erdman, David V. (1939) 'Byron's Stage Fright: The History of his Ambition and Fear of Writing for the Stage', *English Literary History* 6 (September): 219–43.

Foot, Michael (1988) *The Politics of Paradise: A Vindication of Byron*, London: William Collins.

Foster, Richard (1962) *The New Romantics: A Reappraisal of the New Criticism*, Bloomington, Ind.: Indiana University Press.

Franklin, Caroline (1992) *Byron's Heroines*, Oxford: Oxford University Press.

—— (1993) 'Juan's Sea Changes: Class, Race and Gender in Byron's *Don Juan*', in Wood (1993), pp. 56–89.

—— (1997) 'Cosmopolitan Masculinity and the British Female Reader of *Childe Harold's Pilgrimage*', in Richard A. Cardwell (ed.), *Lord Byron the European: Essays from the International Byron Society*, New York, Lampeter and Queenston, Ont.: Edwin Mellen Press, pp. 149–208.

—— (ed.) (1998) *Wellesley Index to Victorian Periodicals 1824–1900: British Romantic Poets*, 5 vols, The Wellesley Series, Nineteenth-Century Sources in the Humanities and Social Sciences, London and Tokyo: Routledge/Thoemmes.

—— (2000) *Byron, A Literary Life*, Basingstoke: Macmillan.

Franklin, Michael (2000) 'The Building of Empire and the Building of Babel', in Martin Procházka (ed.) *Byron: East and West*, Prague: Charles University Press, pp. 63–78.

Fuess, Claude (1912) *Lord Byron as a Satirist in Verse*, New York: Haskell.

Fulford, Tim and Kitson, Peter J. (eds) (1998) *Romanticism and Colonialism 1780–1830*, Cambridge: Cambridge University Press.

Galperin, William H. (1993) *The Return of the Visible in British Romanticism*, Baltimore, Md.: Johns Hopkins University Press.

Garber, Frederick (1988) *Self, Text, and Romantic Irony: The Example of Byron*, Princeton, NJ: Princeton University Press.

Gilmartin, Kevin (1996) *Print Politics: The Press and Radical Opposition in Early Nineteenth-Century England*, Cambridge: Cambridge University Press.

Gleckner, Robert F. (1967) *Byron and the Ruins of Paradise*, Baltimore, Md.: Johns Hopkins University Press.

Gleckner, Robert F. and Beatty, Bernard (eds) (1997) *The Plays of Lord Byron*, Liverpool: Liverpool University Press.

Goldstein, Stephen L. (1975) 'Byron's Cain and the Paineites', *Studies in Romanticism* 14: 391–410.

Graham, Peter W. (1990) *'Don Juan' and Regency England*, Charlottesville, Va.: University Press of Virginia.

Gross, Jonathan David (2001) *Byron: The Erotic Liberal*, Lanham, Md. and Oxford: Rowman & Littlefield.

Haslett, Moyra (1997) *Byron's Don Juan and the Don Juan Legend*, Oxford: Clarendon Press.

Hoagwood, Terence Allan (1993) *Byron's Dialectic: Scepticism and the Critique of Culture*, Lewisburg, Pa.: Bucknell University Press.

Howell, Margaret (1982) *Byron Tonight: A Poet's Place on the Nineteenth-Century Stage*, Windlesham: Springwood.

Johnson, E. D. H. (1944) '*Don Juan* in England', *English Literary History* 11: 135–53.

Jones, Steven E. (1993) 'Intertextual Influences in Byron's Juvenalian Satire', *Studies in English Literature*, 33: 771–83.

Joseph, M. K. (1964) *Byron the Poet*, London: Victor Gollancz.

Jump, John (1973) *Byron*: Childe Harold's Pilgrimage *and* Don Juan: A Casebook, London: Macmillan.

Kelsall, Malcolm (1987) *Byron's Politics*, Brighton: Harvester.

Kernan, Alvin B. (1965) *The Plot of Satire*, New Haven, Conn.: Yale University Press.

Knight, Wilson G. (1939) *The Burning Oracle*, Oxford: Oxford University Press, pp. 197–215.

—— (1957) *Lord Byron's Marriage: The Evidence of Asterisks*, New York: Macmillan.

Kidwai, A. R. (1995) *Orientalism in Lord Byron's 'Turkish tales'*, Lewiston, NY and Lampeter: Edwin Mellen Press.

Lansdown, Richard (1992) *Byron's Historical Dramas*, Oxford: Oxford University Press.

Leask, Nigel (1992) *British Romantic Writers and the East: Anxieties of Empire*, Cambridge: Cambridge University Press.

—— (2004) 'Byron and the Eastern Mediterranean: *Childe Harold* II and the "polemic of Ottoman Greece" ', in Bone (2004), pp. 99–117.

Leavis F. R. (1962) *Revaluation: Tradition and Development in English Poetry*, London: Chatto & Windus.

Levine, Alice and Keane, Robert H. (eds) (1993) *Rereading Byron*, New York: Garland.

Levinson, Marjorie (ed.) (1989) *Rethinking Historicism: Critical Readings in Romantic History*, Oxford: Basil Blackwell.

Looper, Travis (1978) *Byron and the Bible: A Compendium of Biblical Usage in the Poetry of Lord Byron*, Metuchen, NJ: Scarecrow Press.

Lovell, Ernest J. Jr. ed. (1954) *His Very Self and Voice, Collected Conversations of Lord Byron*, London and New York: Macmillan.

—— (1969) *Medwin's Conversations of Lord Byron*, Princeton, NY: Princeton University Press.

Luke, Hugh J., Jr. (1965) 'The Publishing of Byron's *Don Juan*' *PMLA* 80: 199–209.

MacCarthy, Fiona (2002) *Byron: Life and Legend*, London: John Murray.

McGann, Jerome J. (1968) *Fiery Dust: Byron's Poetic Development*, Chicago, Ill: University of Chicago Press.

—— (1976) *Don Juan in Context*, London: John Murray.

—— (1983a) *The Romantic Ideology: A Critical Investigation*, Chicago, Ill. and London: University of Chicago Press.

—— (1983b) *A Critique of Modern Textual Criticism*, Chicago, Ill. and London: University of Chicago Press.

—— (ed.) (1985a) *Textual Criticism and Literary Interpretation*, Chicago, Ill. and London: University of Chicago Press.

—— (1985b) *The Beauty of Inflections: Literary Investigations in Historical Method and Theory*, Oxford: Clarendon Press.

—— (1988) *Social Values and Poetic Acts: The Historical Judgment of Literary Work*, Cambridge, Mass and London: Harvard University Press.

—— (1991) 'On Reading *Childe Harold's Pilgrimage*: Byron and the World of Fact', in Robert F. Gleckner (ed.) *Critical Essays on Lord Byron*, New York: G. K. Hall, pp. 33–58.

—— (1998) 'Lord Byron's Twin Opposites of Truth [*Don Juan*]', in Stabler (1998), pp. 27–51.

—— (2001) *Radiant Textuality: Literature after the World Wide Web*, New York and Basingstoke: Palgrave.

—— (2002) *Byron and Romanticism*, ed. James Soderholm, Cambridge: Cambridge University Press.

Mandrell, James (1992) Don Juan *and the Point of Honor: Seduction, Patriarchal Society, and Literary Tradition*, University Park, Pa.: Pennsylvania State University Press.

Manning, Peter J. (1970) 'Byron's *English Bards and Scotch Reviewers*: The Art of Allusion', *Keats-Shelley Memorial Bulletin*, 21: 7–11.

—— (1978) *Byron and His Fictions*, Detroit, Mich.: Wayne State University Press.

—— (1979) '*Don Juan* and Byron's Imperceptiveness to the English Word', *Studies in Romanticism* 18: 207–33.

—— (1981) 'Tales and Politics: *The Corsair, Lara, The White Doe of Rylstone*', in E. A. Stürzl and James Hogg (eds) *Byron, Poetry and Politics*, Salzburg: Institut für Anglistik und Amerikanistik, Universität Salzburg, pp. 204–30.

—— (1991) 'Childe Harold in the Marketplace: From Romaunt to Handbook', *Modern Language Quarterly*, 52: 170–90.

Marchand, Leslie A. (1957) *Byron: A Biography*, 3 vols, New York: Alfred A. Knopf.

—— (1965) *Byron's Poetry: A Critical Introduction*, Boston, Mass.: Houghton Mifflin Company.

—— (1971) *Byron, a Portrait*, London: John Murray.

—— (1973–94) *Byron's Letters and Journals*, 12 vols, London: John Murray.

Marjarum, E. W. (1938) *Byron as Sceptic and Believer*, Princeton Studies in English no. 16, Princeton, NJ: Princeton University Press.

Marshall, William H. (1960) *Byron, Shelley, Hunt and* The Liberal, Philadelphia, Pa.: University of Pennsylvania Press.

—— (1962) *The Structure of Byron's Major Poems*, Philadelphia, Pa.: University of Pennsylvania Press.

Martin, Philip W. (1982) *Byron: A Poet before his Public*, Cambridge: Cambridge University Press.

—— (1993) 'Reading *Don Juan* with Bakhtin', in Wood (1993), pp. 90–121.

—— (2004) 'Heroism and History: *Childe Harold* I and II and the Tales', in Bone (2004), pp. 77–98.

Massie, Allan (1988) *Byron's Travels*, London: Sidgwick & Jackson.

Medwin, Thomas (1969) *Medwin's Conversations of Lord Byron*, ed. Ernest J. Lovell, Jr., Princeton, NJ: Princeton University Press.

Mellor, Anne K. (1980) *English Romantic Irony*, Cambridge, Mass: Harvard University Press.

Mellown, Muriel (1981) 'Francis Jeffrey, Lord Byron, and *English Bards and Scotch Reviewers*', *Studies in Scottish Literature*, 16: 80–90.

Minta, Stephen (1998) *On a Voiceless Shore: Byron in Greece*, New York: Henry Holt.

Moore, Thomas (1860) *The Life, Letters and Journals of Lord Byron*, London: John Murray.

Moore, Doris Langley (1961) *The Late Lord Byron: Posthumous Dramas*, London: John Murray.

—— (1974) *Lord Byron: Accounts Rendered*, London: John Murray.

Nellist, B. (1988) 'Lyric Presence in Byron from the Tales to Don Juan', in Beatty and Newey (1988), pp. 39–77.

Newey, Vincent (1988) 'Authoring the Self: *Childe Harold III and IV*', in Beatty and Newey (1988), pp. 148–65.

Nicholson, Andrew (ed.) (1991) *Lord Byron, The Complete Miscellaneous Prose*, Oxford: Oxford University Press.

—— (1998) 'Lord Byron', in Michael O'Neill (ed.) *Literature of the Romantic Period: A Bibliographical Guide*, Oxford: Oxford University Press, pp. 90–117.

Origo, Iris (1949) *The Last Attachment*, London: Jonathan Cape.

Oueijan, Naji B. (1996) *The Progress of an Image: The East in English Literature*, New York: Peter Lang.

Paine, Thomas (1969) *The Rights of Man*, Harmondsworth: Penguin. First published 1791–2.

Pratt, Willis W. (1973) *Byron at Southwell: The Making of a Poet*, New York: Haskell House Publishers.

Praz, Mario (1933) *The Romantic Agony*, Oxford: Oxford University Press.

Priestman, Martin (1999) *Romantic Atheism: Poetry and Freethought, 1780–1830*, Cambridge: Cambridge University Press.

Procházka, Martin (ed.) (2000) *Byron: East and West*, Prague: Charles University Press.

Punter, David (1993) '*Don Juan*, or, the Deferral of Decapitation: Some Psychological Approaches', in Wood (1993), pp. 122–53.

Purinton, Marjean D. (1994) *Romantic Ideology Unmasked: The Mentally Constructed Tyrannies in Dramas of William Wordsworth, Lord Byron, Percy Shelley, and Joanna Baillie*, Newark, Del.: University of Delaware Press.

Quennell, Peter (1935) *Byron: The Years of Fame*, London: Faber & Faber.

Quennell, Peter (1941) *Byron in Italy*, New York: Viking.

Rank, Otto (1975) *The Don Juan Legend by Otto Rank*, trans and ed. D. G. Winter, Princeton, NJ: Princeton University Press.

Rawes, Alan (2000) *Byron's Poetic Experimentation: Childe Harold, the Tales and the Quest for Comedy*, Aldershot and Burlington, Va.: Ashgate.

Redpath, Theodore (1973) *The Young Romantics and Critical Opinion 1807–1824*, London: Harrap.

Reiman, Donald H. (ed.) (1972) *The Romantics Reviewed, Part B: Byron and Regency Society Poets*, 5 vols, New York: Garland.

—— (1988) *Intervals of Inspiration: The Sceptical Tradition and the Psychology of Romanticism*, Greenwood, Fla.: Penkevill.

Richardson, Alan (1988) *A Mental Theater: Poetic Drama and Consciousness in the Romantic Age*, University Park, Pa.: Pennsylvania State University Press.

Ridenour, George M. (1960) *The Style of Don Juan*, Yale Studies in English, Vol. 144. New Haven, Conn.: Yale University Press.

Robinson, Charles E. (1976) *Shelley and Byron: The Snake and Eagle Wreathed in Flight*, Baltimore, Md.: John Hopkins University Press.

Roe, Nicholas (2005) *Fiery Heart: The First Life of Leigh Hunt*, London: Pimlico.

Rowse, A. L. (1978) *The Byrons and the Trevanions*, London: Weidenfeld & Nicolson.

Rutherford, Andrew (1961) 'The Influence of Hobhouse on *Childe Harold's Pilgrimage, Canto IV*', *RES*, N.S. 12: 391–7.

—— (1962) *Byron, A Critical Study*, Edinburgh: Oliver & Boyd.

—— (ed.) (1970) *Byron: The Critical Heritage*, London: Routledge.

—— (ed.) (1990) *Byron: Augustan and Romantic*, London: Macmillan.

Saglia, Diego (1996) *Byron and Spain: Itinerary in the Writing of Place*, Lewiston, NY and Lampeter: Edwin Mellen Press.

Said, Edward (1978) *Orientalism*, New York: Pantheon Books.

Santucho, Oscar José and Goode, Clement Tyson (1997) *George Gordon, Lord Byron, Lord Byron: A Comprehensive Bibliography of Secondary Materials in English, 1807–1977*, updated to 1990, Lanham, Md. and London: Scarecrow Press.

Sharafuddin, Mohammed (1994) *Islam and Romantic Orientalism: Literary Encounters with the Orient*, London: I. B. Tauris.

Shilstone, Frederick (1989) *Byron and the Myth of Tradition*, Lincoln, Nebr.: University of Nebraska Press.

Simpson, Michael (1998) *Closet Performances: Political Exhibition and Prohibition in the Dramas of Byron and Shelley*, Stanford, Calif.: Stanford University Press.

Smiles, Samuel (1891) *Memoir and Correspondence of the Late John Murray with an Account of the Origin and Progress of the House, 1768–1843*, 2 vols, London: John Murray.

Stabler, Jane (1998) *Byron. Longman Critical Reader*, London and New York: Longman.

—— (2002) *Byron, Poetics and History*, Cambridge: Cambridge University Press.

—— (2004) 'Byron, Postmodernism and Intertextuality' in Bone (2004), pp. 265–84.

St Clair, William (1972) *That Greece Might Still Be Free*, London and New York: Oxford University Press.

—— (1990) 'The Impact of Byron's Writings: An Evaluative Approach', in Rutherford (1990), pp. 1–25.

—— (2004) *The Reading Nation in the Romantic Period*, Cambridge: Cambridge University Press.

Steffan, Truman Guy (ed.) (1968) *Lord Byron's 'Cain': Twelve Essays and a Text with Variants and Annotations*, Austin, Tex. and London: University of Texas Press.

Steffan, Truman Guy, and Pratt, Willis (eds) (1971) *Byron's Don Juan, A Variorum Edition*, 3 vols, Austin, Tex.: University of Texas Press.

Storey, Mark (1986) *Byron and the Eye of Appetite*, Basingstoke: Macmillan.

Strickland, Margot (1974) *The Byron Women*, London: Owen.

Stürzl, Edwin and Hogg, James (eds) (1981) *Byron: Poetry and Politics*, Salzburg: Institut für Anglistik und Amerikanistik Universität Salzburg.

Taborski, Boleslaw (1972) *Byron and the Theatre*, Saltzburg: Salzburg: Institut für Anglistik und Amerikanistik Universität Salzburg.

—— (1981) 'Byron's Theatre: Private Spleen or Cosmic Revolt. Theatrical Solutions – Stanislavsky to Grotowski', in Edwin Stürzl and James Hogg (eds) *Byron: Poetry and Politics*, Salzburg: Institut für Anglistik und Amerikanistik Universität Salzburg, pp. 356–79.

Thompson, E. P. (1963) *The Making of the English Working Class*, London: Gollancz.

Thorslev, Peter L. Jr. (1962) *The Byronic Hero: Types and Prototypes*, Minneapolis, Minn.: University of Minnesota Press.

Vassallo, Peter (1984) *Byron: The Italian Literary Influence*, London: Macmillan.

Walker, Keith (1979) *Byron's Readers: A Study of Attitudes Towards Byron 1812–1832*, Salzburg: Institut für Anglistik und Amerikanistik, Universität Salzburg.

Watkins, Daniel P. (1987) *Social Relations in Byron's Eastern Tales*, London and Toronto: Associated University Presses.

—— (1993) *A Materialist Critique of English Romantic Drama*, Gainesville, Fla.: University Press of Florida.

West, Paul (1960) *Byron and the Spoiler's Art*, London: Chatto & Windus.

—— (ed.) (1963) *Byron: A Collection of Critical Essays*, Englewood Cliffs, NJ: Prentice-Hall.

Wilkes, Joanne (1999) *Lord Byron and Madame de Staël: Born for Opposition*, Aldershot and Sydney: Ashgate.

Wilkie, Brian (1965) *Romantic Poets and Epic Tradition*, Madison, Wisc.: University of Wisconsin Press.

Wilson, Frances (ed.) (1999) *Byromania: Portraits of the Artist in Nineteenth- and Twentieth-Century Culture*, Basingstoke: Macmillan.

Wolfson, Susan (1987) ' "Their She Condition": Cross-Dressing and the Politics of Gender in *Don Juan*', *ELH*, 58 (Fall): 867–902. Reprinted in Stabler (1998), pp. 94–109.

—— (1997) 'Heroic Form: Couplets, "Self", and Byron's *Corsair*', in *Formal Charges: The Shaping of Poetry in British Romanticism*, Stanford, Calif.: Stanford University Press, pp. 133–63.

Wood, Marcus (1994) *Radical Satire and Print Culture 1790–1822*, Oxford: Oxford University Press.

Wood, Nigel (ed.) (1993) *Don Juan*, Theory in Practice Series, Buckingham and Philadelphia, Pa.: Open University Press.

Index